The Python Companion to Spatial Cluster Analysis with GeoDa

Luc Anselin and Pedro Amaral

ISBN-13: 978-0-9863421-2-7
GeoDa Press LLC, Chicago, IL

LA: to Eli, Lucas and kleine meid, the future!

PA: to Luciana, Miguel, and Paulo, who are the light of my life

Table of Contents

List of Figures

List of Tables

Preface

This book is intended to be a companion to the treatment of spatial clustering methods in the two `GeoDa` books, *An Introduction to Spatial Data Science with GeoDa - Volume 1, Exploring Spatial Data* (Anselin 2024a), and *An Introduction to Spatial Data Science with GeoDa - Volume 2, Clustering Spatial Data* (Anselin 2024b). The goal is to illustrate as much as possible how the functionality of `GeoDa` can be replicated using Python, using the same empirical examples as in the books. Specifically, we take advantage of the functionality incorporated in the specialized `pygeoda` package as well as in the more traditional `scikit-learn`.

The book was formed by editing a series of Jupyter notebooks prepared for a course on *Spatial Cluster Analysis*, offered at the University of Chicago in winter quarter 2025. The original notebooks can be accessed from the course GitHub site, at https://github.com/lanselin/notebooks_for_spatial_clustering.

1 Introduction

The main goal of this book is to serve as a practical companion to the treatment of spatial clustering methods in the two `GeoDa` books by Luc Anselin, *An Introduction to Spatial Data Science with GeoDa - Volume 1, Exploring Spatial Data* (Anselin 2024a), and *An Introduction to Spatial Data Science with GeoDa - Volume 2, Clustering Spatial Data* (Anselin 2024b). In the remainder, these two volumes will be referred to as, respectively, the *GeoDa Explore Book* and the *GeoDa Cluster Book.*

The objective is to illustrate as much as possible how the functionality of `GeoDa` can be replicated using Python, based on the same empirical examples as in the original books. This introduces extensive functionality contained in the specialized package `pygeoda` as well as from the familiar `scikit-learn` ecosystem for machine learning.

The Companion contains only a minimal discussion of the actual methods. Instead, the focus is on replicating the examples in the GeoDa books for the same data sets. It is intended to be used in a lab environment or for self-study.

Very little computing background is assumed, beyond familiarity with basic Python commands and the essentials of `pandas` and `geopandas` data frames. All other functionality is developed from scratch. Each chapter follows a similar organization, starting with a list of the required Python packages and the data sets used in the examples. The remainder of the chapters typically follows the same outline as a matching chapter in the GeoDa books. Each chapter closes with some suggestions for further practice.

Not all the empirical illustrations in the GeoDa books can be fully replicated using Python code. Specifically, the powerful interactive *linking and brushing* of multiple maps and graphs cannot (yet) be implemented in a Python setup. However, counterparts of all the static illustrations have been provided. In almost all situations, the results are identical to those in the matching chapters of the GeoDa books. In a few instances, particularly in the use of `pygeoda`, minor differences in the architecture of the C++ and Python implementations may cause slight discrepancies.

The book is made up of thirteen chapters beyond this introduction. Chapter 2 provides a brief introduction to the mapping functionality that is available with `geopandas`. Chapters 3 and 4 cover local clusters, respectively multivariate local spatial clusters and density-based clustering. Chapters 5 and 6 deal with dimension reduction. The remaining chapters are devoted to so-called unsupervised machine learning in the form of clustering. Chapters 7 to 10 deal with classic (non-spatial) clustering methods, whereas the Chapters 11-13 cover situations where a spatial contiguity constraint is imposed. The book closes with a review of cluster validation measures.

1.1 Required Python Packages

Each chapter provides a list of the Python packages required for the empirical illustrations contained in it. Below, we provide a comprehensive list of all the packages used in the book. If not present, these may need to be installed by means of `pip install -U package_name` (use `-U` to make sure the latest version is obtained).

In the order of when they are first mentioned, the packages are, with their minimal version number and a brief description of the associated functionality:

- `geopandas` (version 1.0.1): spatial data structures , basic maps
- `matplotlib.pyplot` (version 3.9.2): plotting and mapping functions
- `spatial-cluster-helper` (version 0.1.2): utility functions to load data and interpret cluster results
- `numpy` (version 2.0.2): matrix (array) manipulations
- `pygeoda` (version 0.0.8-1): specialized Python interface to `GeoDa` spatial weights , ESDA and clustering functions
- `sklearn.cluster` (version 1.5.1): density-based clusters, hierarchical clusters, partitioning clusters and spectral clustering from scikit-learn
- `matplotlib.lines` (version 3.9.2): line plotting functionality
- `sklearn.preprocessing` (version 1.5.1): data standardization from scikit-learn
- `sklearn.metrics` (version 1.5.1): pairwise distances, silhouette scores , Adjusted Rand Index and mutual information score from scikit-learn
- `sklearn.decomposition` (version 1.5.1): principal components from scikit-learn
- `pandas` (version 2.2.2): generic data frames
- `sklearn.manifold` (version 1.5.1): multi-dimensional scaling and TSNE from scikit-learn
- `libpysal` (version 4.12.1): spatial weights manipulation
- `scipy.cluster.hierarchy` (version 1.14.1): dendrogram for hierarchical clustering
- `kmedoids` (version 0.5.3.1): specialized package to carry out K-Medoids clustering

1.2 Sample Data Sets

The empirical illustrations use the same example data sets as the two GeoDa books. However, whereas for `GeoDa` these are available directly within the software, they must be installed as a working directory to obtain results for the Python code. The book assumes that the relevant data directories are in a **./datasets/** directory.

All the data sets are available for downloading from the GeoDa Center sample data directory at https://geodacenter.github.io/data-and-lab/. In addition, the `spatial_cluster_helper` module contains the `ensure_datasets` function which is used in each chapter to check whether the required data sets are available and in the correct directory. If not present, the files are downloaded and installed.

The respective data sets are, in the order in which they are used:

- **chicago_commpop**: 2000 and 2010 population data for 77 Chicago Community Areas
- **liquor**: 571 liquor store locations in Chicago (2015)
- **Chi-SDOH**: socio-economic determinants of health for 791 Chicago census tracts in 2014, from the study by Kolak et al. (2020)
- **italy_banks**: performance measures for 261 Italian community banks (2011-2017), from Algeri et al. (2022)
- **Chi-CCA**: socio-economic characteristics for 77 Chicago Community Areas
- **spirals**: 300 two-dimensional point data to illustrate the spectral clustering method
- **ceara**: Zika and microcephaly incidence and socio-economic characteristics for 184 *municipios* in the Brazilian state of Ceará, from Amaral et al. (2019)

Further details on the respective data sets can be found in Chapter 1 of the *GeoDa Explore Book*.

2 Creating Thematic Maps

In this Chapter, we briefly introduce functionality to create thematic maps with Python. This provides only a subset of the mapping capabilities in `GeoDa` (e.g., as illustrated in Chapters 4 to 6 of the *GeoDa Explore Book*), but it is sufficient to provide basic visualization for the examples considered in this companion.

There are many ways to create beautiful maps in Python, for example, using packages such as `folium` or `plotly`. Here, the `plot` functionality of `geopandas` is introduced, which is sufficient for most of our purposes. The functionality will be illustrated with the **chicago_commpop** and **liquor** sample data sets. In contrast to what is the case in the other chapters, the examples do not have a direct counterpart in the GeoDa books, since they are focused on the functionality in `geopandas`.

As packages, we will need `matplotlib.pyplot` and `spatial-cluster-helper` in addition to `geopandas`. Note that in the actual `import` statement used in the code, the relevant module is `spatial_cluster_helper` (underlines, *not* dashes).

> Required Packages
>
> geopandas, matplotlib.pyplot, spatial-cluster-helper

> Required Data Sets
>
> chicago_commpop, liquor

2.1 Preliminaries

2.1.1 Import Required Modules

Following standard practice, we import `geopandas` as `gpd` and `matplotlib.pyplot` as `plt`. In addition, we also use the `ensure_datasets` function from the `spatial_cluster_helper` module to load the data.

```
import geopandas as gpd
import matplotlib.pyplot as plt
from spatial_cluster_helper import ensure_datasets
```

2.1.2 Load Data

To illustrate the examples, we assume that the data sets are in a `./datasets/` subdirectory of the main directory from which the code is executed. Alternatively, the `path` variable can be customized.

Before the data are read using the `read_file` command from `geopandas`, `ensure_datasets` is invoked with `"chicago_commpop/chicago_commpop.shp"` as the path for the shape file. If the files are not present in the designated `path` folder, they are downloaded and installed. If they are already present, nothing happens. In the examples below and in the other chapters, the sample data are installed in the proper directory so no downloading is illustrated.

Next, the input files are read into the GeoDataFrame `chi_comm`. The data set contains nine variables for the 77 community areas of Chicago. We will focus on the variable that gives the percentage change in population between 2010 and 2020, `POPPERCH`.

The same process is applied to the liquor store locations data set that is used to illustrate point maps. After `ensure_datasets` is invoked with `"liquor/liq_Chicago.shp"` as the shape file, the data are loaded in the GeoDataFrame `point_df`.

As is our customary approach, we specify all the files and variables in one place, so that it is easy to run the same set of commands for different data sets and/or variables. We load the data and provide a quick check of the contents.

```
# Setting working folder:
#path = "/your/path/to/data/"
path = "./datasets/"
# Select the Chicago community area data:
shpfile1 = "chicago_commpop/chicago_commpop.shp"
# Select the Chicago liquor store data:
shpfile2 = "liquor/liq_Chicago.shp"
# Load the datasets:
ensure_datasets(shpfile1, folder_path = path)
chi_comm = gpd.read_file(path + shpfile1)
print(chi_comm.shape)
print(chi_comm.head(3), "\n")

ensure_datasets(shpfile2, folder_path = path)
```

```
point_df = gpd.read_file(path + shpfile2)
print(point_df.shape)
print(point_df.head(3))
```

```
(77, 9)
      community  NID  POP2010  POP2000  POPCH   POPPERCH  popplus  popneg
0       DOUGLAS   35    18238    26470  -8232 -31.099358        0       1
1       OAKLAND   36     5918     6110   -192  -3.142390        0       1
2   FULLER PARK   37     2876     3420   -544 -15.906433        0       1

                                            geometry
0  POLYGON ((-87.60914 41.84469, -87.60915 41.844...
1  POLYGON ((-87.59215 41.81693, -87.59231 41.816...
2  POLYGON ((-87.6288 41.80189, -87.62879 41.8017...

(571, 3)
   id                      placeid                                  geometry
0   0   ChIJnyLZdBTSD4gRbsa_hRGgPtc   MULTIPOINT ((1161395.91 1928443.285))
1   3  ChIJ5Vdx0AssDogRVjbNIyF3Mr4  MULTIPOINT ((1178227.792 1881864.522))
2   4  ChIJb5I6QwYsDogRe8R4E9K8mkk  MULTIPOINT ((1178151.911 1879212.002))
```

For the polygon layers, the variable of interest is given as `plotvar`, which is set to `POPPERCH`. The point layer does not have a variable since just the location of the liquor stores is of interest.

```
plotvar = 'POPPERCH'
```

2.2 Polygon Maps

Once the data is loaded as a GeoDataFrame, a basic `plot` function can be applied to the object to show the polygons obtained from the shape file, as illustrated in Figure 2.1 on page 8.

```
chi_comm.plot()
```

We can use any variable contained in the GeoDataFrame to create a choropleth map. Before delving into customization, the default choropleth map created by the `plot` function is illustrated. A bare bones implementation only requires the variable to be mapped (the argument `column`) and the argument `legend = True`. Without the latter, there will still be a map, but it will not have a legend, so there will be no guide as to

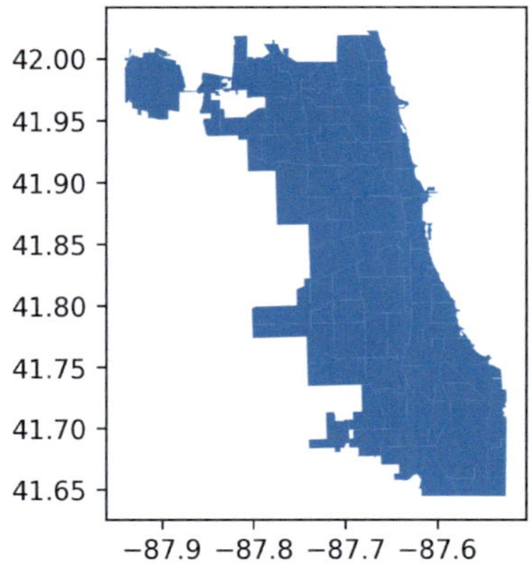

Figure 2.1: Basic map as a plot

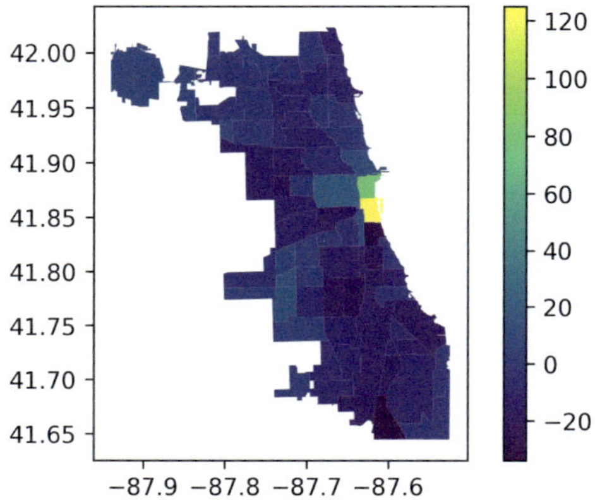

Figure 2.2: Choropleth map as a basic plot with legend

what the colors mean. In the example, we will use the percentage population change, `POPPERCH`, contained in the just-created place-holder variable `plotvar`.

Note that population totals should be avoided in thematic maps. Any total such as population or housing units is a so-called *spatially extensive variable*. All else being the same, one would expect the values for such variables to be larger in larger areas, and thereby provide a false sense of importance. Instead, one should always aim to map *spatially intensive variables*, such as densities, percentages, per capita values, etc. Hence, we use percentage population change in the example instead of total population as in the code below. The result is shown in Figure 2.2.

```
chi_comm.plot(column = plotvar, legend = True)
```

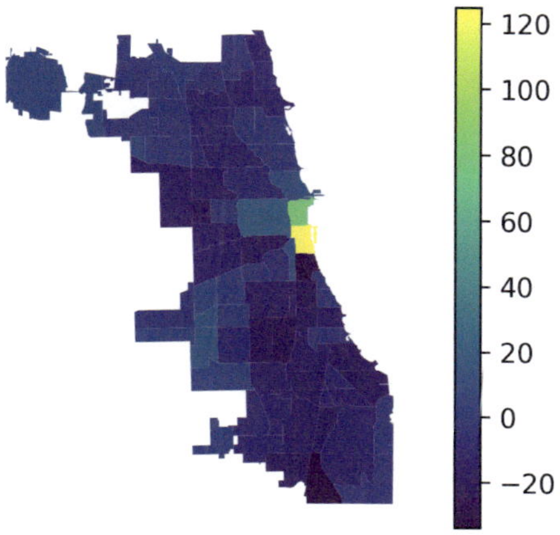

Figure 2.3: Choropleth map without axes

2.2.1 Matplotlib Logic

The `matplotlib` library is extremely powerful and allows just about any type of customized visualization. It starts by setting up the basic parameters and then builds a graphic representation layer by layer. The terminology may seem a bit strange at first, but after a while, it becomes more familiar.

A plot is initialized by assigning some parameters to the tuple `fig , ax`. It is important to realize that `fig` is about the figure makeup and `ax` is about the actual plots. For example, `fig` is used to specify how many subplots there need to be, how they are arranged and what their size is.

Since the examples used here and in later Chapters will mostly produce a single plot, the `fig` aspect can generally be ignored, and only `ax` is needed. In fact, for simple plots such as the maps in our applications, the specification of `ax` as such is not totally necessary and the `plot` function can be applied directly to the GeoDataFrame. However, in general, it remains good practice to refer to the plot object as `ax` in order to allow many further customizations.

An alternative way to set up the default map just shown is to explicitly assign it to an object `ax`, as `ax = chi_comm.plot()` with the same arguments as before. To remove the x-y coordinates and box around the map, the method `set_axis_off()` is applied to the `ax` object. Using this setup also removes any `<Axes: >` listing that may be at the top of the graph. In Figure 2.3, except for the axes, everything is still the same as before.

```
ax = chi_comm.plot(column = plotvar, legend = True)
ax.set_axis_off()
```

2.3 Map Design Characteristics

The purpose of a choropleth or thematic map is to visualize the spatial distribution of a variable over areal units. Choropleth comes from the Greek choros, which stands for region, so it is a map for regions. For our purposes, the proper design of a map has three important characteristics, which each translate into arguments to the `plot` function:

- classification
- color
- legend

2.3.1 Classification

Arguably the most important characteristic is the classification used, i.e., how the continuous distribution of a given variable gets translated into a small number of discrete categories, or bins. This is exactly the same issue as encountered in the design of histogram bins.

The assignment of observations to distinct bins is done by the `mapclassify` library, which is part of the `PySAL` ecoystem. However, this is implemented under the hood by `geopandas` so that no separate `import` statement is needed for `mapclassify` itself.

The classification is set by means of the `scheme` argument. Common options are:

- `Quantiles` (for a quantile map),
- `EqualInterval` (for an equal intervals map),
- `NaturalBreaks` (for a natural breaks map),
- `StdMean` (for a standard deviational map), and
- `BoxPlot` (for a box map).

All but the last two classifications require an additional argument for the number of bins, `k`. This is not needed for the standard deviational map and the box map, for which the breakpoints are derived from the data, respectively the standard deviation and the quartiles/hinge.

The default hinge for the box map is 1.5 times the interquartile range. Other values for the hinge can be specified by setting a different value for the argument `hinge`, but this is typically not necessary.

It is important to note a major difference between the implementation of this option in the underlying `mapclassify` package and its operation as part of `geopandas`. In `mapclassify`, the argument is simply `hinge`, for example, `hinge = 3.0`. In `geopandas`, this argument must be passed as part of a special dictionary, `classification_kwds`. Specifically, to change the hinge value to 3 times the interquartile range would require the argument `classification_kwds = {"hinge": 3.0}`.

The default for the standard deviational map is to show all observations within one standard deviation below and above the mean as one category. To separate observations below and above the mean can be accomplished by setting the argument `anchor` to `True`. Again, this is done by means of the `classification_kwds` dictionary.

Full details on all the classifications available through `mapclassify` and their use in `geopandas` can be found at https://geopandas.org/en/stable/docs/user_guide/mapping.html# and https://pysal.org/mapclassify/api.html.

Each of the five cases is illustrated in turn. We again use the `column` argument to designate the variable to be mapped.

The placement of the legend is managed by means of the `legend_kwds` argument (similar in structure to `classification_kwds`). This is a dictionary that specifies aspects such as the location of the legend and how it is positioned relative to its anchor point. It also makes it possible to set a `title` for the legend, e.g., to set it to the variable that is being mapped.

In the examples, the following arguments are used: `legend_kwds={"loc": "center left", "bbox_to_anchor": (1,0.5), "title": "<variable name>"}`. This is not totally intuitive, but it works. See https://matplotlib.org/stable/api/_as_gen/matplotlib.axes.Axes.legend.html#matplotlib.axes.Axes.legend for details about the various legend customizations.

Also note that the map examples so far use the default color map. More appropriate color maps will be considered in Section 2.3.2.

2.3.1.1 Quantile Map

A simple six category quantile map is illustrated by setting `scheme = "Quantiles"` and `k = 6`, illustrated in Figure 2.4 on page 12. The `legend_kwds` arguments now also include a `title`. In addition, two `ax` methods are used for a minor customization: `ax.set_title` to give the map a title and, as before, `ax.set_axis_off` to get rid of the box with x-y coordinates, shown in the code below.

```
ax = chi_comm.plot(
    column = plotvar,
    scheme = 'Quantiles',
    k = 6,
    legend = True,
```

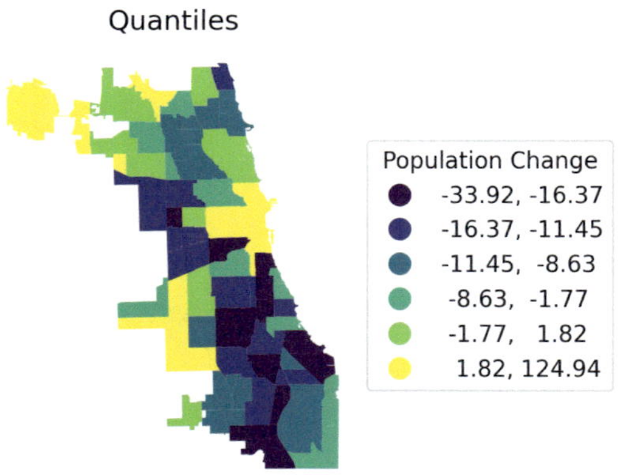

Figure 2.4: Quantile map

```
    legend_kwds = {"loc": "center left", "bbox_to_anchor": (1,0.5),
                   "title": "Population Change"}
)
ax.set_title("Quantiles")
ax.set_axis_off()
```

2.3.1.2 Maps with a Specified Number of Bins

Rather than repeating the single command for each type of map that needs the argument `k`, we construct a small loop that creates each in turn. This is accomplished by putting the name for the respective `scheme` in a list and using that same name as the map title, as shown in the code below. The three types are `Quantiles`, `EqualInterval` and `NaturalBreaks`. They are illustrated in Figure 2.5.

```
schemek = ["Quantiles","EqualInterval","NaturalBreaks"]
for i in schemek:
    ax = chi_comm.plot(
    column = plotvar,
    scheme = i,
    k = 6,
    legend = True,
    legend_kwds = {"loc": "center left", "bbox_to_anchor": (1,0.5),
                   "title": "Population Change"}
    )
    ax.set_title(i)
    ax.set_axis_off()
```

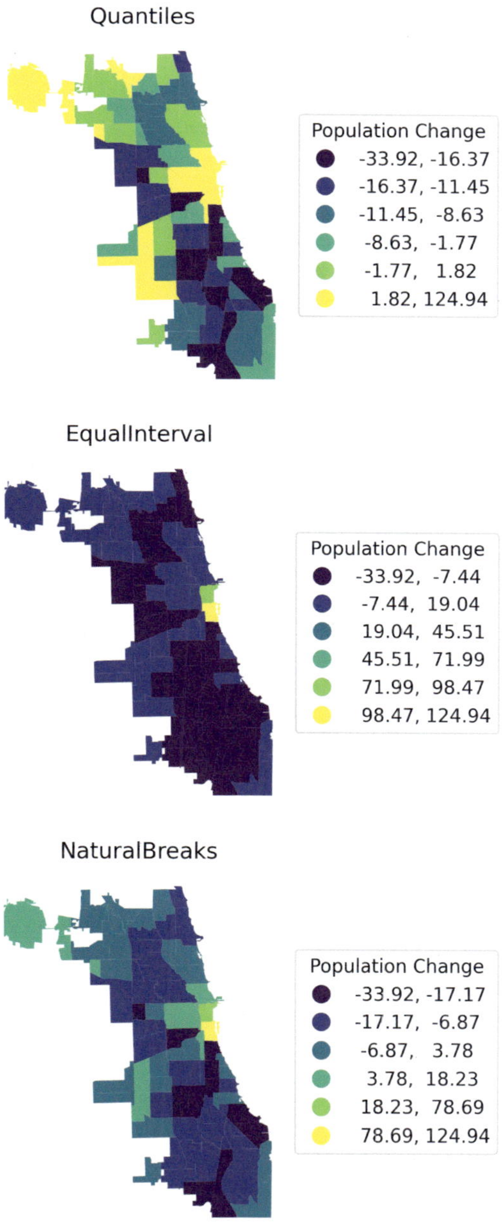

Figure 2.5: Maps with specified number of classifications

Note the contrast in the visualization of the spatial distribution between the different classifications. It is important to keep in mind that each map type has pros and cons. For example, the quantile map yields an equal number of observations in each category, but the range of the categories can vary subtantially, resulting in the grouping of very disparate observations. In the example, this is the case for the top category, which

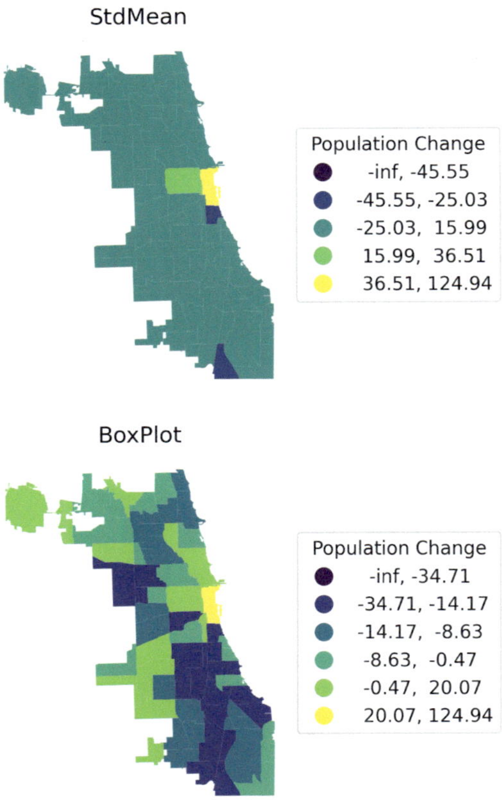

Figure 2.6: Maps with predetermined number of bins

ranges from 1.8 to 124.9.

The range in an equal intervals map is the same for all categories, but as a result some bins may have very few or very many observations, as is the case here for the lowest bins.

Finally, a natural breaks map uses an optimization criterion (essentially equivalent to k-means on one variable) to determine the grouping of observations. Both the number of observations in each bin and the range of the bins is variable.

2.3.1.3 Maps with a Predetermined Number of Bins

The standard deviational map and box map have a pre-set number of bins, depending on, respectively, standard deviational units and quantiles/interquantile range. Again, they are illustrated using a small loop and shown in Figure 2.6.

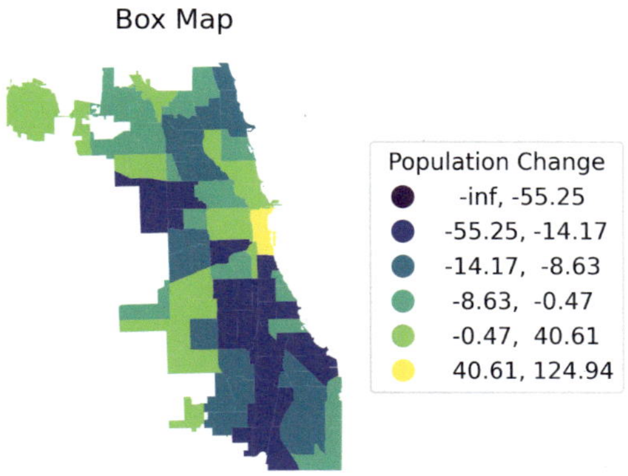

Figure 2.7: Box map with anchor

```
schemenok = ["StdMean","BoxPlot"]
for i in schemenok:
    ax = chi_comm.plot(
    column = plotvar,
    scheme = i,
    legend = True,
    legend_kwds = {"loc": "center left", "bbox_to_anchor": (1,0.5),
                   "title": "Population Change"}
    )
    ax.set_title(i)
    ax.set_axis_off()
```

Both types of maps are designed to highlight outliers. In the standard deviational map, these are observations more than two standard deviations away from the mean, in the box map, the outliers are outside the hinge (1.5 times the interquartile range from the median). As mentioned, the defaults can be customized by setting a different value for the hinge through the `classification_kwds` argument. For example, selecting only the most extreme observations is achieved by setting `classification_kwds = {"hinge": 3.0}`, as illustrated in the code below. Note that since the bins are created based on deviations from the mean or median, the low ranges can start at -inf, as in Figure 2.7, which doesn't really make sense.

```
ax = chi_comm.plot(
    column = plotvar,
    scheme = 'BoxPlot',
    k = 6,
    classification_kwds = {'hinge': 3.0},
```

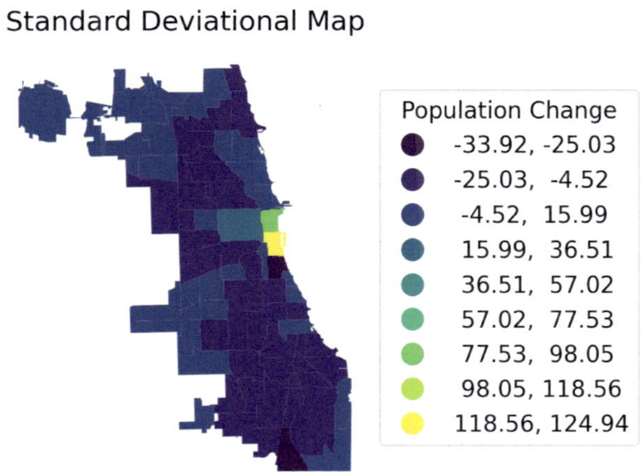

Figure 2.8: Standard deviational map with anchor

```
    legend = True,
    legend_kwds = {"loc": "center left", "bbox_to_anchor": (1,0.5),
                   "title": "Population Change"}
)
ax.set_title("Box Map")
ax.set_axis_off()
```

To avoid the negative bins, we can use the argument `classification_kwds = {"anchor" : True}` to ensure the lower boundary of the classification starts at 0 or the minimum value in the data. A standard deviational map with the categories below and above the mean shown is implemented with `classification_kwds = {"anchor" : True}`, as shown in the code below and illustrated in Figure 2.8.

```
ax = chi_comm.plot(
    column = plotvar,
    scheme = 'StdMean',
    k = 6,
    classification_kwds = {'anchor': True},
    legend = True,
    legend_kwds = {"loc": "center left", "bbox_to_anchor": (1,0.5),
                   "title": "Population Change"}
)
ax.set_title("Standard Deviational Map")
ax.set_axis_off()
```

Whereas the first three types of classifications have a color scheme that suggests a progression from low to high values, a so-called *sequential* legend, the standard deviational map and box map focus on differences from a central value. This requires a color map that highlights the move away from the center, a so-called *diverging* legend. In the examples shown so far, the categories were visualized with the default sequential color map, which is not the best choice. The needed customizations are considered next.

2.3.2 Color Map

The color scheme for the map is set by means of the `cmap` argument. This refers to a `matplotlib` color map, i.e., a pre-determined range of colors optimized for a particular purpose. For example, this allows for a different color map to represent a sequential vs. a diverging legend.

The full range of color maps can be found at https://matplotlib.org/stable/users/explain/colors/colormaps.html.

For our purposes, a good sequential color map uses a gradation that goes from light to dark, either in the same color, such as `cmap = "Blues"`, or moving between colors, such as `cmap = "YlOrRd"`. For a diverging legend, going from one extreme color to another is preferred, e.g., dark blue to light blue and then to light red and dark red, as in `cmap = "bwr"`, or even more extreme, as in `cmap = "seismic"`.

Some examples are shown in the code blocks below. The first two examples are for two sequential color maps, illustrated in Figures 2.9 and 2.10 on page 18. The code only differs in the `cmap` argument.

```
ax = chi_comm.plot(
    column = plotvar,
    scheme = 'Quantiles',
    k = 6,
    cmap = 'Blues',
    legend = True,
    legend_kwds = {"loc": "center left", "bbox_to_anchor": (1,0.5),
                   "title": "Population Change"}
)
ax.set_title("Quantiles")
ax.set_axis_off()
```

```
ax = chi_comm.plot(
    column = plotvar,
    scheme = 'Quantiles',
    k = 6,
    cmap = 'YlOrRd',
```

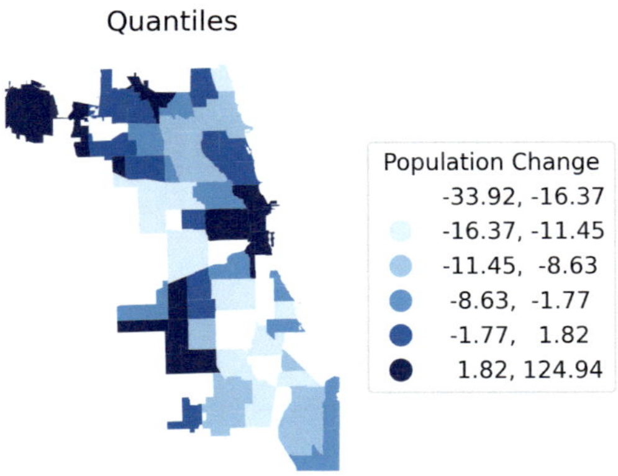

Figure 2.9: Quantile map with Blues color map

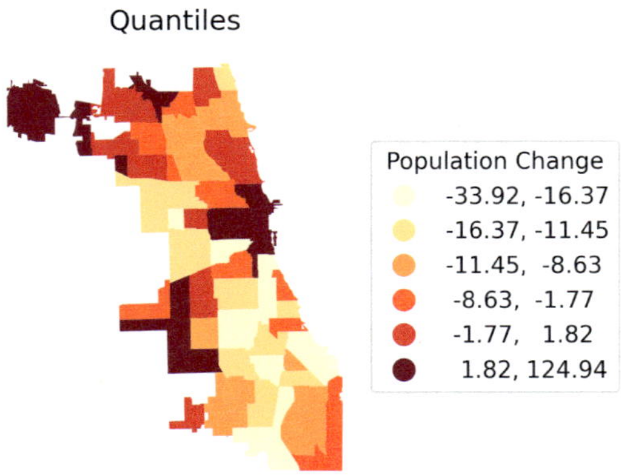

Figure 2.10: Quantile map with YlOrRd color map

```
    legend = True,
    legend_kwds = {"loc": "center left", "bbox_to_anchor": (1,0.5),
                   "title": "Population Change"}
)
ax.set_title("Quantiles")
ax.set_axis_off()
```

The final example is for a diverging legend, illustrated in Figure 2.11.

```
ax = chi_comm.plot(
    column = plotvar,
    scheme = 'BoxPlot',
    cmap = 'seismic',
```

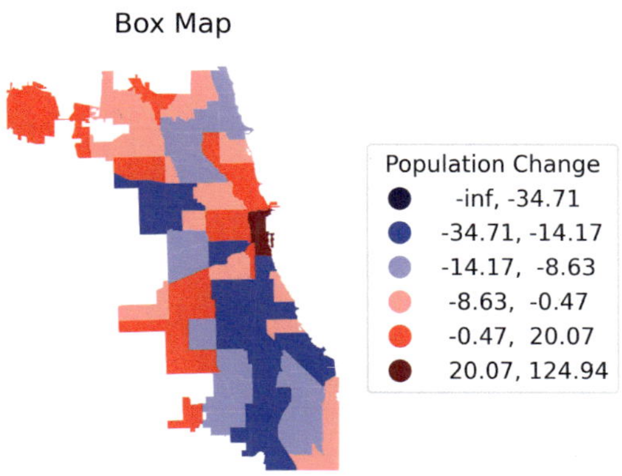

Figure 2.11: Box map with seismic color map

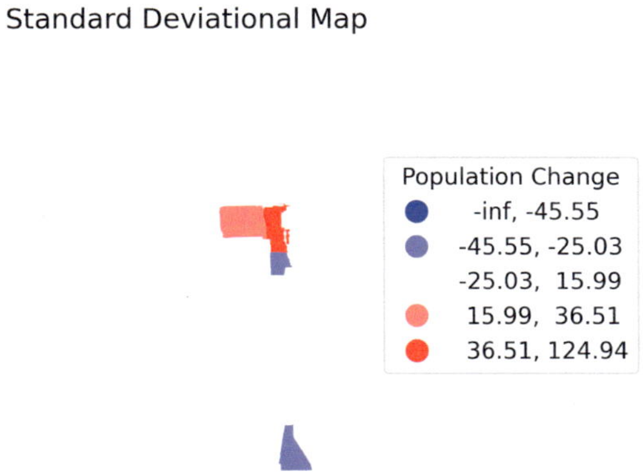

Figure 2.12: Standard deviational map without area outlines

```
    legend = True,
    legend_kwds={"loc":"center left","bbox_to_anchor":(1,0.5),
                 "title": "Population Change"}
)
ax.set_title("Box Map")
ax.set_axis_off()
```

However, notice what happens when this is applied to the standard deviational map with `cmap = bwr` and the conventional classification (i.e., no `anchor` argument).

The corresponding Figure 2.12 is not exactly what we had in mind. Other than the classification being strange, the community areas cannot be distinguished. The reason is that there is no borderline specified for the map in the code below.

```
ax = chi_comm.plot(
    column = plotvar,
    scheme = 'StdMean',
    cmap = 'bwr',
    legend = True,
    legend_kwds = {"loc": "center left", "bbox_to_anchor": (1,0.5),
                  "title": "Population Change"}
)
ax.set_title("Standard Deviational Map")
ax.set_axis_off()
```

2.3.3 Areal Outlines

As mentioned, the full range of `matplotlib` customizations is available to manipulate legends, colors and placement. For our purposes, one more map-specific element is of interest. As seen in the previous examples, the border between polygons is not visible.

This can be fixed by setting the `edgecolor` and associated `linewidth` attributes. For example, with `edgecolor = "Black"` and `linewidth = 0.2`.

With the code below, which yields Figure 2.13, the standard deviational map becomes somewhat more informative.

```
ax = chi_comm.plot(
    column = plotvar,
    scheme = 'StdMean',
    cmap = 'bwr',
    edgecolor = "Black",
    linewidth = 0.2,
    legend = True,
    legend_kwds = {"loc": "center left", "bbox_to_anchor": (1,0.5),
                  "title": "Population Change"}
)
ax.set_title("Standard Deviational Map")
ax.set_axis_off()
```

2.3.4 Saving the Map to a File

So far, the maps are generated in the interface, but are not separately available. To save a specific map to a file, the `matplotlib.pyplot.savefig` command is used (in our examples, abbreviated to `plt.savefig`).

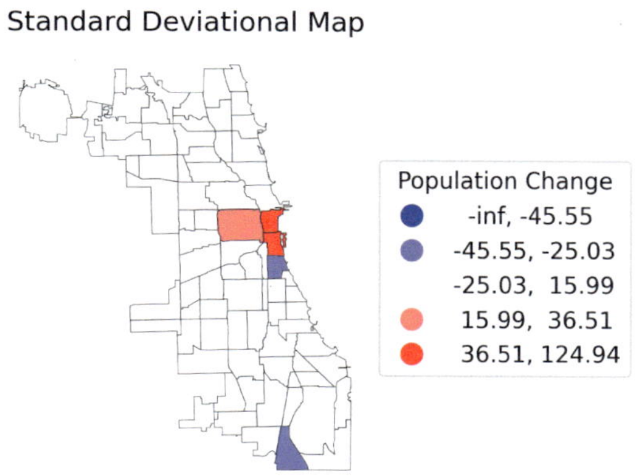

Figure 2.13: Standard deviational map with edgecolor

For example, to save the standard deviational map (or any other map) to a png format file, only the filename needs to be specified as an argument to `plt.savefig`. Optionally, to get higher quality figures, the number of dots per inch can be set by means of `dpi`.

This is illustrated in the code below for the standard deviational map where a border line is obtained as before by setting the thickness with `linewidth = 0.2`. The quality is set to `dpi = 600`.

The file will typically be in the current working directory, unless a full path is passed to the `savefig` function. In our example, the generated map in the file will be identical to Figure 2.14 on page 22.

```
ax = chi_comm.plot(
    column = plotvar,
    scheme = 'StdMean',
    classification_kwds = {'anchor': True},
    cmap = 'bwr',
    edgecolor = "Black",
    linewidth = 0.2,
    legend = True,
    legend_kwds = {"loc": "center left", "bbox_to_anchor": (1,0.5),
                   "title": "Population Change"}
)

ax.set_title("Standard Deviational Map")
ax.set_axis_off()
plt.savefig("popchange_stdmean.png", dpi = 600)
```

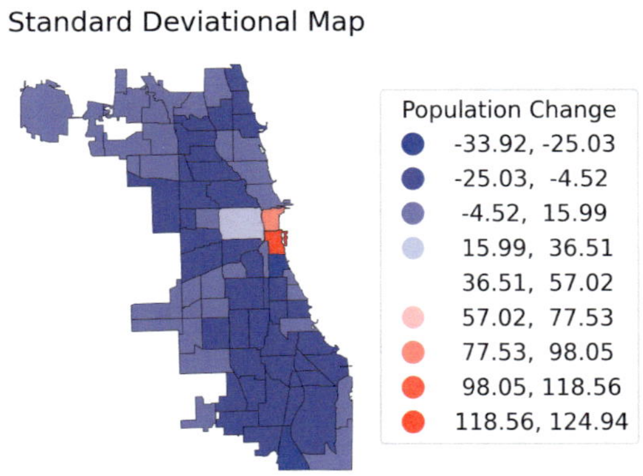

Figure 2.14: Saving the map to a file

2.4 Mapping Polygon Boundaries

A map with just the community area borders is obtained with the `boundary.plot` command, where the color of the border line is controlled by `edgecolor` and the line thickness by `linewidth`, as in the code below.

```
ax = chi_comm.boundary.plot(
    edgecolor = "Black",
    linewidth = 0.2,
)
ax.set_title("Community Area Boundaries")
ax.set_axis_off()
```

The map is as in Figure 2.15.

2.5 Mapping Point Data

So far, in this example, we used a shape file containing polygon or areal spatial data. Alternatively, we can plot point data, indexpoint layer which can be loaded the same way as before from a shape file, or from a spreadsheet as a .CSV file.

In the following examples, we will use the location of liquor stores in Chicago, IL, contained in the `point_df` GeoDataFrame we loaded in Section 2.1.2.

As before, a simple visualization of the data can be obtained with the `.plot` function. Here, we add two optional arguments: `markersize = 4` and `color = 'blue'`, which control the size of the dots on the map and their color.

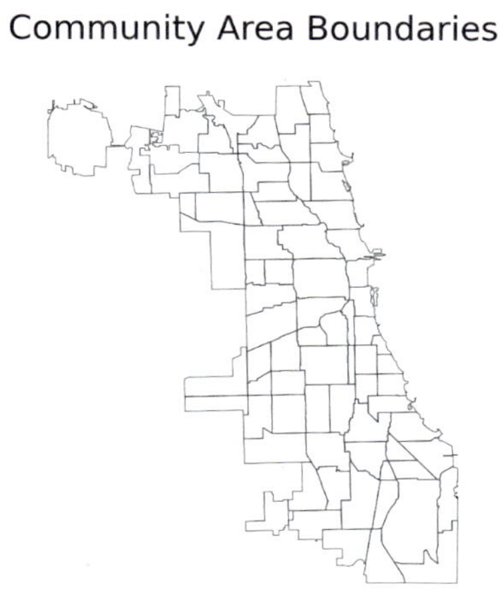

Figure 2.15: Boundary plot

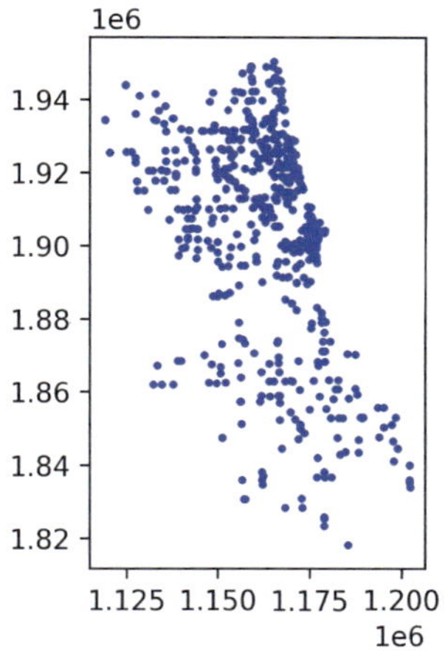

Figure 2.16: Simple plot of point data

```
point_df.plot(markersize = 4, color = 'blue')
```

The result is the simple point plot in Figure 2.16.

2.5.1 Points with Polygons

The simple visualization of points in space lacks context and is often not that meaningful. One typically wants to show the points on a background of polygons, such as the Chicago community areas in this example. By using the ax parameter, it becomes straightforward to combine different graphs in one figure, in this case a point map and a polygon map.

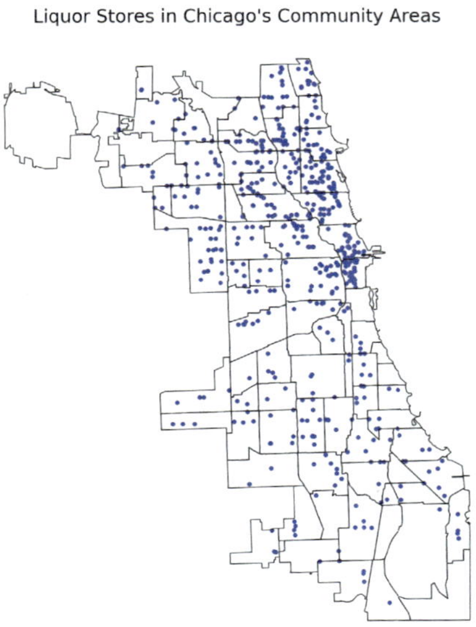

Figure 2.17: Multilayer map

However, an important consideration is to make sure the two layers are in the same projection. As it turns out, in our example, they are not. In fact, the community areas are not projected (latitude-longitude decimal degrees), but the point data have a projection of UTM zone 16N.

Whereas an in-depth discussion of projections is well beyond our scope (for specifics, see Chapter 3 of the *GeoDa Explore Book*), it is useful to know that `geopandas` contains a simple way to synchronize the projections of two layers in the form of `to_crs`. In our example, we set the projection of the community areas to that of the point layer by means of `chi_comm.to_crs(point_df.crs)`.

To overlay the points on the community areas, we can use the `ax` parameter in the `plot()` function to specify the same axes for both plots. We specify the size of the figure and then apply the `plot` function to the polygon layer (`chi_comm`) and the point layer (`point_df`) in turn. We just draw the outlines for the polygon map (as illustrated above) with a customized `linewidth` and use `markersize` and `color` for the points. indexcolor

The result of the code below is a map of the liquor locations liquor store locations overlayed on the community area outlines, shown in Figure 2.17.

```
# Converting the layers to the same projection (CRS)
chi_comm = chi_comm.to_crs(point_df.crs)


# Plotting the figure with both layers
```

```
fig, ax = plt.subplots(figsize = (6, 8))
chi_comm.boundary.plot(ax = ax, edgecolor = 'black', linewidth = 0.5)
point_df.plot(ax = ax, markersize = 4, color = 'blue')
ax.set_title("Liquor Stores in Chicago's Community Areas")
ax.set_axis_off()
plt.show()
```

2.6 Practice

Use your own data set or one of the GeoDa Center or PySAL sample data sets to load a spatial data frame and experiment with various map types, color schemes and other customizations. Save each map to a file for inclusion in papers, reports, etc.

3 Multivariate Local Spatial Clusters

The detection of clusters using local indicators of spatial autocorrelation (LISA) statistics is arguably one of the most common applications of spatial data exploration. As argued in Chapter 18 of the *GeoDa Explore Book*, extending the familiar univariate measures like the Local Moran statistic to the multivariate domain is fraught with difficulties. The local neighbor match test, outlined in Anselin and Li (2020) and illustrated in Chapter 18 of the *GeoDa Explore Book*, is a new approach to visualize and quantify the trade-off between geographical and attribute similarity. The basic idea is to assess the extent of overlap between k-nearest neighbors in geographical space and k-nearest neighbors in multi-attribute space. This is illustrated with functionality from the specialized `pygeoda` package.

The local neighbor match test will be illustrated using the **Chi-SDOH** sample data set.

In addition to the `pygeoda` package mentioned, we will also need the familiar `geopandas`, `numpy` and `matplotlib.pyplot` packages, as well as `spatial-cluster-helper` to check on the presence of the sample data.

> Required Packages
>
> geopandas, numpy, matplotlib.pyplot, pygeoda, spatial-cluster-helper

> Required Data Sets
>
> Chi-SDOH

3.1 Preliminaries

3.1.1 Import Required Modules

We import the relevant modules.

```
import geopandas as gpd
import numpy as np
import matplotlib.pyplot as plt
import pygeoda
from spatial_cluster_helper import ensure_datasets
```

3.1.2 Load Data

We use the same approach as in the previous Chapter and assume that the data are contained in a `./datasets/` directory off the main directory. We use `ensure_datasets` to load the sample data if not already present.

We read the `Chi-SDOH.shp` shape file into the `chi_sdoh` GeoDataFrame and provide a quick check of its contents.

```
# Setting data folder:
#path = "/your/path/to/data/"
path = "./datasets/"
# Select the Chicago census tract data:
shpfile = "Chi-SDOH/Chi-SDOH.shp"
# Load the data:
ensure_datasets(shpfile, folder_path = path)
chi_sdoh = gpd.read_file(path + shpfile)
print(chi_sdoh.shape)
print(chi_sdoh.head(3))
```

```
(791, 56)
   OBJECTID   Shape_Leng    Shape_Area  TRACTCE10       geoid10  commarea
0         1  22777.477721  2.119089e+07   842400.0  1.703184e+10      44.0
1         2  16035.054986  8.947394e+06   840300.0  1.703184e+10      59.0
2         3  15186.400644  1.230614e+07   841100.0  1.703184e+10      34.0

   ChldPvt14  EP_CROWD  EP_UNINSUR  EP_MINRTY  ...  ForclRt  EP_MUNIT
0       30.2       2.0        18.6      100.0  ...      0.0         6
1       38.9       4.8        25.2       85.9  ...      0.0         2
2       40.4       4.9        32.1       95.6  ...      0.0        42

   EP_GROUPQ  SchHP_Mi  BrownF_Mi  card  cpval      COORD_X      COORD_Y
0        0.0  0.323962   0.825032   0.0    0.0  1176.183467  1849.533205
1        0.0  2.913039   0.833580   0.0    0.0  1161.787888  1882.078567
2        0.1  1.534987   0.245875   0.0    0.0  1174.481923  1889.069999
```

```
                                            geometry
0  POLYGON ((1177796.742 1847712.428, 1177805.261...
1  POLYGON ((1163591.927 1881471.238, 1163525.437...
2  POLYGON ((1176041.55 1889791.988, 1176042.377 ...

[3 rows x 56 columns]
```

3.1.3 Variables

Following our standard practice, we specify the variable names to be used in the neighbor match test here.

For the neighbor match test example, we will use the percentage children in poverty in 2014 (`ChldPvt14`), a crowded housing index (`EP_CROWD`), and the percentage without health insurance (`EP_UNINSUR`). These are specified in the list `nbrvars`.

```
# Variables for neighbor match test:
nbrvars = ['ChldPvt14','EP_CROWD','EP_UNINSUR']
```

3.2 Local Neighbor Match Test

The *Local Neighbor Match Test* is based on an intersection operation between two k-nearest neighbor weights matrices. One matrix is derived from the distances in multi-attribute space, the other using geographical distance. With the intersection in hand, the probability that an overlap occurs between the two neighbor sets can be quantified. This corresponds to the probability of drawing v common neighbors from the k out of $n - 1 - k$ possible choices as neighbors, a straightforward combinatorial calculation.

Specifically, the probability of v shared neighbors out of k is:

$p = C(k, v).C(N - k, k - v)/C(N, k),$

where $N = n - 1$ (one less than the number of observations), k is the number of nearest neighbors considered in the connectivity graphs, v is the number of neighbors in common, and C is the combinatorial operator. Details can be found in Chapter 18 of the *GeoDa Explore Book*.

The Local Neighbor Match Test is carried out by means of the `neighbor_match_test` function from `pygeoda`.

3.2.1 pygeoda Logic

The pygeoda package forms an interface between Python and a subset of the C++ code in GeoDa, contained in the libgeoda library. It implements basic data extraction functions, as well as the construction of spatial weights , computation of local spatial autocorrelation statistics and spatial clustering . The full API can be found at https://geodacenter.github.io/pygeoda/api.html.

pygeoda uses its own internal data structure, so before any analysis can be carried out, an existing DataFrame or GeoDataFrame must be loaded by means of the pygeoda.open command. After this step, variables are extracted in the same manner as for data frames, i.e., by specifying the variable name in quotes or as a list of quoted variable names. In our example, this will be the nbrvars list created in Section 3.1.3.

The return object of a pygeoda analysis is an instance of a specialized class, with a range of properties accessible as attributes. It is important to check the API for the specific structure in each function. The spatial_cluster_helper module used to check on the data set also contains a set of helper functions to simplify the extraction of results from the pygeoda return object. However, for the neighbor_match_test, this is not needed.

3.2.2 neighbor_match_test Function

The pygeoda.neighbor_match_test function has three *required* arguments:

- geoda_obj (geoda): An instance of geoda class
- data (list or dataframe): A list of numeric vectors of selected variable or a data frame of selected variables
- k (int): A positive integer as the number of k-nearest neighbors.

In our example, the geoda_obj chi_sdoh_g will be created from the chi_sdoh GeoDataFrame using the open function, which converts it to a geoda class object. The list of variables is in nbrvars. The value of k is set to 12.

Additional optional arguments that can be provided to the function are:

- scale_method (str, optional): One of the scaling methods ('raw', 'standardize', 'demean', 'mad', 'range_standardize', 'range_adjust') to apply on input data. Default is 'standardize' (Z-score normalization).
- distance_method (str, optional): The type of distance metric used to measure the distance between input data. Options are ('euclidean', 'manhattan'). Default is 'euclidean'.
- power (float, optional): The power used in an inverse distance calculation, default is 1.0.

- `is_inverse` (bool, optional): False (default) or True, apply inverse on distance value.
- `is_arc` (bool, optional): False (default) or True, compute arc distance between two observations.
- `is_mile` (bool, optional) True (default) or False, distance units used.

The function returns a *dictionary* with two keys : `Cardinality` and `Probability`. The cardinalities indicate for each location how many neighbors the two weights matrices have in common, whereas the probability shows the associated p-value. Different p-value cut-offs can be employed to select the significant locations, i.e., where the probability of a given number of common neighbors falls below the chosen p.

The example below consists of four steps:

- create the geoda data object `chi_sdoh_g`
- extract the variables into `data`
- return the result object to `nmt`
- print the `keys` of the dictionary

```
chi_sdoh_g = pygeoda.open(chi_sdoh)
data = chi_sdoh_g[nbrvars]
nmt = pygeoda.neighbor_match_test(chi_sdoh_g, data, 12)
print(nmt.keys())
```

```
dict_keys(['Cardinality', 'Probability'])
```

3.2.3 Neighbor Cardinality Map

We can now use `matplotlib` to create a `categorical` map to plot the neighbor cardinalities for each location. First, we need to add the `Cardinality` values to the existing `chi_sdoh` GeoDataFrame, to which we can then apply the `plot` functionality.

In the code below, we use the commands covered in Chapter 2 to set the `column` to `Cardinality`, specify the map type as `categorical`, and choose a color map, edgecolor and linewidth.

```
chi_sdoh['Cardinality'] = nmt['Cardinality']

fig, ax = plt.subplots(figsize = (6, 6))

chi_sdoh.plot(ax = ax,
              column = 'Cardinality',
```

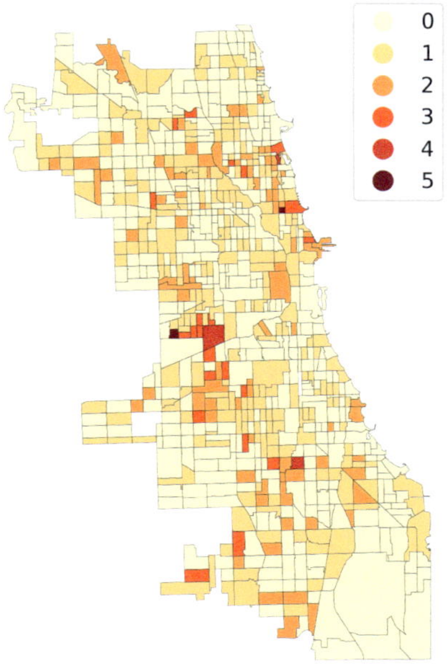

Figure 3.1: Neighbor cardinality map

```
            legend = True,
            categorical = True,
            cmap = 'YlOrRd',
            edgecolor = 'black',
            linewidth = 0.1)

ax.set_axis_off()
plt.show()
```

The result is shown in Figure 3.1. The matches range from 1 to 5 (out of a possible 12). There are three locations with four matches and two locations with five matches. Five matches is extremely rare, with a p-value less than 0.0000001. Four matches has a p-value less than 0.000014. These suggest locations of *multivariate local spatial clusters*.

3.3 Practice

Use your own data set or one of the GeoDa Center or PySAL sample data sets to load a multivariate data file. Compute the Local Neighbor Match Test and assess the impact of varying number of neighbors.

4 Density Based Clustering

Density-based cluster methods are designed to identify meaningful groupings in point data. `GeoDa` supports three familiar methods: DBSCAN, DBSCAN* and HDBSCAN . They are discussed in Chapter 20 of the *GeoDa Explore Book*. DBSCAN and HDBSCAN are implemented in the `sklearn.cluster` package, but not DBSCAN*.

To illustrate these methods, we follow Chapter 20 of the *GeoDa Explore Book* and use the locations of Italian community banks contained in the **italy_banks** sample data set.

In addition to the `sklearn.cluster` package mentioned, we will also need the familiar `geopandas` and `numpy` packages. As before, we will be using specialized helper functions developed to support the illustration and visualization of spatial clusters, contained in the `spatial-cluster-helper` package.

> Required Packages
>
> geopandas, numpy, sklearn.cluster, spatial-cluster-helper

> Required Data Sets
>
> italy_banks

4.1 Preliminaries

4.1.1 Import Required Modules

We import the relevant modules as mentioned above. Specifically, from `sklearn.cluster`, we import `DBSCAN` and `HDBSCAN`, and from `spatial_cluster_helper`, we import `ensure_datasets`, `cluster_stats` and `cluster_map`.

```
import geopandas as gpd
import numpy as np
from sklearn.cluster import DBSCAN, HDBSCAN
```

```
from spatial_cluster_helper import ensure_datasets,\
                                   cluster_stats, cluster_map
```

4.1.2 Load Data

We continue to use the same approach as before and assume that the data are contained in a `./datasets/` directory off the main directory. We use `ensure_datasets` to check on the presence of the data and then read the `italy_banks.shp` shape file into `dfs`.

```
# Setting data folder:
#path = "/your/path/to/data/"
path = "./datasets/"
# Select the Italy community banks point data:
shpfile = "italy_banks/italy_banks.shp"
# Load the data:
ensure_datasets(shpfile, folder_path = path)
dfs = gpd.read_file(path + shpfile)
print(dfs.shape)
print(dfs.head(3))
```

```
(261, 102)
   idd                                           BankName     City   latitud
0  1.0  Banca di Andria di Credito Cooperativo SocietÃ...   ANDRIA  41.226694
1  8.0  Banca di Credito Cooperativo di Napoli-BCC di ...  NAPLES  40.841020
2  9.0  Banca Adria Credito Cooperativo del Delta s.c....    ADRIA  45.052882

   longitud       COORD_X          XKM       COORD_Y          YKM   ID  ...
0  16.302685  1.112303e+06  1112.303366  4.589794e+06  4589.793823  1.0  ...
1  14.250822  9.427720e+05   942.771983  4.534476e+06  4534.475758  8.0  ...
2  12.056720  7.407057e+05   740.705695  4.993464e+06  4993.464408  9.0  ...

    EXPE_16   EXPE_17   SERV_11   SERV_12   SERV_13   SERV_14   SERV_15
0  0.027966  0.025114  0.793877  0.775691  0.745046  0.630469  0.611941
1  0.023624  0.018840  0.770019  0.562623  0.540712  0.522125  0.601549
2  0.013770  0.012745  0.790542  0.626628  0.515733  0.358735  0.483700

    SERV_16   SERV_17                          geometry
0  0.640208  0.666425  POINT (1112303.366 4589793.823)
1  0.502599  0.625220   POINT (942771.983 4534475.758)
2  0.567946  0.608880   POINT (740705.695 4993464.408)

[3 rows x 102 columns]
```

4.1.3 Variables

The density-based cluster methods use the point coordinates . In the **italy_banks** sample data set, with projected coordinates, these are converted to kilometers in the variables `XKM` and `YKM` for easier interpretation (the original coordinates are in meters). The scikit-learn functions require these as a numpy input array. In order to keep the code generic, we specify `coords_array` here. Using `numpy.vstack`, we create a 2 by n array, which we subsequently transpose (`T`) to get the input as a n by 2 array.

```
coords_array = np.vstack([dfs["XKM"], dfs["YKM"]]).T
print(coords_array[:3])
```

```
[[1112.30336594 4589.79382325]
 [ 942.77198327 4534.47575791]
 [ 740.70569453 4993.46440835]]
```

4.2 A Quick Introduction to scikit-learn

The most comprehensive Python library for classical machine learning is scikit-learn, imported as `sklearn`. Among its extensive functionality, it supports many methods for so-called *unsupervised learning*, which includes a wide range of clustering techniques. In this Companion, we will be using scikit-learn for all classic non-spatial clustering methods. The complete user guide for scikit-learn can be found at https://scikit-learn.org/stable/user_guide.html.

As it turns out, most spatially constrained clustering methods are currently not included in scikit-learn. For the latter methods, we will continue to rely on `pygeoda`, which supports a subset of the clustering functionality in GeoDa desktop.

Scikit-learn can be a bit overwhelming at first. Also, the interface may seem a bit strange, but it is fully consistent throughout (not a mean feat when supporting so many different methods). Once the basic principles become more familiar, the elegance of the framework becomes obvious. For our purposes, we can get away with only some basic knowledge.

The distinguishing characteristic of the scikit-learn design is that it is fully object oriented. Each type of clustering is represented by a class, which needs to be instantiated, i.e., a specific object of that class is generated. The class supports a range of methods and creates attributes. The main method, common to all classes in scikit-learn, is `fit`. In essence, this applies the clustering algorithm. The results are available as attributes of the object. For example, for all the clustering methods considered in scikit-learn, this is the attribute `labels_` (don't forget the underline), a simple numpy array with a label for each observation. It is then up to you to translate this into meaningful information, such as a cluster map. It is also important to remember that all input to scikit-learn consists of numpy arrays, **not** pandas DataFrames. This typically requires some additional work up front to get the data into the proper format.

Later, we will also see how `sklearn.preprocessing` supports a range of data transformations, including standardization. However, here we only consider clustering of point data, which should **not** be standardized. This is because standardization yields new coordinates with the same unit variance in the vertical and horizontal dimension. Unless the original dimensions are square, this will distort the distances. For example, in Italy, which has a much longer vertical dimension than horizontal dimension, distances computed from standardized coordinates will tend to compress vertical separation. This should be avoided, hence the use of coordinates in their original scale.

We return to the topic of standardization in Chapter 5.

4.3 DBSCAN

The principles of density-based clustering were formulated in the DBSCAN algorithm, originally described in Ester et al. (1996) and Sander et al. (1998), and more recently elaborated upon in Gan and Tao (2017) and Schubert et al. (2017). The method is discussed in detail in Chapter 20 of the *GeoDa Explore Book*.

The essence of the algorithm is to identify high-density subsets of the data, as an application of so-called *bump hunting*. This results in a classification of points as *core*, *border* and *noise* points, depending on how far they are from each other and how many points are contained within a critical distance (the *density*). These two concepts are critical parameters for the method.

The critical distance band is referred to as *Epsilon distance*. It plays a role similar to what the bandwidth achieves in a uniform kernel function and defines the area within which the frequency of points will be assessed.

On the other hand, the *minimum points* criterion corresponds to the smallest number of points contained within the critical distance band to consider the spatial distribution to be *dense*. Note that in DBSCAN, the center point (around which the Epsilon distance is considered) is part of the minimum points. In other words, a minimum points criterion of 4 implies 3 nearest neighbors.

In our illustration, we will use the `DBSCAN` functionality from `sklearn.cluster`. Full details can be found at https://scikit-learn.org/stable/modules/clustering.html#dbscan.

4.3.1 Data Input

As mentioned, scikit-learn expects its input to consist of numpy arrays. In Section 4.1.3, we created `coords_array` as a n by 2 array, which we will use as the input to the `fit` method of `DBSCAN`.

4.3.2 Cluster Instance

Before we can carry out any analysis, we must create an instance of an object of the class `DBSCAN`. This takes two *required* arguments, `eps`, the *Epsilon distance*, and `min_samples`, the minimum number of points. In our example, matching the illustration of DBSCAN in the *GeoDa Explore Book*, we set `eps = 124.66` and `min_samples = 4` and create the object `db_results`. The result is an instance of the class DBSCAN, as revealed by a `type` command. In a typical application, the creation of the object and the application of the `fit` method can be chained, but we keep them separate for now.

```
db_results = DBSCAN(eps = 124.66, min_samples = 4)
print(type(db_results))
```

```
<class 'sklearn.cluster._dbscan.DBSCAN'>
```

4.3.3 Cluster `fit` Method

So far, we don't have any actual results. These are obtained by applying the `fit` method to the cluster object. The `fit` method takes the numpy array with the x and y coordinates as input. After applying this method, a large number of attributes will be included in the cluster object. At this point, our main interest is in the attribute `labels_`, which contains the clustering designation of each of the community bank locations. As in Chapter 20 of the *GeoDa Explore Book*, this example does not contain any **noise** points (those would be labeled as -1). We only have labels 0 and 1, respectively with 242 and 19 members.

We use the `numpy unique` function to find the (unique) cluster labels and the respective size of the associated clusters.

```
db_results = db_results.fit(coords_array)
# at this point the cluster object contains many methods and attributes
print(dir(db_results))
# the cluster labels
print(type(db_results.labels_))
# a brief summary of the cluster categories
```

```
totclust,clustcount = np.unique(db_results.labels_, return_counts = True)
print(totclust)
print("number of different cluster categories (noise points included): ",
      len(totclust))
print("cluster member size: ", clustcount)
```

```
['__annotations__', '__class__', '__delattr__', '__dict__',
'__dir__',  ...,
'core_sample_indices_', 'eps', 'fit', 'fit_predict',
'get_metadata_routing', 'get_params', 'labels_', 'leaf_size',
'metric', 'metric_params', 'min_samples', 'n_features_in_',
'n_jobs', 'p', 'set_fit_request', 'set_params']
<class 'numpy.ndarray'>
[0 1]
number of different cluster categories (noise points included):  2
cluster member size:  [242  19]
```

4.3.4 Cluster Statistics

It would be useful to create a small DataFrame that lists the labels for each cluster and the number of observations that belong to them. To accomplish this, we use the `cluster_stats` helper function from the `spatial_cluster_helper` module. We will reuse this for all future cluster methods, since scikit-learn will consistently put the cluster labels in the `labels_` attribute (all scikit-learn computed results are labeled with a trailing underline character).

We can now apply `cluster_stats` to the output of our DBSCAN DBSCAN application. The only input is the array with cluster labels. The results shows the distribution of the cluster sizes for clusters 0 and 1. Note that unlike what holds for the `GeoDa` clustering methods, the cluster labels are given in no particular order (in `GeoDa`, they are sorted by size).

```
c_stats = cluster_stats(db_results.labels_)
```

Labels	Cardinality
0	242
1	19

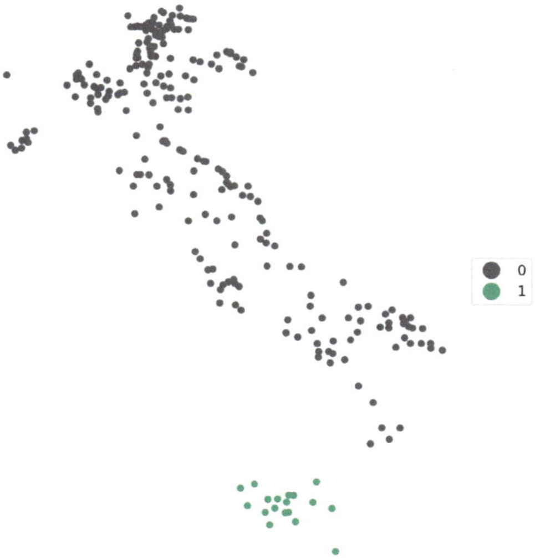

Figure 4.1: DBScan cluster map

4.3.5 Cluster Map

The results of a cluster exercise are best visualized in a so-called cluster map. Again, to save us time later, we use the `cluster_map` helper function to create a categorical point map for the cluster labels.

The arguments to `cluster_map` are the target layer that will show the label categories (in this case, the point layer contained in `dfs`), the array with cluster labels (`labels_`), an optional title, an optional `baselayer` (useful to provide context to a categorical point map), and an optional color map (`cmap`)

In our example, we use `cmap = 'Dark2_r'`. We have no base layer. Note that `cluster_map` assumes that the point and area layers are in the same projection (there is no check), which should be ensured by reprojection, if necessary, see Chapter 2.

The result of the call below is shown in Figure 4.1.

```
cluster_map(dfs, db_results.labels_, title="",
            cmap='Dark2_r', legend_fontsize=8)
```

4.3.6 Sensitivity Analysis

The results of DBSCAN are very sensitive to the choice of the parameters `eps` and `min_samples`. When changing either one of these parameters in the DBSCAN function, the resulting clusters are typically affected.

In the code below, we set `eps = 50` and `min_samples = 10` (following the example in Chapter 20 of the *GeoDa Explore Book*). Note how we now combine the instantiation of the DBSCAN class with the `fit` method in one line.

The result is quite different, with seven clusters identified, as well as 70 noise points, as shown by the cluster statistics and visualized in Figure 4.2.

```
db_results = DBSCAN(eps = 50, min_samples = 10).fit(coords_array)
c_stats = cluster_stats(db_results.labels_)
```

Labels	Cardinality
-1	70
0	19
1	110
2	14
3	11
4	16
5	10
6	11

```
cluster_map(dfs, db_results.labels_, title="", cmap='Dark2_r',
            legend_fontsize=8)
```

4.4 HDBSCAN

The DBSCAN algorithm lacks some flexibility due to the use of the same critical distance for all points. This turns out to be problematic when the density of the points is very uneven. To remedy this issue, the DBSCAN* method introduced the concepts of *core distance* and *mutual reachability distance*. The core distance is the k-nearest neighbor distance for each point. The inverse of this concept ($\lambda = 1/d_{core}$) corresponds with the notion of *density*. The mutual reachability distance is a transformation of these core distances that pushes points in low-density regions further away. More specifically, the mutual reachability distance between points A and B is defined as:

$$d_{mr}(A, B) = max[d_{core}(A), d_{core}(B), d(AB)].$$

In DBSCAN, the mutual reachability distance takes on the role of the critical distance. DBSCAN* is outlined in detail in Chapter 20 of the *GeoDa Explore Book*, but is currently not supported by `sklearn`.

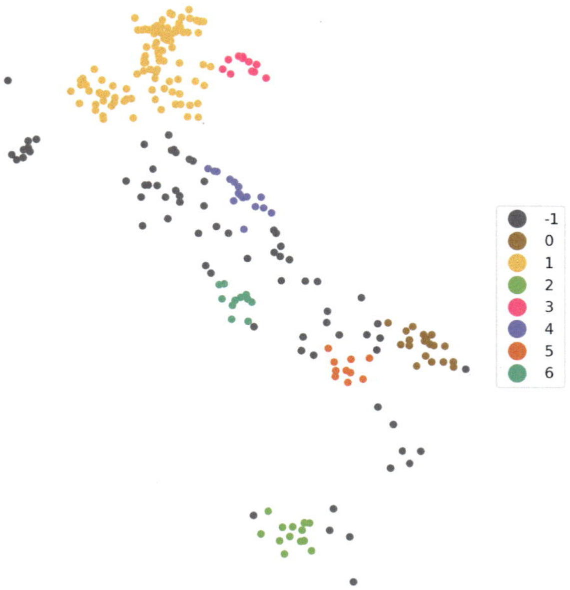

Figure 4.2: DBScan cluster map (sensitivity analysis)

A further refinement was implemented in HDBSCAN, where a flexible distance cut-off was introduced. As a result, only the minimum points criterion must be specified. The distance cut-off is based on a concept of *persistence*, an indication of the stability of each potential cluster. HDBSCAN was originally proposed by Campello, Moulavi, and Sander (2013) and more recently elaborated upon by Campello et al. (2015) and McInnes and Healy (2017). Extensive technical detail and a toy example are given in Chapter 20 of the *GeoDa Explore Book*.

The algorithm is implemented in the `HDBSCAN` class of `sklearn.cluster` (see https://scikit-learn.org/stable/modules/generated/sklearn.cluster.HDBSCAN.html). To instantiate an object of this class, the only required argument is the `min_cluster_size` argument, the minimum number of points in a cluster neighborhood. As before, we apply the `fit` method with as argument the numpy array of point coordinates. The cluster labels are again contained in the `labels_` attribute.

We illustrate this using `min_cluster_size = 10`. We combine the class instantiation and `fit` method in one line and reuse our `cluster_stats` and `cluster_map` functions to summarize the results.

As shown by the cluster cardinalities, the results are quite reasonable, yielding seven clusters with sizes ranging from 10 to 67, as well as 69 noise points. As in the DBSCAN case, some experimentation with different parameter settings is highly recommended.

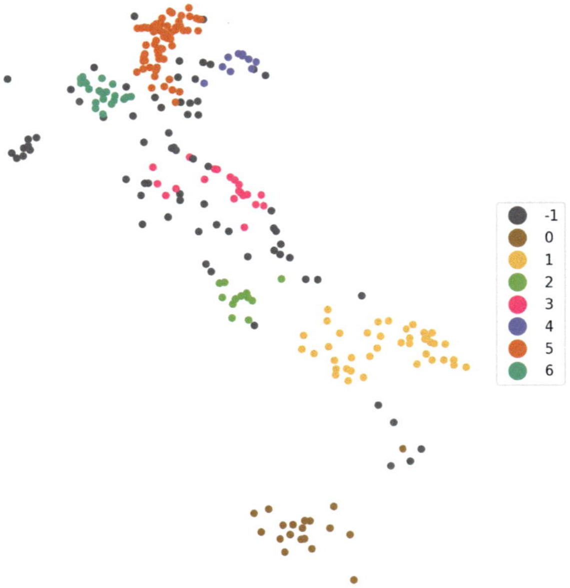

Figure 4.3: HDBSCAN cluster map

```
hdb_results = HDBSCAN(min_cluster_size = 10).fit(coords_array)
c_stats = cluster_stats(hdb_results.labels_)
```

Labels	Cardinality
-1	69
0	20
1	41
2	12
3	20
4	10
5	67
6	22

The cluster map shows more interesting patterns as well, illustrated in Figure 4.3.

```
cluster_map(dfs, hdb_results.labels_, title="", cmap='Dark2_r',
            legend_fontsize=8)
```

4.5 Practice

Use your own data set or one of the GeoDa Center or PySAL sample data sets to load a point data file. Compare the results between DBSCAN and HDBSCAN, and assess the impact of changing the relevant parameters.

5 Principal Component Analysis

In this Chapter, we consider Principal Component Analysis (PCA), a core method of both multivariate statistics and machine learning, used for dimension reduction. Dimension reduction is particularly relevant in situations where many variables are available that are highly intercorrelated. In essence, the original variables are replaced by a smaller number of proxies that represent them well in terms of their statistical properties. PCA is discussed in detail in Chapter 2 of the *GeoDa Cluster Book*.

To illustrate this method, we will again use the **italy_banks** sample data set.

Principal component analysis is implemented in `sklearn.decomposition`. The required variable standardization is contained in `sklearn.preprocessing`. In addition to the usual `numpy`, `pandas`, `geopandas` and `matplotlib.pyplot` requirements, we will also use `matplotlib.lines`, as well as `spatial-cluster-helper` to check on the data. Finally, we implement some local spatial autocorrelation analysis by means of `pygeoda`.

> Required Packages
>
> numpy, pandas, geopandas, matplotlib.pyplot, matplotlib.lines, sklearn.decomposition, sklearn.preprocessing, spatial-cluster-helper, pygeoda

> Required Data Sets
>
> italy_banks

5.1 Preliminaries

5.1.1 Import Required Modules

```
import numpy as np
import pandas as pd
import geopandas as gpd
import matplotlib.pyplot as plt
```

```
import matplotlib.lines as pltlines
from sklearn.preprocessing import StandardScaler
from sklearn.decomposition import PCA
from spatial_cluster_helper import ensure_datasets
import pygeoda
```

5.1.2 Load Data

We follow the usual practice of setting a path (if needed), and reading the data from the Italian banks shape file (`italy_banks.shp`) into a GeoDataFrame (`dfs`). We also carry out a quick check of its contents using `head`. The data set has 261 point locations and 102 variables in UTM Zone 32 projection. The output is the same as in the previous Chapter and will not be repeated here.

```
# Setting data folder:
#path = "/your/path/to/data/"
path = "./datasets/"
# Select the Italy community banks point data:
shpfile = "italy_banks/italy_banks.shp"
# Load the data:
ensure_datasets(shpfile, folder_path = path)
dfs = gpd.read_file(path + shpfile)
print(dfs.shape)
print(dfs.head(3))
```

5.1.3 Variables

We follow the example in Chapter 2 of the *GeoDa Cluster Book* and select ten variables for 2013 from the Italian banks sample data set, listed in Table 5.1.

The variables are stored in the `varlist` list for future use. If you want to use a different set of variables, only `varlist` needs to be updated.

```
varlist = ['CAPRAT13', 'Z_13', 'LIQASS_13', 'NPL_13', 'LLP_13',
           'INTR_13', 'DEPO_13', 'EQLN_13', 'SERV_13', 'EXPE_13']
```

5.1.3.1 Descriptive statistics

We create a subset of our original data set with just the selected variables as `data_pca`. Correlations among these variables are computed by applying the `corr` method to this

Table 5.1: PCA Variables

Column Name	Variable Description
CAPRAT13	Ratio of capital over risk-weighted assets
Z_13	Z-score of return on assets (ROA) + leverage over the standard deviation of ROA
LIQASS_13	Ratio of liquid assets over total assets
NPL_13	Ratio of non-performing loans over total loans
LLP_13	Ratio of loan loss provision over customer loans
INTR_13	Ratio of interest expense over total funds
DEPO_13	Ratio of total deposits over total assets
EQLN_13	Ratio of total equity over customer loans
SERV_13	Ratio of net interest income over total operating revenues
EXPE_13	Ratio of operating expenses over total assets

Table 5.2: Correlations Among Selected Variables

	CAPRAT	Z	LIQASS	NPL	LLP	INTR	DEPO	EQLN	SERV	EXPE
CAPRAT	1.00	-0.03	0.21	-0.08	-0.10	-0.39	0.18	0.87	0.32	0.14
Z	-0.03	1.00	-0.08	-0.28	-0.16	-0.02	-0.15	-0.02	-0.04	-0.14
LIQASS	0.21	-0.08	1.00	-0.00	-0.05	-0.14	0.23	0.09	0.01	0.18
NPL	-0.08	-0.28	-0.00	1.00	0.64	0.33	-0.09	-0.10	-0.20	0.15
LLP	-0.10	-0.16	-0.05	0.64	1.00	0.41	-0.19	-0.14	-0.39	-0.04
INTR	-0.39	-0.02	-0.14	0.33	0.41	1.00	-0.43	-0.48	-0.40	-0.18
DEPO	0.18	-0.15	0.23	-0.09	-0.19	-0.43	1.00	0.18	0.17	0.16
EQLN	0.87	-0.02	0.09	-0.10	-0.14	-0.48	0.18	1.00	0.39	0.12
SERV	0.32	-0.04	0.01	-0.20	-0.39	-0.40	0.17	0.39	1.00	0.07
EXPE	0.14	-0.14	0.18	0.15	-0.04	-0.18	0.16	0.12	0.07	1.00

data frame. The results, rounded to two decimals, are shown in Table 5.2 (the year subscript is dropped for simplicity).

```
data_pca = dfs[varlist]
round(data_pca.corr(), 2)
```

Note that the correlations are all rather low, which will constitute a challenge for dimension reduction.

5.2 Steps in a Principal Components Analysis

Before illustrating the application of PCA by means of `sklearn.decomposition`, we first examine in detail the computational steps that are carried out under the hood. These steps consist of:

- standardizing the variables
- constructing the correlation matrix
- computing eigenvalues and eigenvectors of the correlation matrix

Table 5.3: Descriptive Statistics for Standardized Variables

	0	1	2	3	4	5	6	7	8	9
count	261.00	261.00	261.00	261.00	261.00	261.00	261.00	261.00	261.00	261.00
mean	-0.00	-0.00	-0.00	0.00	-0.00	-0.00	0.00	-0.00	-0.00	-0.00
std	1.00	1.00	1.00	1.00	1.00	1.00	1.00	1.00	1.00	1.00
min	-1.42	-0.76	-1.27	-1.94	-1.68	-2.28	-2.34	-1.33	-3.07	-2.34
25%	-0.64	-0.54	-0.75	-0.76	-0.69	-0.70	-0.74	-0.67	-0.66	-0.73
50%	-0.29	-0.29	-0.24	-0.11	-0.16	-0.04	-0.06	-0.28	-0.01	-0.10
75%	0.48	0.08	0.41	0.64	0.45	0.68	0.80	0.44	0.68	0.55
max	5.49	5.97	3.66	2.76	3.90	2.07	2.40	4.92	2.51	3.41

- deriving principal component loadings from the eigenvectors
- computing the variance decomposition from the eigenvalues

5.2.1 Standardized Variables

The first step in the PCA analysis is to standardize the data, which is accomplished using the `StandardScaler` class in `sklearn.preprocessing`. Recall how everything in scikit-learn is a class to which specific methods are applied, or from which specific attributes are extracted.

The method used for standardization to a mean of zero and variance of one is `fit_transform` applied to a `StandardScaler` object (additional arguments can be passed to `StandardScaler` to select different transformations, etc., but here we take the default settings). We use the `data_pca` data frame as input.

Descriptive statistics of the resulting data frame, computed by means of `describe` are listed in Table 5.3. This reveals that indeed the mean is zero and the standard deviation is one.

Note that `StandardScaler` uses a consistent estimate of the variance, i.e., the sum of squared deviations from the mean is divided by the number of observations. In contrast, in `GeoDa`, an unbiased estimate is used in which the same sum is divided by the number of observations less one (for the estimated mean). This does not affect the principal component analysis, but it will be relevant in the later cluster analyses carried out with `sklearn`.

```
# Standardize the data
X = StandardScaler().fit_transform(data_pca)
pd.DataFrame(X).describe().round(2)
```

5.2.2 Correlation Matrix

The next step is to compute the associated correlation matrix, as the cross product of the transpose of the matrix of standardized data, `X.T` with `X`, divided by the number of observations. Note that this gives the same result as computed above using data_pca.corr(). In our calculation, n corresponds with the number of observations (rows of X). Note how these values are the same as in Table 5.2 on page 47.

```
n = X.shape[0]
C = np.dot(X.T, X)/n
C.round(2)
```

```
array([[ 1.  , -0.03,  0.21, -0.08, -0.1 , -0.39,  0.18,  0.87,  0.32,
         0.14],
       [-0.03,  1.  , -0.08, -0.28, -0.16, -0.02, -0.15, -0.02, -0.04,
        -0.14],
       [ 0.21, -0.08,  1.  , -0.  , -0.05, -0.14,  0.23,  0.09,  0.01,
         0.18],
       [-0.08, -0.28, -0.  ,  1.  ,  0.64,  0.33, -0.09, -0.1 , -0.2 ,
         0.15],
       [-0.1 , -0.16, -0.05,  0.64,  1.  ,  0.41, -0.19, -0.14, -0.39,
        -0.04],
       [-0.39, -0.02, -0.14,  0.33,  0.41,  1.  , -0.43, -0.48, -0.4 ,
        -0.18],
       [ 0.18, -0.15,  0.23, -0.09, -0.19, -0.43,  1.  ,  0.18,  0.17,
         0.16],
       [ 0.87, -0.02,  0.09, -0.1 , -0.14, -0.48,  0.18,  1.  ,  0.39,
         0.12],
       [ 0.32, -0.04,  0.01, -0.2 , -0.39, -0.4 ,  0.17,  0.39,  1.  ,
         0.07],
       [ 0.14, -0.14,  0.18,  0.15, -0.04, -0.18,  0.16,  0.12,  0.07,
         1.  ]])
```

5.2.3 Eigenvalues and Eigenvectors

The coefficient loadings that are used to transform the original variables into principal components are obtained as the eigenvectors of the correlation matrix. We use the eig function from numpy.linalg to compute both eigenvalues and eigenvectors. Note how the linalg.eig function returns a tuple, with two arrays. The first is a vector with the eigenvalues, the second is a $p \times p$ matrix with the eigenvectors as columns, where p is the number of variables. More precisely, the first column of this matrix is the eigenvector for the first eigenvalue, etc.

Keep in mind that the eigenvalues will not necessarily be sorted. So we will also need to sort them from the greatest value to the smallest. This is accomplished by means of numpy.argsort (the order needs to be reversed, hence the use of [::-1])

In our code, we first compute the arrays for the tuple of eigenvalues and eigenvectors as `E_values` and `E_vectors`. We obtain the `sorted_indices` from the eigenvalues in `E_values` so that we can re-order the arrays for both eigenvalues and eigenvectors.

```
# Compute the eigenvalues and eigenvectors to use as loadings
E_values, E_vectors = np.linalg.eig(C)

# Sort eigenvalues and eigenvectors in descending order
sorted_indices = np.argsort(E_values)[::-1]
E_values = E_values[sorted_indices]
E_vectors = E_vectors[:, sorted_indices]

print('Eigenvalues:\n',E_values.round(3))
print('Eigenvectors:\n',E_vectors.round(3))
```

```
Eigenvalues:
 [2.987 1.763 1.263 0.961 0.843 0.738 0.607 0.424 0.304 0.11 ]
Eigenvectors:
 [[ 0.417 -0.289  0.4    0.201  0.054  0.035  0.178 -0.218  0.021  0.677]
 [ 0.014  0.42   0.236  0.565 -0.292 -0.392 -0.452 -0.068  0.04   0.003]
 [ 0.148 -0.229 -0.39   0.639  0.203  0.507 -0.205  0.129 -0.    -0.094]
 [-0.264 -0.546  0.081 -0.106 -0.07  -0.121 -0.409  0.063  0.65   0.032]
 [-0.333 -0.453  0.222  0.094  0.124 -0.234 -0.17   0.234 -0.687 -0.004]
 [-0.454 -0.03   0.14   0.082 -0.015  0.31  -0.013 -0.807 -0.083 -0.109]
 [ 0.277 -0.133 -0.483 -0.064  0.382 -0.542 -0.164 -0.443 -0.068 -0.024]
 [ 0.438 -0.241  0.44   0.068  0.027 -0.049  0.144 -0.085  0.06  -0.719]
 [ 0.363  0.066  0.091 -0.443 -0.114  0.35  -0.676 -0.068 -0.247  0.037]
 [ 0.131 -0.321 -0.348  0.026 -0.831 -0.065  0.151 -0.112 -0.164 -
0.02 ]]
```

5.2.4 Component Loadings

We combine the eigenvectors into a DataFrame `pdvec`, using the variable names (`columns` of `data_pca`) as the `index` (in `pandas`, these will become the row names). The eigenvectors are the component loadings of each of the original variables. Note that there are ten components in total, the same number as there are original variables. Dimension reduction will result by replacing the ten variables by a *smaller* number of principal components, such that a target *explained variance* is obtained. The smaller the resulting number of needed components, the greater the dimension reduction.

The loadings show us the weight of each original variable in the newly created components. This allows us to interpret and, potentially, label these new components, although that typically takes considerable creativity.

```
# Combine eigenvectors into a data frame
L = E_vectors
pdvec = pd.DataFrame(L, index = data_pca.columns)

print('Component Loadings:')
print(pdvec)
```

```
Component Loadings:
                  0         1         2         3         4         5
CAPRAT13   0.416651 -0.289011  0.400281  0.200754  0.054467  0.034624
Z_13       0.013973  0.420044  0.235984  0.564699 -0.291502 -0.392045
LIQASS_13  0.147681 -0.229038 -0.390257  0.638757  0.202743  0.506880
NPL_13    -0.264109 -0.546288  0.081384 -0.105872 -0.069770 -0.120596
LLP_13    -0.332622 -0.452568  0.221917  0.094127  0.124286 -0.234403
INTR_13   -0.454442 -0.030416  0.139912  0.081664 -0.015137  0.309591
DEPO_13    0.277034 -0.133345 -0.483049 -0.064276  0.381635 -0.541985
EQLN_13    0.438027 -0.240695  0.440113  0.068469  0.026698 -0.048546
SERV_13    0.362998  0.066494  0.090886 -0.443382 -0.113546  0.349947
EXPE_13    0.130787 -0.321352 -0.347914  0.025643 -0.831361 -0.065367

                  6         7         8         9
CAPRAT13   0.177808 -0.218361  0.020765  0.677092
Z_13      -0.451626 -0.067665  0.039630  0.002815
LIQASS_13 -0.204524  0.129197 -0.000251 -0.094164
NPL_13    -0.408614  0.063170  0.650065  0.032139
LLP_13    -0.169731  0.234213 -0.687286 -0.004423
INTR_13   -0.013168 -0.807004 -0.083059 -0.109131
DEPO_13   -0.163713 -0.443464 -0.067723 -0.023698
EQLN_13    0.143620 -0.084699  0.059671 -0.719291
SERV_13   -0.675579 -0.068169 -0.247354  0.036992
EXPE_13    0.151014 -0.111648 -0.163775 -0.019992
```

5.2.5 Variance Decomposition

An important property of the principal components is how much of the original variance each explains. Since the ten variables are standardized, the total variance equals 10. We verify that this is also the sum of the eigenvalues of $X'X$. Then we compute the share of the total variance associated with each principal component as the ratio of its eigenvalue to the total variance.

```
# Variance decomposition
totvar = np.sum(E_values)
print('Total variance:',totvar)

# Variance share
varshare = E_values / totvar
print('Share of total variance in each component:\n', varshare)
```

```
Total variance: 10.000000000000007
Share of total variance in each component:
 [0.2986745  0.17631768 0.12628661 0.09612748 0.08433105 0.07383474
  0.06074807 0.04237308 0.03035229 0.01095451]
```

In addition to the individual variance share, the cumulative variance share is an important property. This provides a measure of how much the components contribute up to a given number of components. This can then be used as a criterion to select the number of components. We compute this by applying `numpy.cumsum` to the array of variance shares, `varshare`.

```
cumvarshare = np.cumsum(varshare)
print('Cumulative variance share:\n', cumvarshare)
```

```
Cumulative variance share:
 [0.2986745  0.47499218 0.60127878 0.69740626 0.78173731 0.85557205
  0.91632012 0.9586932  0.98904549 1.        ]
```

A common criterion to select the number of components is the 95% threshold. In our example, this is reached after seven components, not exactly much in terms of dimension reduction. An alternative criterion is the so-called *Kaiser criterion*, which selects components with an eigenvalue larger than one. The rationale for this is that the variance associated with these components is larger than that for the original variables (standardized to variance one). In our example, the Kaiser criterion would yield three components, a much more reasonable result.

5.3 Principal Components Analysis With Scikit-Learn

In scikit-learn, principal component analysis is implemented through the PCA class of sklearn.decomposition. This operates in the same fashion as the earlier examples of sklearn that we considered: first an instance of the PCA class is created, to which then a fit method is applied. As we have seen, these operations can be chained.

In contrast to the procedure outlined in Section 5.2, the sklearn implementation uses a singular value decomposition (SVD) to obtain the relevant eigenvalues and eigenvectors. SVD is applied directly to the n by p matrix X instead of to the cross product. A detailed discussion is given in Chapter 2 of the *GeoDa Cluster Book*. SVD is also the default method used in GeoDa.

The PCA results are obtained in a single line command by applying fit to a PCA object, with as argument the standardized matrix X. The result is assigned here to pca_res, an instance of the PCA class that now contains several useful attributes.

```
pca_res = PCA().fit(X)
print(type(pca_res))
```

```
<class 'sklearn.decomposition._pca.PCA'>
```

5.3.1 PCA Result Properties

an application of the fit method, our pca_res result object has several important attributes:

- components_: the factor loadings as an array of rows (not columns as in the example above), one for each component. So, the first row contains the loadings for the first PC, etc.
- explained_variance_: the explained variance by each component. As shown above, this corresponds to the matching eigenvalue of $X'X$.
- explained_variance_ratio_: the share of the total variance explained by each component,

as well as several other, more technical attributes.

We again collect the component loadings into a data frame, but now organize it differently, with the original variables as columns and the labeled components (from 1 to 10) as rows (we name the rows as sequence numbers using range passed to index). The resulting table is exactly the transpose of the table in Section 5.2.4.

```
# Component loadings, row by row
pdload = pd.DataFrame(pca_res.components_,
             index = range(1, pca_res.components_.shape[0] + 1),
             columns = data_pca.columns)
print(pdload)
```

```
    CAPRAT13      Z_13  LIQASS_13    NPL_13    LLP_13   INTR_13   DEPO_13
1  -0.416651 -0.013973  -0.147681  0.264109  0.332622  0.454442 -0.277034
2   0.289011 -0.420044   0.229038  0.546288  0.452568  0.030416  0.133345
3  -0.400281 -0.235984   0.390257 -0.081384 -0.221917 -0.139912  0.483049
4   0.200754  0.564699   0.638757 -0.105872  0.094127  0.081664 -0.064276
5  -0.054467  0.291502  -0.202743  0.069770 -0.124286  0.015137 -0.381635
6  -0.034624  0.392045  -0.506880  0.120596  0.234403 -0.309591  0.541985
7  -0.177808  0.451626   0.204524  0.408614  0.169731  0.013168  0.163713
8   0.218361  0.067665  -0.129197 -0.063170 -0.234213  0.807004  0.443464
9  -0.020765 -0.039630   0.000251 -0.650065  0.687286  0.083059  0.067723
10 -0.677092 -0.002815   0.094164 -0.032139  0.004423  0.109131  0.023698

     EQLN_13   SERV_13   EXPE_13
1  -0.438027 -0.362998 -0.130787
2   0.240695 -0.066494  0.321352
3  -0.440113 -0.090886  0.347914
4   0.068469 -0.443382  0.025643
5  -0.026698  0.113546  0.831361
6   0.048546 -0.349947  0.065367
7  -0.143620  0.675579 -0.151014
8   0.084699  0.068169  0.111648
9  -0.059671  0.247354  0.163775
10  0.719291 -0.036992  0.019992
```

The explained variance of each component (i.e., the sorted eigenvalues of $X'X$) are contained in `explained_variance_`. These are the same results as in Section 5.2.5. The explained variance share does not have to be computed explicitly, since it is contained in the array `explained_variance_ratio_`. However, the cumulative explained variance share still needs to be calculated by means of `numpy.cumsum`. The results are again identical to those above.

```
# Explained variance of each component
pca_res.explained_variance_
```

```
array([2.99823249, 1.76995822, 1.26772324, 0.96497201, 0.84655397,
```

```
       0.74118715, 0.60981717, 0.42536058, 0.30469032, 0.10996639])
```

```
# Explained variance share
print("Explained variance share:", pca_res.explained_variance_ratio_)
print("\nCumulative variance share:",
np.cumsum(pca_res.explained_variance_ratio_))
```

```
Explained variance share: [0.2986745  0.17631768 0.12628661 0.09612748
     0.08433105 0.07383474 0.06074807 0.04237308 0.03035229 0.01095451]

Cumulative variance share: [0.2986745  0.47499218 0.60127878 0.69740626
      0.78173731 0.85557205 0.91632012 0.9586932  0.98904549 1.        ]
```

5.3.2 Principal Components

The actual components are found by applying `transform(X)` to the PCA result object. This yields a n by p numpy array with the observations as rows and the component scores as columns. To illustrate this, we show the first five rows of the array.

```
# The actual principal components
pcomps = pca_res.transform(X)
pcomps[0:5,:]
```

```
array([[-2.26679046,  0.43413755,  3.41152327,  0.96571188,  1.04437104,
        -1.16371188,  0.08190058,  0.14667044,  0.63028628,  0.04197353],
       [-1.17912038,  1.97789286,  1.42306193,  2.61503026, -0.2044251 ,
        -1.16313925, -1.11227835,  0.43890689, -0.034723  , -0.43096847],
       [ 1.51954157,  0.67741483,  1.03804823,  0.89012655, -0.9791715 ,
         0.13891672, -0.31238392,  1.06950892, -0.7985399 ,  0.03163169],
       [ 2.31900576,  0.92853046,  0.19192593,  0.3382497 , -0.32122236,
         0.20426167, -0.30377276, -0.84063078,  0.1894053 ,  0.15740099],
       [ 2.36956218, -0.24021829, -0.47730339,  0.33135428, -0.28279248,
        -0.46963886, -0.42419014,  0.29410648, -0.37962959,  0.13039031]])
```

5.4 Scree Plot

The choice of how many components to keep is not an easy one. There are several shortcut criteria, but they often yield different recommendations. For example, one

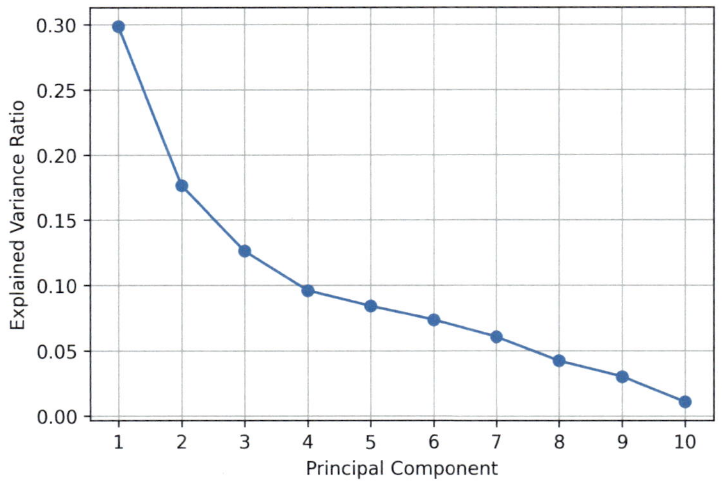

Figure 5.1: Scree plot

would suggest to keep all the components until the explained variance is 95% of the original. In our example, that would mean keeping seven or eight components (out of ten, depending on how the criterion is imposed), which is not exactly dimension reduction.

The Kaiser criterion suggests keeping the principal components with eigenvalues larger than one. This would yield three components, a more reasonable reduction.

A graphical method to assess the number of components is the so-called *scree plot*, a plot of explained variance against the number of components. The goal is to identify a *kink* in this plot, which then suggests the proper number of components. In practice, this is not as easy as it sounds, as the example below illustrates.

We implement a scree plot by means of a simple `matplotlib` line plot with the explained variance ratio (`explained_variance_ratio_`) on the vertical axis and a simple counter on the horizontal axis.

As the graph in Figure 5.1 shows, it is not easy at all to identify the *kink*.

```
#Screeplot of variance
plt.figure(figsize = (6, 4))
plt.plot(range(1, len(pca_res.explained_variance_ratio_) + 1),
        pca_res.explained_variance_ratio_, marker= 'o' ,
        linestyle = '-')

plt.xlabel('Principal Component')
plt.ylabel('Explained Variance Ratio')
plt.xticks(np.arange(1, len(pca_res.explained_variance_ratio_) + 1))
```

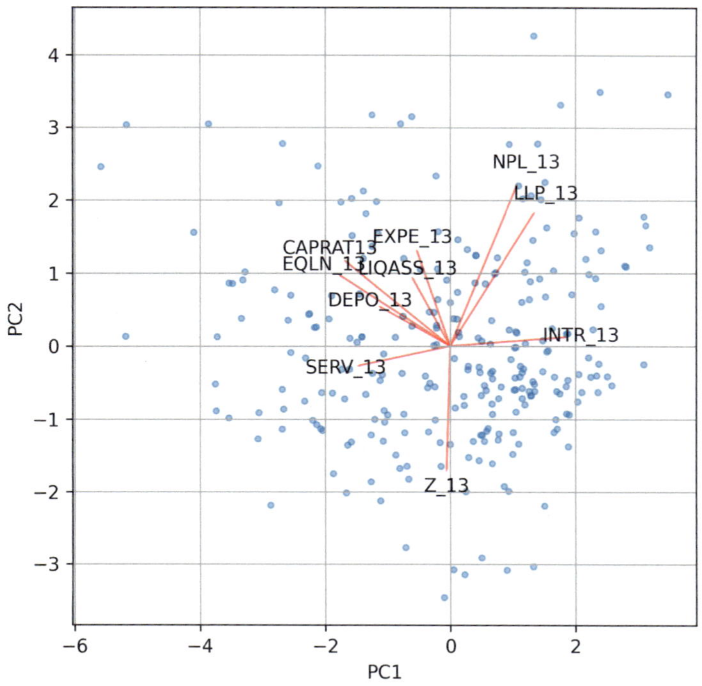

Figure 5.2: Biplot

```
plt.grid(True)
plt.show()
```

5.5 Visualizing Principal Components

5.5.1 Biplot

A classic visualization of the relative contribution of the original variables to the principal components is a so-called *biplot*. For any pair of components, it consists of a scatter plot of the component values, with superimposed line plots that show the relative contribution of each variable to each of the components.

For example, a line plot that points to the upper-right quadrant in the scatter plot (e.g., `LLP_13`) would indicate that the variable in question contributes positively to both components (note that the results may yield different signs for the loadings, depending on the method used). On the other hand, a line plot that points to the upper-left quadrant (e.g., `CAPRAT13`) would suggest a negative contribution to the first component, but a positive contribution to the second (on the y-axis).

In Figure 5.2 on page 57, we illustrate the biplot by means of a simple function using a number of basic `matplotlib` plotting operations. The first two principal components are contained in the first two columns of the `pcomps` array constructed in Section 5.3.2.

In the biplot code listed below, we have re-scaled the loadings by multiplying them by 4 just so they get more visible in the graph.

```
# Biplot
def biplot(score, coeff, labels = None):
    plt.figure(figsize = (6, 6))
    plt.scatter(score[:, 0], score[:, 1], alpha = 0.5, s=10)
    for i in range(len(coeff)):
        plt.arrow(0, 0, coeff[i, 0], coeff[i, 1], color = 'r',
                       alpha = 0.5)
        if labels is None:
            plt.text(coeff[i, 0]*1.15, coeff[i, 1]*1.15,
"                        Var" + str(i+1),
                     color = 'black', ha = 'center', va = 'center')
        else:
            plt.text(coeff[i, 0]*1.15, coeff[i, 1]*1.15, labels[i],
                     color = 'black', ha = 'center', va = 'center')
    plt.xlabel("PC1")
    plt.ylabel("PC2")
    plt.grid()
    plt.show()

biplot(pcomps[:, :2], pca_res.components_.T*4,
       labels = data_pca.columns)
```

Other visualizations, such as the ones illustrated in the *GeoDa Cluster Book* can be pursued as well, including a parallel coordinate plot showing the contributions of different variables to a component. This is not further pursued here.

5.6 Spatializing the PCA

As described in the *GeoDa Cluster Book*, there are several ways in which the spatial characteristics of the results of a principal components calculation can be visualized. The basic idea is that a component (typically the first or second principal component) summarizes several underlying variables and therefore can be used as a proxy for multivariate relationships. In essence then, a univariate spatial visualization of a principal component provides insight into *multivariate spatial patterns*.

All the usual visualizations can be applied, such as various thematic maps and cluster maps based on indicators of local spatial autocorrelation. Care must be taken in interpreting these results, since the sign of the loadings is indeterminate (so high can become low and vice versa). In addition, one can assess the similarity in results of a full multivariate approach, such as a multivariate local Geary or a neighbor match map and the univariate results for the principal component. This is not further pursued here (for extensive examples, see Chapter 2 of the *GeoDa Cluster Book*).

We close the overview with an illustration of a Box Map and a Local Moran cluster map for the first principal component.

The strongest loadings (absolute values > 0.3) in PC1 are:

```
Negative:
    CAPRAT13 (-0.42) → Capital adequacy
    EQLN_13 (-0.44) → Equity over loans
    SERV_13 (-0.36) → Net interest income over revenues
Positive:
    LLP_13 (0.33) → Loan loss provisions
    INTR_13 (0.45) → Interest expenses
```

Therefore, PC1 contrasts capital adequacy and profitability (negative loadings on CAPRAT13, EQLN_13, and SERV_13) with credit risk and funding costs (positive loadings on LLP_13 and INTR_13). Low PC1 values represent banks with higher capital adequacy, more equity, and stronger deposit bases. High PC1 values represent banks with higher credit risk, loan loss provisions, and funding costs, indicating capital inadequacy and financial strain. As a result, an appropriate label for PC1 could be "Credit Risk & Funding Costs vs. Capital Adequacy". Remember that the signs of the loadings may be inverted. The interpretation — and therefore the labelling of the coefficients — must be adjusted accordingly, depending on the signs of the loadings.

5.6.1 Box Map

The first component is the first column of the array `pcomps`. It is added to our GeoDataFrame `dfs` so that the `plot` function can be applied. We use the by now familiar options from Chapter 2. The code below yields the box map shown in Figure 5.3.

```
# Box map of Component 1:
dfs['Comp.1'] = pcomps[:, 0]

ax = dfs.plot(
    column = 'Comp.1',
```

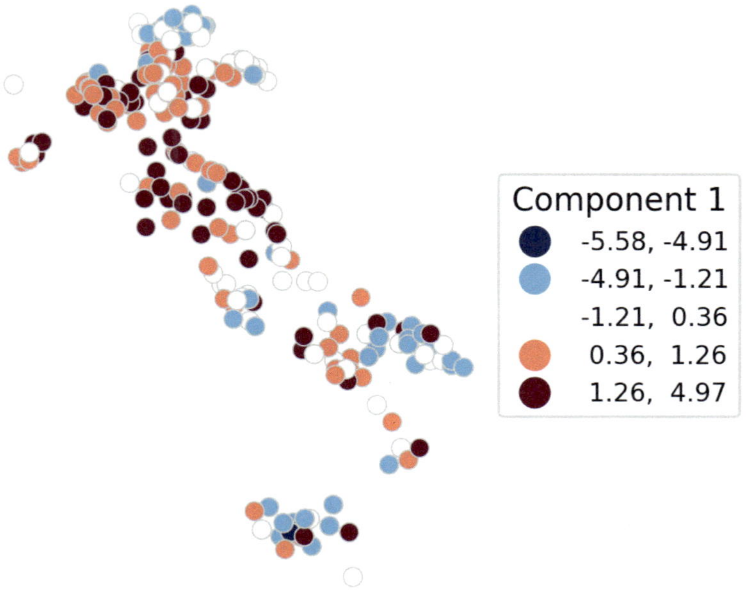

Figure 5.3: Box plot of first principal component

```
    scheme = 'BoxPlot',
    cmap = 'RdBu_r',
    linewidth = 0.5,
    edgecolor = '0.8',
    legend = True,
    legend_kwds = {"loc": "center left", "bbox_to_anchor": (1,0.5),
                   "title": "Component 1", "fontsize":8}
)

ax.set_axis_off()
```

5.6.2 Local Moran Cluster Map

We use `pygeoda` to compute the Local Moran statistic. This requires three steps:

- `open` the GeoDataFrame and turn it into a `pygeoda` data object
- create `queen_weights` from the geoda data object
- compute a `local_moran` object by passing the weights and the variable

- optional arguments are `permutations` for the number of permutations (default is 999), `seed` for the random seed (default is 1234567), and `significance_cutoff` for the p-value that determines significance (default is 0.05)

In our illustration, we use the first principal component with 9999 permutations and a p-value cut-off of 0.01.

The code below yields a `lisa object` with the statistics, `lisa_values`, associated p-values, `lisa_pvalues`, the neighbor cardinality, `lisa_num_nbrs`, the cluster classification, based on the specified p-value, `lisa_clusters`, labels, `lisa_labels`, and associated colors, `lisa_colors`.

```
dfs_g = pygeoda.open(dfs)
queen_w = pygeoda.queen_weights(dfs_g)
lm = pygeoda.local_moran(queen_w, dfs_g['Comp.1'],
                         permutations = 9999, seed = 1234567,
                         significance_cutoff = 0.01)
lm
```

```
lisa object:

    lisa_values(): [0.005296951235279905, -0.3184600483378756,
                    0.36298009350110183, 1.109043986529309,
                    1.1710899759593107, 1.056924984131107,
                   -1.3445446406378438, 0.055015911773549774,
                   -0.1488976211105254, 0.2916115206147433, ...]
    lisa_pvalues(): [0.4801, 0.1814, 0.0859, 0.019, 0.0077, 0.0422,
                     0.0716, 0.0966, 0.021, 0.2121, ...]
    lisa_num_nbrs(): [6, 4, 10, 5, 6, 6, 5, 8, 5, 5, ...]
    lisa_clusters(): [0, 0, 0, 0, 1, 0, 0, 0, 0, 0, ...]
    lisa_labels(): ('Not significant', 'High-High', 'Low-Low',
                    'Low-High', 'High-Low', 'Undefined', 'Isolated')
    lisa_colors(): ('#eeeeee', '#FF0000', '#0000FF', '#a7adf9',
                    '#f4ada8', '#464646', '#999999')
```

Note that this listing is actually a bit misleading, since all methods except `lisa_pvalues()` return *tuples*, not *lists*. In practice, this doesn't matter much, since they are typically converted to numpy arrays or pandas series anyway.

In addition, there are two functions to obtain the Bonferroni bound p cut-off and the False Discovery Rate (FDR) p-value, respectively as `lm.lisa_bo(pvalue)` and `lm.lisa_fdr(pvalue)`, where p-value is typically 0.05. Note that smaller values may not yield a feasible cut-off given the maximum number of permutations. However, in

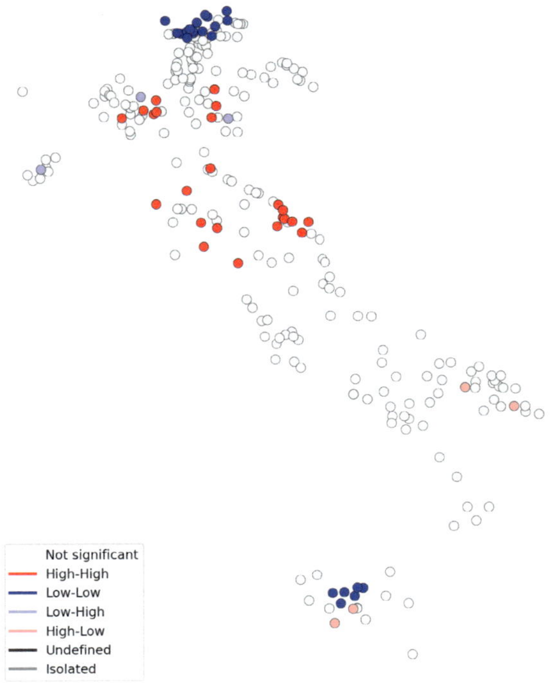

Figure 5.4: Local Moran map for first principal component

contrast to what is the case for desktop GeoDa, the pygeoda implementation allows any value for the number of permutations. We illustrate this for a target p-value of 0.05.

```
print("Bonferroni bound:", np.round(lm.lisa_bo(0.05), 6))
print("FDR:", np.round(lm.lisa_fdr(0.05), 6))
```

```
Bonferroni bound: 0.000192
FDR: 0.009962
```

With the usual commands, contained in the code block below, we create a custom local cluster map using the lisa_colors and lisa_labels. This yields the cluster map in Figure 5.4.

```
fig, ax = plt.subplots(figsize = (8,8))
lisa_colors = lm.lisa_colors()
lisa_labels = lm.lisa_labels()
dfs['LISA'] = lm.lisa_clusters()
for ctype, data in dfs.groupby('LISA'):
```

```
    color = lisa_colors[ctype]
    lbl = lisa_labels[ctype]
    data.plot(color = color,
        ax = ax,
        label = lbl,
        edgecolor = 'black',
        linewidth = 0.2)
lisa_legend = [pltlines.Line2D([0], [0],
                color = color, lw = 2) for color in lisa_colors]
ax.legend(lisa_legend, lisa_labels, loc = 'lower left',
        fontsize = 8, frameon = True)
ax.set_axis_off()
```

5.7 Practice

Use a different set of variables from the **italy_banks** data set (or any other sample data set) to compute a set of principal components. Assess the extent to which true dimension reduction is achieved. Experiment with different spatial and non-spatial visualization techniques.

6 Distance Preserving Methods

In this Chapter, we consider a second class of dimension reduction techniques, based on the preservation of relative distances in high-dimensional attribute space. We cover two different approaches:

- *multi-dimensional scaling* (MDS), and
- *stochastic neighbor embedding* (SNE)

Whereas MDS uses the actual multi-attribute distance between pairs of observations, SNE is based on information-theoretic concepts of the similarity between probability distributions as the criterion for embedding. The two sets of techniques are covered in Chapters 3 and 4 of the *GeoDa Cluster Book*.

We continue with the **italy_banks** sample data for the empirical illustration.

In addition to the usual `numpy`, `pandas`, `geopandas` and `matplotlib.pyplot`, we also import several specialized packages from scikit-learn. Specifically, to carry out variable standardization, we import `StandardScaler` from `sklearn.preprocessing`, and to compute the distance matrix we need `pairwise_distances` from `sklearn.metrics`.

The specific methods are `MDS` and `TSNE` from `sklearn.manifold`, and, as used before, `PCA` from `sklearn.decomposition` and `HDBSCAN` from `sklearn.cluster`. To characterize the results, we use several helper functions from `spatial-cluster-helper`, namely `ensure_datasets`, `cluster_stats`, `stress_value`, `distcorr` and `common_coverage`. We implement some of the *spatialization* of these methods employing `KNN` and `w_intersection` from `libpysal.weights` as well as the local spatial autocorrelation functionality from `pygeoda`.

> Required Packages
>
> numpy, pandas, geopandas, matplotlib.pyplot, sklearn.decomposition, sklearn.preprocessing, sklearn.manifold, sklearn.metrics, sklearn.cluster, spatial-cluster-helper, libpysal, pygeoda

> Required Data Sets
>
> italy_banks

6.1 Preliminaries

6.1.1 Import Required Modules

```
import geopandas as gpd
import pandas as pd
import numpy as np
import matplotlib.pyplot as plt
from sklearn.preprocessing import StandardScaler
from sklearn.metrics import pairwise_distances
from sklearn.manifold import MDS, TSNE
from sklearn.decomposition import PCA
from sklearn.cluster import HDBSCAN
from libpysal.weights import KNN, w_intersection
from spatial_cluster_helper import ensure_datasets, cluster_stats, \
    stress_value, distcorr, common_coverage
import pygeoda
```

6.1.2 Load Data

We follow the usual practice of setting a path (if needed), and read the data from the Italian banks shape file (`italy_banks.shp`). Since this is the same input as in previous Chapters, we provide the relevant code block, but skip the output.

```
# Setting data folder:
#path = "/your/path/to/data/"
path = "./datasets/"
# Select the Italy community banks point data:
shpfile = "italy_banks/italy_banks.shp"
# Load the data:
ensure_datasets(shpfile, folder_path = path)
dfs = gpd.read_file(path + shpfile)
print(dfs.shape)
print(dfs.head(3))
```

6.1.3 Variables

We continue to use the same selection of bank performance indicators for 2013 as in Chapter 5, listed in Table 5.1 on page 47 .

We again specify `varlist` as a list with the respective variables names.

```
varlist = ['CAPRAT13', 'Z_13', 'LIQASS_13', 'NPL_13', 'LLP_13',
           'INTR_13', 'DEPO_13', 'EQLN_13', 'EXPE_13', 'SERV_13']
```

We also create a subset of the original GeoDataFrame with just the selected variables, as `data_mds`.

```
data_mds = dfs[varlist]
```

6.2 Classic MDS

Classic MDS is based on the Gramm matrix XX' when the full data set is available (as is the case here). Alternatively, it can also be computed directly from a double-centered squared distance matrix, which is useful when that is the only information available (i.e., no full set of observations X):

$$XX' = -(1/2)(I - M)D^2(I - M),$$

where D is the matrix of pairwise distances, and M is a matrix consisting of elements $1/n$. The result of the $(I - M)$ operation is to compute values as deviations from the mean. Pre- and post-multiplying the squared distance matrix with $(I - M)$ is referred to as *double centering*.

6.2.1 Gramm Matrix

We start by comparing the Gramm matrix and the double centered squared distance matrix. As before, we first standardize the variables using `StandardScaler`, to which we apply `fit_transform` with the original data `data_mds` as argument. In the example below, the matrix $(I - M)$ is used as H.

```
# Pre-processing: standardize the data
X = StandardScaler().fit_transform(data_mds)

# Compute pairwise distances
dist_matrix = pairwise_distances(X)

# Double-center the distance matrix
n_samples = dist_matrix.shape[0]
# Matrix I - M
```

```
H = np.eye(n_samples) - np.ones((n_samples, n_samples)) / n_samples
B = -0.5 * H @ (dist_matrix ** 2) @ H

# Compare to XX
XXp = X @ X.T

print("B:\n", B[0:5,0:5])
print("XXp:\n", XXp[0:5,0:5])
```

```
B:
 [[ 2.07700836e+01  1.19850381e+01 -3.04437191e-01 -4.46754435e+00
  -6.75815062e+00]
 [ 1.19850381e+01  1.71772980e+01  4.22260221e+00 -1.76067198e-02
  -1.91990000e+00]
 [-3.04437191e-01  4.22260221e+00  7.49594112e+00  4.04560929e+00
   4.20339927e+00]
 [-4.46754435e+00 -1.76067198e-02  4.04560929e+00  7.39569901e+00
   5.11760413e+00]
 [-6.75815062e+00 -1.91990000e+00  4.20339927e+00  5.11760413e+00
   6.73823232e+00]]
XXp:
 [[ 2.07700836e+01  1.19850381e+01 -3.04437191e-01 -4.46754435e+00
  -6.75815062e+00]
 [ 1.19850381e+01  1.71772980e+01  4.22260221e+00 -1.76067198e-02
  -1.91990000e+00]
 [-3.04437191e-01  4.22260221e+00  7.49594112e+00  4.04560929e+00
   4.20339927e+00]
 [-4.46754435e+00 -1.76067198e-02  4.04560929e+00  7.39569901e+00
   5.11760413e+00]
 [-6.75815062e+00 -1.91990000e+00  4.20339927e+00  5.11760413e+00
   6.73823232e+00]]
```

Clearly, it doesn't matter whether we use the Gramm matrix or the double centered squared distance matrix. In our example, since we have the full matrix X, we will use the Gramm matrix to compute the eigenvalues and eigenvectors.

6.2.2 Eigendecomposition

In classic MDS, the coordinates of the observations in two dimensions are obtained from the eigenvalues and eigenvectors of the Gramm matrix. To compute these, we use the `eigh` function from `numpy.linalg` because we know that XX' is real and symmetric. Note that the eigenvalues are not necessarily in any given order, so that we need to apply `argsort` to get them in decreasing order (the ordering given by `argsort` is always in increasing order, hence the additional argument `[::-1]`).

```
# Eigendecomposition
eigvals, eigvecs = np.linalg.eigh(XXp)
sorted_indices = np.argsort(eigvals)[::-1]
eigvals = eigvals[sorted_indices]
eigvecs = eigvecs[:, sorted_indices]

print("Leading eigenvalues:", np.round(eigvals[0:2],4))
```

```
Leading eigenvalues: [779.5404 460.1891]
```

6.2.3 MDS Dimensions

We obtain the first two dimensions as $VG^{1/2}$, i.e., we multiply the first two eigenvectors with the square root of the matching eigenvalue. We add the result to a DataFrame (`mds_classic_df`) for easy plotting.

```
# Compute the embedding
k = 2  # Number of dimensions
top_eigvals = eigvals[:k]
top_eigvecs = eigvecs[:, :k]
embedding = top_eigvecs * np.sqrt(top_eigvals)
mds_classic_df = pd.DataFrame(embedding,
    columns=['Dimension 1', 'Dimension 2'])
print(mds_classic_df.head(10))
```

```
   Dimension 1  Dimension 2
0    -2.266790     0.434138
1    -1.179120     1.977893
2     1.519542     0.677415
3     2.319006     0.928530
4     2.369562    -0.240218
5    -2.548597    -0.089174
6     3.475160     3.461779
7     0.214755    -0.683837
8     0.273706     1.325170
9     1.427797     0.922841
```

6.2.4 Characteristics of the MDS Solution

6.2.4.1 Stress function

A measure of how well the higher-dimension distances have been reflected in the embedding is given by the *stress function*, the squared difference between the pairwise distances in higher dimension and in the embedded space.

To compute the stress value, we need the `pairwise_distances` for the embedded coordinates. We then compute the sum of squares of the differences between the two distances (raw stress), and normalize this by dividing by the sum of squares of the original distance matrix.

This operation is implemented in the `stress_value` function imported from the `spatial_cluster_helper` module. The function only requires two arguments, the original pairwise distance matrix, here `dist_matrix`, and the n by 2 matrix of embedded coordinates, here `embedding`. The return is a tuple consisting of the raw stress measure (not standardized) and the normalized stress.

```
r1, nr1 = stress_value(dist_matrix, embedding)
print("Raw Stress:", np.round(r1, 4))
print("Normalized Stress:", np.round(nr1, 4))
```

```
Raw Stress: 105792.7325
Normalized Stress: 0.3941
```

The normalized stress value obtained here is identical to the measure shown in Figure 3.3. of the *GeoDa Spatial Cluster* book.

6.2.4.2 Rank correlation

Another common measure to indicate the quality of the MDS embedding is the rank correlation between the original and embedded distance matrices.

The small function `distcorr` from the `spatial_cluster_helper` module computes the Spearman rank correlation using the `spearmanr` function from `scipy.stats`. To avoid duplication in the computation (since the distance matrix is symmetric and has a zero diagonal), the function first extracts the upper diagonal elements from each distance matrix and turns them into a numpy array. It again takes the original pairwise distance matrix, `dist_matrix` and the embedded coordinate array, `embedding`, as arguments.

In our example, the rank correlation is 0.804. This is again identical to the result shown in Figure 3.3 of the *GeoDa Spatial Cluster* book.

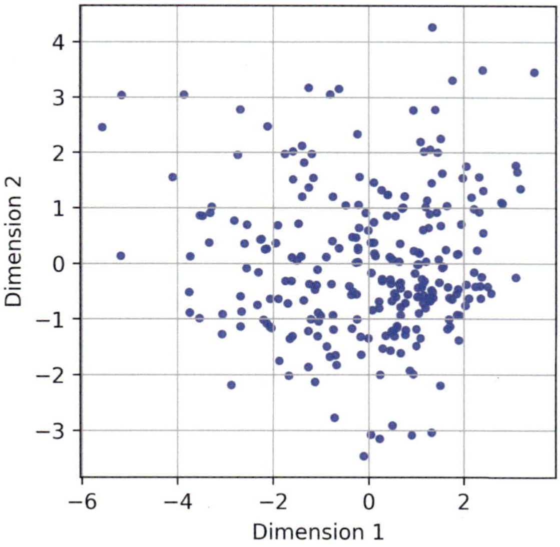

Figure 6.1: Scatter plot for Classic MDS

```
print("Rank correlation: ", np.round(distcorr(dist_matrix,embedding), 3))
```

```
Rank correlation:  0.804
```

6.2.5 Visualizing MDS Results

We illustrate the locations of the observations in the two-dimensional MDS space by means of a simple scatter plot applied to the dimension coordinates contained in the `mds_classic_df` DataFrame just created. In the code below, we add labels for the x and y axes. A final customization is to set the `color` as `blue`, the transparency `alpha = 0.7` and the size of the points as `s=10`.

The resulting graph is shown in Figure 6.1.

```
plt.figure(figsize = (4, 4))
plt.scatter(mds_classic_df['Dimension 1'], mds_classic_df['Dimension 2'],
            color = 'blue', alpha = 0.7, s=10)

plt.xlabel("Dimension 1")
plt.ylabel("Dimension 2")
plt.grid(True)
plt.show()
```

6.3 Classic MDS and PCA

6.3.1 Comparing Two Dimensions

Since the Classic MDS solution is based on the eigenvalues and eigenvectors of XX', the dimensions provide the same information as the first two principal components. We illustrate this by showing the associated scatter plots side by side.

In the code block below, we first compute the principal components using the `PCA` class from `sklearn.decomposition` with `fit_transform`, as illustrated in Chapter 5. We add the first two components (the first two columns of `pca_res`) to a data frame `pca_df` for plotting. We then apply the same routines as in Section 6.2.5 for the scatter plot of MDS dimensions (using `mds_classic_df`) and the principal components (using `pca_df`) and ensure the figures are side by side by means of `subplots`.

The resulting plots are identical, as evidenced by Figure 6.2.

```
#Compare with PCA
pca_res = PCA(n_components = 2).fit_transform(X)

pca_df = pd.DataFrame(pca_res[:, :2],
                      columns = ['Component 1', 'Component 2'])
fig, axes = plt.subplots(1, 2, figsize = (8, 4))

# Plot MDS results
axes[0].scatter(mds_classic_df['Dimension 1'],
                mds_classic_df['Dimension 2'],
                color = 'blue', alpha = 0.7, s=10)
axes[0].set_title("Classic MDS")
axes[0].set_xlabel("Dimension 1")
axes[0].set_ylabel("Dimension 2")
axes[0].grid(True)

# Plot PCA results
axes[1].scatter(pca_df['Component 1'], pca_df['Component 2'],
                color = 'blue', alpha = 0.7, s=10)
axes[1].set_title("PCA")
axes[1].set_xlabel("Component 1")
axes[1].set_ylabel("Component 2")
axes[1].grid(True)

plt.show()
```

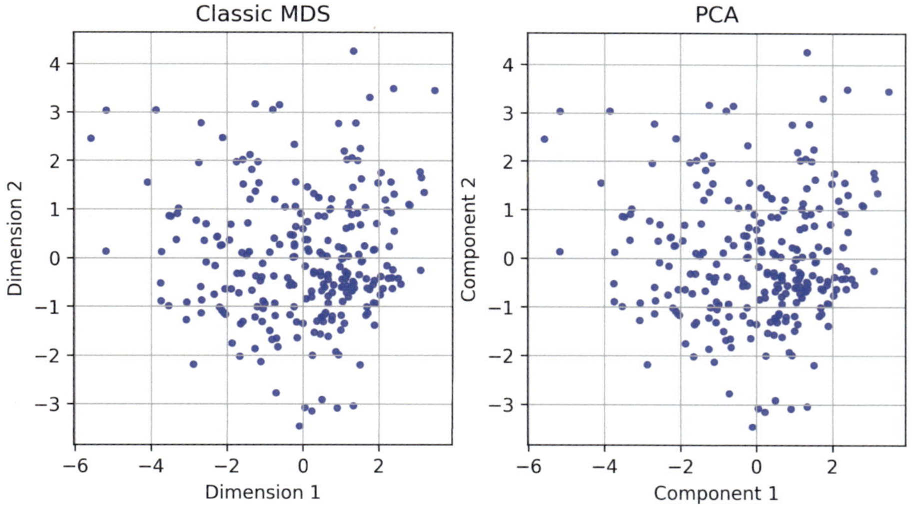

Figure 6.2: Comparing MDS-Classic dimensions and PCA

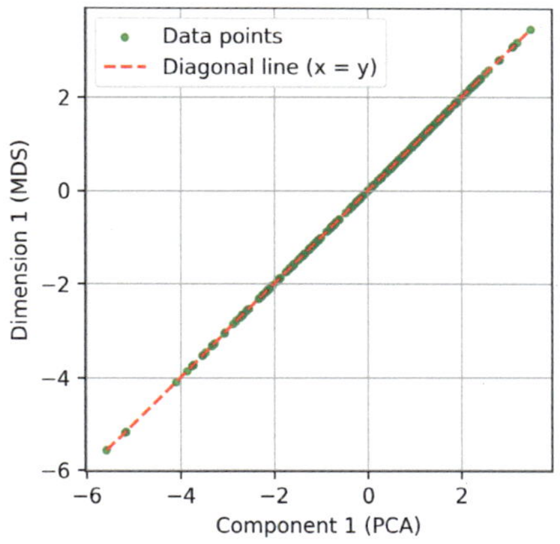

Figure 6.3: Comparison of first MDS dimension and first principal component

6.3.2 Comparing the First Dimension

Finally, we show a scatter plot of the first principal component against the first MDS dimension. We extract these from their respective data frames, i.e, the just created `pca_df` and `mds_classic_df`. We carry out some utility manipulations with the minima and maxima to create the graph. The result, in Figure 6.3, shows a perfect linear relationship between the two concepts.

```
# Combine MDS and PCA results into one DataFrame
comparison_df = pd.DataFrame({
                    'Component 1': pca_df['Component 1'],
```

```
                   'Dimension 1': mds_classic_df['Dimension 1']
})

x = comparison_df['Component 1']
y = comparison_df['Dimension 1']

# Get the range for the axes
x_min, x_max = x.min(), x.max()
y_min, y_max = y.min(), y.max()

# Determine the limits for the diagonal line (x = y)
min_val = min(x_min, y_max)  # Smallest value considering the inverted y
max_val = max(x_max, y_min)  # Largest value considering the inverted y

# Create the plot
plt.figure(figsize = (4, 4))
plt.scatter(comparison_df['Component 1'], comparison_df['Dimension 1'],
            color = 'green', alpha = 0.7, label = 'Data points', s=10)
plt.plot([min_val, max_val], [min_val, max_val], color = 'red',
         linestyle = '--', label = 'Diagonal line (x = y)')

plt.xlabel("Component 1 (PCA)")
plt.ylabel("Dimension 1 (MDS)")
plt.grid(True)
plt.legend()
plt.show()
```

6.4 MDS Analysis With Scikit-Learn

6.4.1 SMACOF

The `MDS` class in `sklearn.manifold` does not support the classic MDS solution, but instead implements the SMACOF method due to de Leeuw (1977) and de Leeuw and Mair (2009) (SMACOF stands for "scaling by majorizing a complex function"). Technical details are provided in Section 3.3 of the *GeoDa Cluster Book*.

The implementation works as all others in scikit-learn: first an object of the proper class is created, and then a method of the class (typically `fit` or `fit_transform`) is applied to find a solution. There are two basic ways to accomplish this with an object of the MDS class. One is to apply the `fit_transform` method, to which the standardized X matrix is passed. This yields a $n \times 2$ numpy array with the embedded coordinates.

A second, more comprehensive approach is to apply the generic `fit` method. This yields an object that contains several characteristics of the solution as attributes, such as the coordinates in `embedding_` (don't forget the underscore), the stress value in `stress_` and the number of iterations in `n_iter_`. One attribute is `dissimilarity_matrix_`, the distance matrix for the original data - note that this is NOT the distance matrix for the MDS solution. For `metric` distance, the stress value is not normalized. We can use the `stress_value` function from the `spatial_cluster_helper` module to compute the normalized measure.

The stress is the only measure of fit provided by the `MDS` class. To compute a rank correlation, we again use our `distcorr` function.

The `MDS` call takes as arguments the number of desired components, `n_components` - default 2 -, the type of distance, `metric = True` by default, a random number seed to ensure reproducibility, `random_state`, as well as some other arguments. In most cases the default settings are fine and only the `random_state` should be set to get the same results each time (the initialization is random, so that different results can be obtained depending on the starting values). Full details are given at https://scikit-learn.org/stable/modules/generated/sklearn.manifold.MDS.html.

We first create an MDS object as `mds_est` and then apply `fit_transform` to obtain a $n \times 2$ array of embedded coordinates as `mds_res`. We next turn that array into a data frame (`mds_df`) for later plotting. The only argument needed is `random_state`. We set it to `123456789`, the same as the `GeoDa` default. For all the other arguments, the default values are fine (e.g., `n_components = 2`).

We can safely ignore any warning.

```
# Perform MDS using scikit-learn
mds_est = MDS(random_state = 123456789)
mds_res = mds_est.fit_transform(X)

mds_df = pd.DataFrame(mds_res, columns = ['Dimension 1', 'Dimension 2'])
print(mds_df.head(10))
```

```
   Dimension 1  Dimension 2
0     4.366106     1.063019
1     4.060755    -1.026445
2    -0.177011    -2.509416
3    -1.042375    -2.565401
4    -2.059762    -1.746349
5     1.046476     5.701215
6    -0.391955    -5.548806
7    -0.814223     0.428391
```

```
8     2.420641    -2.200385
9    -1.233516    -2.275464
```

By using the `fit_transform` method, several attributes were added to the original `mds_est` object. This is in addition to returning an array with coordinates. For example, the same coordinates are contained in `mds_est.embedding_`.

```
mds_est.embedding_[0:10, :]
```

```
array([[ 4.36610569,  1.06301919],
       [ 4.06075516, -1.02644466],
       [-0.17701083, -2.50941605],
       [-1.0423754 , -2.56540099],
       [-2.05976176, -1.74634883],
       [ 1.0464762 ,  5.70121531],
       [-0.39195529, -5.54880556],
       [-0.81422257,  0.42839149],
       [ 2.42064085, -2.20038499],
       [-1.2335157 , -2.27546384]])
```

If the method `fit` were used, the output would be an MDS object with the attributes attached, but not a numpy array. Otherwise, there is no distinction between the two approaches.

6.4.2 Visualizing MDS (SMACOF)

As in the case of classic MDS, we can use the columns in the new data frame (`mds_df`) to create a scatter plot of the coordinates, by means of the same commands as in Section 6.2.5. This yields Figure 6.4.

```
plt.figure(figsize = (4, 4))
plt.scatter(mds_df['Dimension 1'], mds_df['Dimension 2'],
            color = 'blue', alpha = 0.7, s=10)

plt.xlabel('Dimension 1')
plt.ylabel('Dimension 2')
plt.grid(True)
plt.show()
```

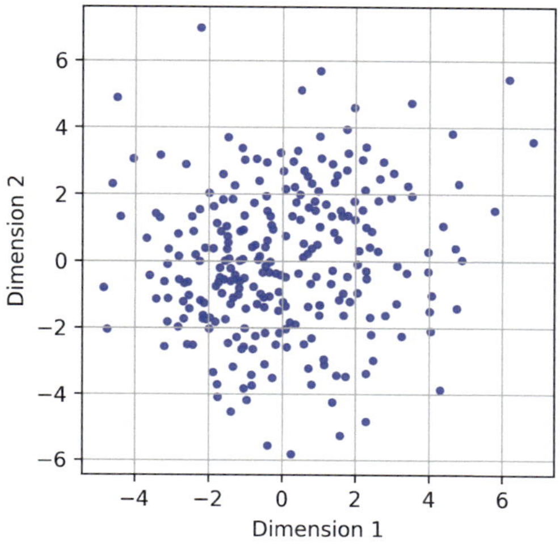

Figure 6.4: MDS SMACOF scatter plot

6.4.3 Measures of Fit

The MDS object contains a stress measure in the `stress_` attribute. However, for metric scaling, this result is not normalized. Also, there is no rank correlation. As mentioned, we can use the `stress_value` and `dist_corr` functions from the `spatial-cluster-helper` module to obtain those properties.

```
print(np.round(mds_est.stress_, 0))
```

```
40675.0
```

```
r2, nr2 = stress_value(dist_matrix, mds_res)
print("Raw Stress:", np.round(r2, 0))
print("Normalized Stress:", np.round(nr2, 4))
```

```
Raw Stress: 40675.0
Normalized Stress: 0.2444
```

```
print("Rank correlation: ", np.round(distcorr(dist_matrix, mds_res), 4))
```

```
Rank correlation:  0.8686
```

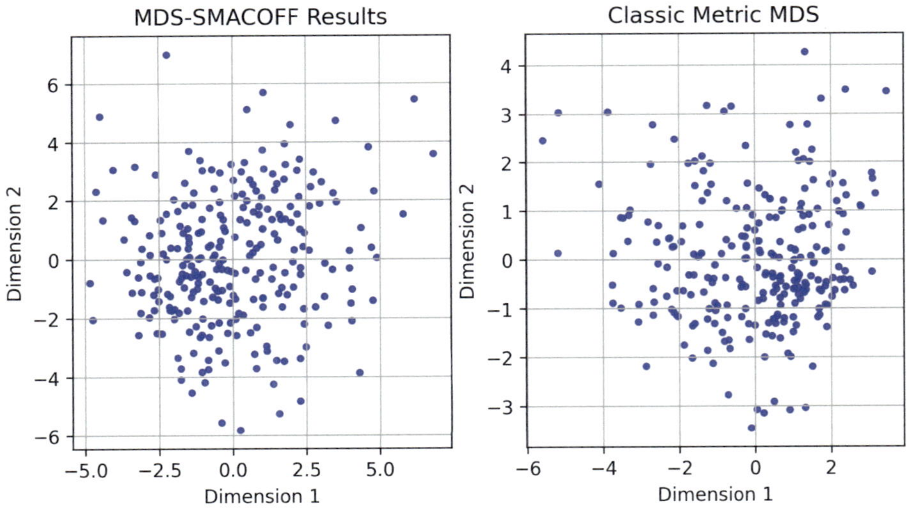

Figure 6.5: MDS Classic vs SMACOF

6.5 SMACOF vs classic MDS

6.5.1 Comparing Two Dimensions

To compare the layout obtained by SMACOF MDS to the one from classic MDS, we take the relevant columns from the `mds_df` (for SMACOF) and `mds_classic_df` (for classic MDS) DataFrames and apply the same matplotlib commands as in Section 6.3.1 to set the plots side by side. The corresponding code is given in the code block below.

The scatter plots in Figure 6.5 reveal quite a bit of discrepancies.

```
fig, axes = plt.subplots(1, 2, figsize = (8, 4))

# Plot MDS SMACOFF results
axes[0].scatter(mds_df['Dimension 1'], mds_df['Dimension 2'],
                color = 'blue', alpha = 0.7, s=10)
axes[0].set_title('MDS-SMACOFF Results')
axes[0].set_xlabel('Dimension 1')
axes[0].set_ylabel('Dimension 2')
axes[0].grid(True)

# Plot Classic MDS results
axes[1].scatter(mds_classic_df['Dimension 1'],
                mds_classic_df['Dimension 2'],
                color = 'blue', alpha = 0.7, s=10)
```

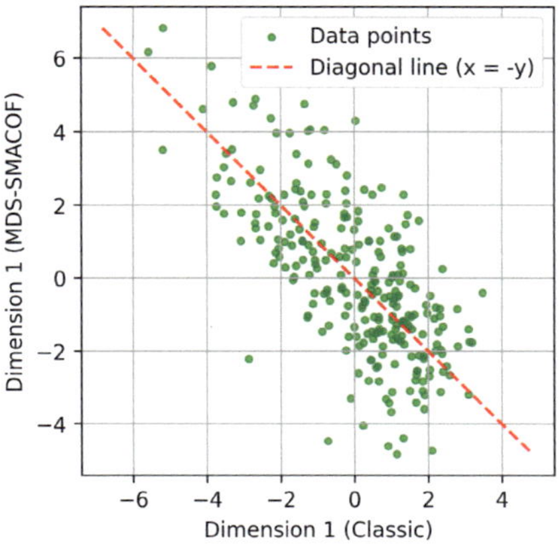

Figure 6.6: First dimension of MDS Classic and SMACOF

```
axes[1].set_title('Classic Metric MDS')
axes[1].set_xlabel('Dimension 1')
axes[1].set_ylabel('Dimension 2')
axes[1].grid(True)

plt.show()
```

6.5.2 Comparing the First Dimension

A closer comparison follows from a scatter plot of the first dimensions against each other, as in Section 6.3.2. The relevant columns are from `mds_df` and `mds_classic_df`.

The graph in Figure 6.6 clearly illustrates how the two methods result in different lower-dimensional embeddings.

```
# Combine MDS classic and SMACOF results into one DataFrame
comparison_df = pd.DataFrame({
    'Dimension 1C': mds_classic_df['Dimension 1'],
    'Dimension 1S': mds_df['Dimension 1']
})

x = comparison_df['Dimension 1C']
y = comparison_df['Dimension 1S']

# Get the range for the axes
x_min, x_max = x.min(), x.max()
```

```
y_min, y_max = y.min(), y.max()

# Determine the limits for the diagonal line (x = -y)

min_val = min(x_min, -y_max)  # Smallest value considering the inverted y
max_val = max(x_max, -y_min)  # Largest value considering the inverted y

# Create the plot
plt.figure(figsize = (4, 4))
plt.scatter(comparison_df['Dimension 1C'], comparison_df['Dimension 1S'],
            color = 'green', alpha = 0.7, label = 'Data points',s = 10)
plt.plot([min_val, max_val], [-min_val, -max_val], color = 'red',
         linestyle = '--', label = 'Diagonal line (x = -y)')

plt.xlabel('Dimension 1 (Classic)')
plt.ylabel('Dimension 1 (MDS-SMACOF)')
plt.grid(True)
plt.legend()
plt.show()
```

6.6 Spatializing MDS

A distinctive characteristics of the presentation of dimension reduction methods in the *GeoDa Cluster Book* is the introduction of different ways to *spatialize* the results of an MDS. This exploits the coordinates of the points in the embedded space as a shortcut for points in higher-dimensional space. In other words, clustering on the MDS points becomes a proxy for multi-dimensional clustering.

This is particularly relevant for multivariate *spatial* clustering, which we have seen is a challenge. Instead of tackling this as a multivariate problem, it is approached as an application of the analysis of point clusters in two dimensions.

We consider two specific applications: a neighbor match test and HDBScan, both computed with the MDS coordinates as variables.

6.6.1 Neighbor Match Test

One straightforward application is the computation of a *neighbor match test* on the MDS coordinates. In our current example, this can then be compared to the results of a neighbor match test in 10-dimensional space. As mentioned, it becomes computationally

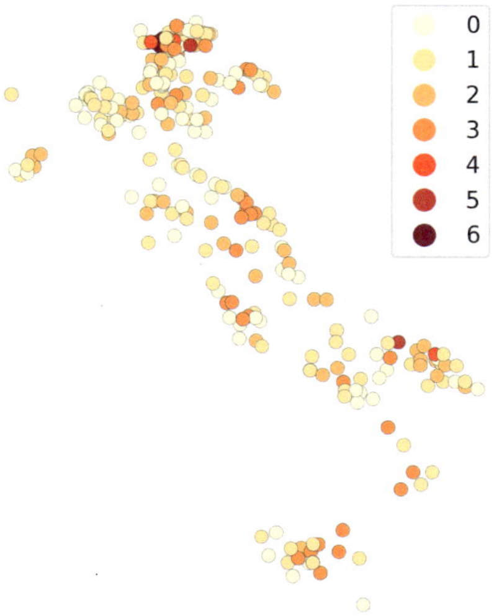

Figure 6.7: MDS Neighbor Match Test

quite challenging to obtain k-nearest neighbors in higher-dimensional spaces, so this provides an easy proxy.

We compute the neighbor match test by means of `pygeoda.neighbor_match_test`, as covered in Chapter 3. We first create a new DataFrame as a concatenation of the original point data with the coordinates from classic MDS, contained in `mds_classic_df`. We set $k = 12$ and plot the resulting neighbor cardinality in Figure 6.7. These results can then be compared to a neighbor match test applied to the original 10 variables (not shown here).

The code is given below.

```
#Neighbor Match Test
dfs_mds = pd.concat([dfs.reset_index(drop = True),
                     mds_classic_df.reset_index(drop = True)], axis = 1)
dfs_mds_g = pygeoda.open(dfs_mds)
nmt = pygeoda.neighbor_match_test(dfs_mds_g,
                      dfs_mds_g[['Dimension 1', 'Dimension 2']], 12)
dfs_mds['Cardinality'] = nmt['Cardinality']
fig, ax = plt.subplots(figsize = (5, 5))
dfs_mds.plot(column = 'Cardinality',
             ax = ax,
             legend = True,
             categorical = True,
             cmap = 'YlOrRd',
```

```
              edgecolor = 'black',
              linewidth = 0.1)

ax.set_axis_off()
```

We observe that there are several locations (banks) with considerable overlap between the neighbors in attribute space and the geographical neighbors. These represent multivariate spatial clusters.

6.6.2 HDBScan

Another alternative to a full multidimensional clustering exercise is to carry out density-based clustering on the MDS coordinate points. In other words, close points in MDS space represent close points in the higher-dimensional attribute space. Clusters in the MDS points detected by a method such as HDBScan thus become a proxy for full multivariate clustering.

We illustrate this with the `HDBSCAN` approach from scikit-learn, covered in Chapter 4. We set `min_cluster_size` to 7 and extract the dimensions from the `dfs_mds` data frame. We also add the cluster labels to the data frame as `hdb_labels`.

```
#HDBSCAN
hdb_results = HDBSCAN(min_cluster_size = 7).fit(dfs_mds[['Dimension 1',
                                                         'Dimension 2']])
hdb_labels = [str(label) for label in hdb_results.labels_]
n_clusters_ = len(set(hdb_labels)) - (1 if '-1' in hdb_labels else 0)
n_noise_ = hdb_labels.count('-1')
print("Estimated number of clusters: %d" % n_clusters_)
print("Estimated number of noise points: %d" % n_noise_)
dfs_mds['hdb_cluster'] = hdb_labels
```

```
Estimated number of clusters: 2
Estimated number of noise points: 54
```

We can now use the `cluster_stats` function imported from the `spatial_cluster_helper` module to provide a succint summary of the cluster results. As before, we pass the `labels_` array to this function. The result reveals 54 noise points and two remaining clusters, one large (199 banks) and one much smaller (8 banks). As mentioned in Chapter 4, for a realistic analysis considerable sensitivity analysis would be in order.

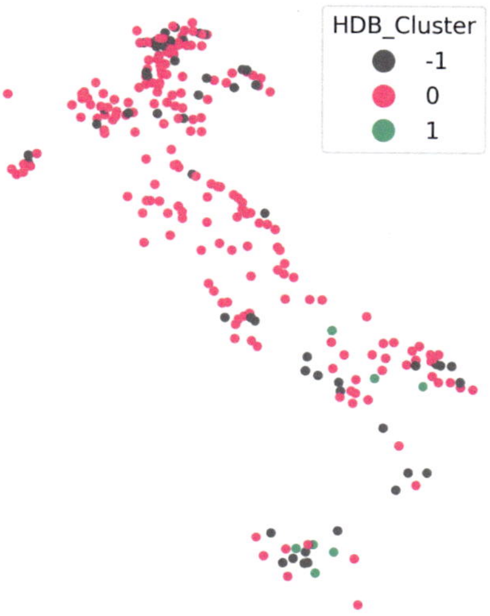

Figure 6.8: HDBSCAN on MDS coordinates

```
c_stats = cluster_stats(hdb_results.labels_)
```

```
 Labels  Cardinality
     -1           54
      0          199
      1            8
```

Finally, we also generate the associated cluster map in the usual way. The result is shown in Figure 6.8.

```
fig, ax = plt.subplots(figsize = (5, 5))
dfs_mds.plot(column = 'hdb_cluster', ax = ax, cmap = 'Dark2_r',
          legend = True, markersize = 10,
          legend_kwds = {'loc': 'upper right', 'title': 'HDB_Cluster'})
ax.set_axis_off()
plt.show()
```

6.6.3 Common Coverage Percentage

The *GeoDa Cluster Book* introduces the *common coverage percentage* as a measure to quantify the extent of *local* overlap between MDS solutions. This is based on a comparison of k-nearest neighbor *spatial weights* constructed from the respective coordinates. A special case is to compare the MDS solution to geographical spatial weights, similar in spirit to the principle behind the nearest neighbor match test.

A number of different applications are possible. First, one can assess the *intersection* between two spatial weights and the extent to which this matches the overall coverage. For example, if the weights are k-nearest neighbor with k = 6, then the number of non-zero elements in the weights matrix is $n_{max} = n \times k$. We can use the `w_intersection` method from `libpysal.weights` to find the number of common non-zero elements between the two spatial weights as the `nonzero` attribute of the intersection, say $n_{nonzero}$. Then the ratio of $n_{nonzero}/n_{max}$ or $n_{nonzero}/n^2$ gives a scale-free measure of the *common coverage* between the two weights. This is a quantitative measure of the commonality of nearest neighbors between the two sets of coordinates, which is easier to interpret than a visual assessment of the two scatter plots.

We first illustrate the measures for the classic MDS solution relative to the geographical k-nearest neighbors and then extend this to comparing the classic and SMACOF solutions. We start by going through the different steps in detail to illustrate the logic. Afterwards, we will be using the `common_coverage` function from the `spatial_cluster_helper` module.

The first step is to create spatial weights objects from the geographical coordinates, using `libpysal.weights.KNN.from_dataframe`, and from the embedded coordinates, using `libpysal.weights.KNN.from_array` (the coordinates are passed as a $n \times 2$ numpy array). We show the number of `nonzero` cells as an attribute of the weight object.

```
# knn spatial weights for geographical coordinates
w_pts = KNN.from_dataframe(dfs, k = 6)
print("Nonzero weights - geographical coordinates:", w_pts.nonzero)
w_mds_classic = KNN.from_array(embedding, k = 6)
w_mds_classic.nonzero
print("Nonzero weights - MDS:", w_mds_classic.nonzero)
```

```
Nonzero weights - geographical coordinates: 1566
Nonzero weights - MDS: 1566
```

Of course, the number of non-zero weights is nothing but $n \times k$, or 261 x 6. The *density* of these weights can be compared to a complete coverage (ignoring the diagonals, taking n^2 for simplicity) as the ratio nonzero/n^2. In this example, this yields about 2.3%.

```
n = embedding.shape[0]
print(np.round((100.0 * w_pts.nonzero) / n**2,4))
```

```
2.2989
```

The intersection between the two weights is obtained with the `w_intersection` method from `libpysal.weights`. We can then take the ratio of the non-zero elements to the complete coverage or to the maximum obtained for the specific value of k.

```
w_mds_knn = w_intersection(w_mds_classic, w_pts, silence_warnings = True)
nn_mds = w_mds_knn.nonzero
print("Nonzero elements in intersection:", nn_mds)
print("Absolute common coverage (percent):",
      np.round(100.0*nn_mds/n**2,4))
print("Relative common coverage (percent):",
      np.round(100.0*nn_mds/w_pts.nonzero,4))
```

```
Nonzero elements in intersection: 97
Absolute common coverage (percent): 0.1424
Relative common coverage (percent): 6.1941
```

If not silenced as in this example, the intersection operation yields some warnings for unconnected observations, which can be safely ignored in this context. The results show 97 overlapping non-zero weights, which yield an absolute common coverage percent (relative to the complete connection) of 0.14% and a relative common coverage percent of 6.19%.

The common coverage percentage between the point pattern and classic MDS can also be computed by means of the `common_coverage` function. The two arguments are the point GeoDataFrame (`dfs`), the n by 2 array with the embedded coordinates (`embedding`), and the number of nearest neighbors (`k = 6`). The result is a tuple, containing the number of overlapping neighbors, the common coverage percentage relative to the size of the weights and the common coverage percentage relative to the total number of neighbors.

```
comm_pt_classic = common_coverage(dfs, embedding, k = 6,
      silence_warnings = True)
print(np.round(comm_pt_classic,4))
```

```
[97.      0.1424  6.1941]
```

We similarly compute the common coverage percentage between classic MDS and MDS SMACOF. In this case, the first argument is the numpy array with classic MDS coordinates, `embedding`, and the second argument is the numpy array obtained from `MDS`, `mds_res`. The number of nearest neighbors is the default (`k = 6`) and therefore not specified. The result is again a tuple.

```
comm_class_smac = common_coverage(embedding, mds_res,
    silence_warnings = True)
print(np.round(comm_class_smac,4))
```

```
[587.        0.8617   37.484 ]
```

Relative to the match between the geographic coordinates and MDS, the two MDS solutions show 37.5% overlap in their non-zero intersections.

6.7 Stochastic Neighbor Embedding (SNE)

A drawback of the MDS approach is that it employs squared distances in the objective function, and thus emphasizes the impact of points that are far apart. As a consequence, MDS tends to do less well to keep the low-dimensional representation of *close* data points in high dimension also close together in the embedded space. A different approach is offered by *stochastic neighbor embedding* (SNE) developed by Hinton and Roweis (2003) and van der Maaten and Hinton (2008). Instead of basing the alignment between high and low-dimensional representations on a stress function that includes the actual distances, the problem is reformulated as one of matching two different probability distributions. These distributions replace the explicit distance measure by a probability that any point j is a neighbor of a given point i, with this probability as an inverse function of distance.

The essence of SNE then boils down to matching the probability distribution in high dimensional space to a distribution in low-dimensional embedded space, similar to how distances were matched in MDS. This is based on information-theoretic concepts, such as the Kullback-Leibler Information Criterion (KLIC) measure of fit. Technical details are given in Chapter 4 of the *GeoDa Cluster Book*.

6.7.1 Implementation

Stochastic Neighbor Embedding (SNE or t-SNE) is implemented as `TSNE` in `sklearn.manifold`. The overall interface is very similar to that of `MDS`, even though the algorithm is totally different. In addition, the results of `TSNE` are very sensitive to various parameter settings, so that just using the defaults is typically not satisfactory. This is also illustrated with the examples using `GeoDa` in Chapter 4 of the *GeoDa Cluster Book*.

Important arguments in the creation of an object of class `SNE` are:

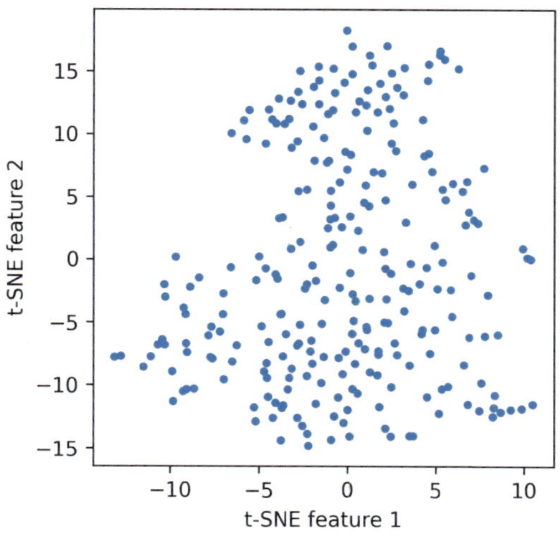

Figure 6.9: TSNE dimensions

- `n_components`: the dimension of the embedding, default = 2
- `perplexity`: a measure of the number of nearest neighbors considered, related to the entropy of the distribution, default = 30.0
- `learning_rate`: multiplier used in the optimization routine, default = 'auto'
- `max_iter`: the number of iterations, default = 1000
- `metric`: distance metric, default = 'euclidean'
- `random_state`: random seed to ensure replication, default = None

Of these, the perplexity turns out to be a critical parameter. It should be adjusted in a sensitivity analysis. Also, as mentioned before, it is good practice to set `random_state` to a fixed value so that the results can be reproduced.

Important attributes of a `TSNE` object are:

- `embedding_`: the resulting coordinate vectors
- `kl_divergence_`: the Kullback-Leibler divergence between the original distribution and the final point distribution
- `learning_rate_`: the effective learning rate
- `n_iter_`: the number of iterations used

As in the case of `MDS`, we can use either `fit` or `fit_transform` to compute a solution.

Further details can be found at https://scikit-learn.org/stable/modules/generated/sklearn.manifold.TSNE.html.

We implement `TSNE` using `fit_transform` with the matrix `X` as argument. We use the familiar matplotlib commands to plot the resulting coordinate scatter plot, shown in Figure 6.9. The only argument is `random_state`, which we again set to the same value as in GeoDa. Nevertheless, there are several small differences between the implementation of the highly nonlinear algorithm so that it becomes near impossible to replicate the results exactly. Also, the type of animation possible with GeoDa cannot be achieved in a static Python environment.

```
#stochastic neighbor embedding
tsne = TSNE(random_state = 123456789)
tsne_res = tsne.fit_transform(X)


plt.figure(figsize = (4, 4))
plt.scatter(tsne_res[:, 0], tsne_res[:, 1],s=10)

plt.xlabel('t-SNE feature 1')
plt.ylabel('t-SNE feature 2')
plt.show()
```

Some characteristics of the solution.

```
print("Kullback-Leibler divergence:", np.round(tsne.kl_divergence_,4))
print("Number of iterations:", tsne.n_iter_)
print("Learning rate:", tsne.learning_rate_)
```

```
Kullback-Leibler divergence: 0.7582
Number of iterations: 999
Learning rate: 50.0
```

It cannot be emphasized enough that considerable experimentation is needed to assess the sensitivity of the results to the various tuning parameters. This is beyond our current scope.

6.7.2 Solution characteristics

The t-SNE object created by scikit-learn only contains the Kullback_Leibler divergence as a measure of fit. Alternatives, such as the rank correlation coefficient, can be computed by means of the distcorr function defined above. The two arguments are the original pairwise distance matrix, dist_matrix and the coordinates of the embedded points, contained in tsne_res.

```
print("Rank correlation:", np.round(distcorr(dist_matrix, tsne_res), 4))
```

```
Rank correlation: 0.6275
```

6.7.3 Spatializing t-SNE

We can apply the same visualization and spatial analysis of the t-SNE coordinates as illustrated above for MDS. This includes a nearest neighbor match test, HDBScan on the t-SNE coordinates, and an assessment of the common coverage percentage. This is not further pursued here.

6.8 Practice

Given the sensitivity of the results to various starting values for the parameters, considerable experimentation is in order. For example, different random seeds can be considered, and the important parameters of t-SNE adjusted. The results can be compared in terms of their fit with the helper functions `stress_value` or `distcorr`, and their degree of overlap assessed visually as well as by means of `common_coverage`.

7 Hierarchical Clustering Methods

In this Chapter, we begin our overview of traditional clustering methods by considering techniques that build up the clusters step-by-step, in a *hierarchical* fashion. There are two approaches. One, *agglomerative* clustering, starts from the bottom and works its way up. More precisely, initially, each observation forms a separate cluster. Subsequently, pairs of observations are systematically grouped into larger entities, until the whole data set forms one cluster. In the other approach, *divisive* clustering, the opposite path is taken. One starts with the full set of observations as one cluster, and subsequently splits this into subclusters until each observation is again its own cluster. In the current Chapter, we only consider agglomerative clustering. A form of divisive clustering is included in the discussion of spatially constrained clustering in Chapter 12. Hierarchical clustering methods are covered in Chapter 5 of the *GeoDa Cluster Book*.

There are two important elements to be considered in the grouping of observations:

- *linkage* option, i.e., how to decide which observations/clusters are *closest*
- *update* function, i.e., how to compute the *distance* between clusters once they are formed from different observations

The main methods are characterized by different linkage options. We consider the four most common ones, i.e., *Ward's* method, *single linkage*, *complete linkage* and *average linkage*.

An important aspect of hierarchical clustering is the so-called *dendrogram*, which visualizes the process of grouping observations/entities into larger entities and the associated distance criterion. The number of clusters is not set initially, but is determined by a *cut* of the dendrogram.

We focus mostly on Ward's method, which is arguably the most robust and most commonly used method. However, it only works for a squared distance criterion, whereas other measures work with any distance.

Hierarchical clustering is in implemented through `AgglomerativeClustering` from `sklearn.cluster`. An alternative method to obtain hierarchical clusters, which is somewhat easier to visualize, is contained in `scipy.cluster.hierarchy`. As before, we will also need `StandardScaler` from `sklearn.preprocessing` to standardize the data. In order to implement some of the *spatialization* of these methods, we import several functions from the `spatial-cluster-helper` package:

- ensure_datasets
- cluster_stats
- plot_dendrogram
- cluster_center
- cluster_fit
- cluster_map

As before, we will also need numpy, geopandas and matplotlib.pyplot.

To illustrate these methods, we will use the **Chi-CCA** sample data set with socio-economic determinants of health for Community Areas in 2020 in Chicago, IL. It has only 77 observations, which facilitates the drawing of a dendrogram. The latter becomes difficult for larger data sets.

> Required Packages
>
> numpy, geopandas, matplotlib.pyplot, sklearn.cluster, sklearn.preprocessing, scipy.cluster.hierarchy, spatial-cluster-helper

> Required Data Sets
>
> Chi-CCA

7.1 Preliminaries

7.1.1 Import Required Modules

```
import geopandas as gpd
import numpy as np
import matplotlib.pyplot as plt

from sklearn.cluster import AgglomerativeClustering
from sklearn.preprocessing import StandardScaler

from scipy.cluster.hierarchy import dendrogram, linkage

from spatial_cluster_helper import ensure_datasets,cluster_stats, \
               plot_dendrogram, cluster_center, cluster_fit, cluster_map
```

Table 7.1: Partial Contents of CCA Sample Data Set

	area_num_1	community	shape_area	shape_len	districtno	district	TOT_POP
0	35.0	DOUGLAS	4.600462e+07	31027.054510	7.0	South Side	21325.0
1	36.0	OAKLAND	1.691396e+07	19565.506153	7.0	South Side	7227.0
2	37.0	FULLER PARK	1.991670e+07	25339.089750	7.0	South Side	2394.0

Table 7.2: Variables for Hierarchical Clustering

Column Name	Variable Description
INCPERCAP	Per capita income
Und20	Population share aged < 20
Ov65	Population share aged > 65
Minrty	Percentage of minority population
Unemprt	Unemployment rate
Noveh	Percentage of households with no vehicle
Lt_high	Percentage of population without high school education
Rentocc	Percentage of renter-occupied housing
Rntburd	Rent burden
Noeng	Percentage of population with limited English proficiency

7.1.2 Load Data

We follow the usual practice of setting a path (if needed), read the data from the `Chicago_2020_sdoh` shape file and carry out a quick check of its contents (only partially shown in Table 7.1).

```
# Setting working folder:
#path = "/your/path/to/data/"
path = "./datasets/"

# Select the Chicago community area data:
shpfile = "Chi_CCA/Chicago_2020_sdoh.shp"

# Load the data:
ensure_datasets(shpfile, folder_path = path)
dfs = gpd.read_file(path + shpfile)

print(dfs.shape)
dfs.head(3)
```

```
(77, 233)
```

Table 7.3: Socio-Economic Determinants of Health – Descriptive Statistics

	Incpercap	Und20	Ov65	Minrty	Unemprt	Noveh	Lt_high	Rentocc	Rntburd	Noeng
count	77.00	77.00	77.00	77.00	77.00	77.00	77.00	77.00	77.00	77.00
mean	32501.26	24.56	13.69	72.05	10.56	12.73	16.00	45.20	25.71	33.38
std	19482.12	6.35	4.61	26.91	6.87	8.01	9.63	15.75	8.26	26.73
min	11857.00	8.90	4.80	16.79	0.37	1.93	1.73	9.13	11.23	2.19
25%	19842.00	20.25	10.12	51.74	5.01	6.04	9.12	31.70	20.40	7.38
50%	25944.00	25.08	12.82	85.51	8.74	10.53	14.69	48.36	23.94	26.71
75%	36736.00	29.41	16.09	96.37	15.74	19.92	21.70	56.20	29.80	55.36
max	101727.00	44.28	26.52	99.50	30.42	34.31	44.65	76.92	49.85	86.53

7.1.3 Variables

We replicate the illustration in Chapter 5 of the *GeoDa Cluster Book* and use a subset of socio-economic determinants of health from the study by Kolak et al. (2020) that included all the U.S. census tracts. The variables and a brief description are listed in Table 7.2 on page 93. The selected variables are included in `varlist`, as before. We also create a separate `data_cluster` DataFrame with just those variables and provide some descriptive statistics, listed in Table 7.3.

```
varlist = ['INCPERCAP', 'Und20', 'Ov65', 'Minrty', 'Unemprt',
           'Noveh', 'Lt_high', 'Rentocc', 'Rntburd', 'Noeng']
data_cluster = dfs[varlist]

np.round(data_cluster.describe(), 2)
```

7.2 Ward's method

We start by considering Ward's method. We illustrate four important aspects of the solution: computing the clusters (cluster labels), visualizing the dendrogram, calculating characteristics of a cluster solution, and visualizing the clusters in a *cluster map*.

7.2.1 Cluster Computation

One approach to obtain the cluster computation is with the `AgglomerativeClustering` class of scikit-learn. For details, see https://scikit-learn.org/stable/modules/generated/sklearn.cluster.AgglomerativeClustering.html. The second option, using `scipy.cluster.hierarchy` is considered in the discussion of the dendrogram in Section 7.2.2.

The main arguments to create an instance of the `AgglomerativeClustering` class are the number of clusters, `n_clusters`, the `linkage` option, as well as an option to compute the distances from an initial array of inputs, `compute_distances = True`. As before, the input data frame is first standardized using `fit_transform` from `StandardScaler`. Once an instance of the class is created, the `fit` method returns the results, with the cluster labels contained in the `labels_` attribute. Other attributes are provided as well, but the labels are our main interest here (see the extended documentation for details). We summarize the results with our `cluster_stats` utility function.

We illustrate this for Ward's method with a for k=5.

```
# Select the desired number of clusters and linkage method
n_clusters = 5
method = 'ward'

# Standardize the data
X = StandardScaler().fit_transform(data_cluster)

# Fit Agglomerative Clustering
agg_clust = AgglomerativeClustering(n_clusters = n_clusters,
                    linkage = method, compute_distances = True)
agg_clust.fit(X)
cluster_labels = agg_clust.labels_
c_stats = cluster_stats(cluster_labels)
```

Labels	Cardinality
0	21
1	15
2	15
3	13
4	13

The resulting clusters are labeled from 0 to 4. They are relatively balanced, with 21 observations in the largest cluster, two clusters with 15 and two clusters with 13.

An interesting piece of information is contained in the `distances_` attribute. This shows the distances at which each cluster is formed, increasing from the smallest distance (here 0.36) to the one between the final two clusters that form the full data set (here 20.3).

```
agg_clust.distances_
```

```
array([ 0.36274015,  0.53936027,  0.68178409,  0.71372655,  0.78778369,
        0.79647585,  0.84125925,  0.84297015,  0.85370346,  0.8831146 ,
        0.88675916,  0.92955806,  0.98841925,  1.05998996,  1.06438798,
        1.07255791,  1.0765715 ,  1.1538963 ,  1.21130411,  1.25532594,
```

```
       1.27768021,  1.32193569,  1.35293476,  1.36454495,  1.37498667,
       1.37632845,  1.39756016,  1.41986327,  1.42228951,  1.42756184,
       1.46881725,  1.51405012,  1.52158604,  1.53340115,  1.5670125 ,
       1.73174358,  1.73496471,  1.78386891,  1.84018742,  1.89045915,
       1.91123968,  1.94707456,  1.95727687,  1.99076458,  2.00088467,
       2.04991017,  2.14413004,  2.28039251,  2.31301355,  2.41508411,
       2.43475984,  2.47209374,  2.5891719 ,  2.63945666,  2.70434923,
       2.85506842,  3.01764305,  3.08092386,  3.10174269,  3.14956205,
       3.2148449 ,  4.25006606,  4.29530368,  4.56351567,  4.97645808,
       5.18803816,  5.32611836,  5.50111751,  5.85655264,  6.29068946,
       6.77711462,  7.92611783, 11.16248439, 12.85337461, 17.02788825,
      20.30116606])
```

7.2.2 Dendrogram

The scikit-learn functionality does not return a dendrogram as such. It can be constructed from various attributes of the cluster object, but this is not straightforward. Therefore, in order to visualize the hierarchy of grouping decisions, we use an alternative implementation, which is part of `scipy.cluster`, namely `scipy.cluster.hierarchy`.

The setup is somewhat different from the scikit-learn approach and provides functions to compute hierarchical cluster results, specifically through the `linkage` command. The function returns a hierarchical cluster as a numpy array, which can then be visualized as a `dendrogram`. In addition, other summaries are available as well, see https://docs.scipy.org/doc/scipy-1.16.0/reference/cluster.hierarchy.html for details.

We illustrate this for our example. In a first step, we create the cluster result by applying `linkage` to the array `X` with the standardized values (the same as used above). A second argument is the method, again `"ward"`. The function returns a numpy array with all the linkage information expressed in a n-1 by 4 matrix. In each row, the first two elements refer to cluster indices that are being combined, with values less than n (starting at 0) referring to original observations, and values of n and larger referring to clusters that are combinations of earlier clusters. The third column gives the inter-cluster distance, and the last column shows the number of original observations contained in the cluster.

The inter-cluster distance shown in the third column is the same as what we had in the `distances_` attribute of the cluster constructed with scikit-learn in Section 7.2.1.

To illustrate this for our example, we list the first five rows. In the first row, individual observations 59 and 62 are combined to yield a cluster of two (element in column 4). In the third row, observation 50 is combined with 77, which is the first cluster (or 59 and 62). As a result, it now consists of 3 elements (shown in the fourth column).

```
Z = linkage(X, method = 'ward')
print(Z.shape)
print(Z[0:5,:])
```

```
(76, 4)
[[59.         62.          0.36274015  2.        ]
 [13.         21.          0.53936027  2.        ]
 [50.         77.          0.68178409  3.        ]
 [18.         20.          0.71372655  2.        ]
 [ 5.         22.          0.78778369  2.        ]]
```

The full set of distances (column 2) is identical to the values contained in `distances_` above.

```
Z[:,2]
```

```
array([ 0.36274015,  0.53936027,  0.68178409,  0.71372655,  0.78778369,
        0.79647585,  0.84125925,  0.84297015,  0.85370346,  0.8831146 ,
        0.88675916,  0.92955806,  0.98841925,  1.05998996,  1.06438798,
        1.07255791,  1.0765715 ,  1.1538963 ,  1.21130411,  1.25532594,
        1.27768021,  1.32193569,  1.35293476,  1.36454495,  1.37498667,
        1.37632845,  1.39756016,  1.41986327,  1.42228951,  1.42756184,
        1.46881725,  1.51405012,  1.52158604,  1.53340115,  1.5670125 ,
        1.73174358,  1.73496471,  1.78386891,  1.84018742,  1.89045915,
        1.91123968,  1.94707456,  1.95727687,  1.99076458,  2.00088467,
        2.04991017,  2.14413004,  2.28039251,  2.31301355,  2.41508411,
        2.43475984,  2.47209374,  2.5891719 ,  2.63945666,  2.70434923,
        2.85506842,  3.01764305,  3.08092386,  3.10174269,  3.14956205,
        3.2148449 ,  4.25006606,  4.29530368,  4.56351567,  4.97645808,
        5.18803816,  5.32611836,  5.50111751,  5.85655264,  6.29068946,
        6.77711462,  7.92611783, 11.16248439, 12.85337461, 17.02788825,
       20.30116606])
```

We can now proceed and graph the dendrogram. The `dendrogram` function takes the linkage array (Z) as well as several other arguments to fine tune the looks of the graph. The most important of these is `color_threshold`, which is the cut-off distance to define the clusters. Since the distances in Z are sorted from smallest to largest, the top distance corresponds to a single cluster, the next to last to a result with two clusters, etc. As a result, the cut-off distance for `n_clusters` is contained in position - (n_clusters - 1), or 1 - n_clusters from the end (a negative entry for the element). We pass this distance to

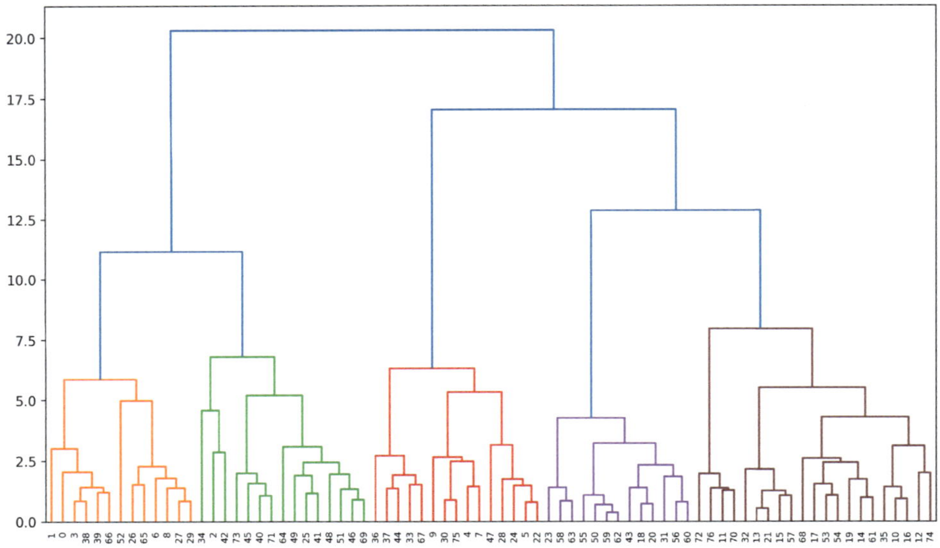

Figure 7.1: Dendrogram

`color_threshold` so that all the branches corresponding to each cluster are colored the same in the graph.

Other arguments are `orientation` (`top` for a top-down graph), `leaf_rotation` (90 for the top-down graph), and `leaf_font_size` (size of the font of the observation label, here 7). Some experimentation with these may be needed for each particular instance.

We use `plt` to set the `figsize` and plot the graph. There are also options to create a dendrogram for larger data sets, where the full graph is no longer practical. This is not further considered (see the detailed documentation).

The `dendrogram` function returns a dictionary that contains all the details necessary to construct the graph. Typically, this is not needed, except for the `"leaves_color_list"` item, which can be used to compute the `cluster_stats`.

In the code block below, we first create the dendrogram and then plot it. The resulting graph is shown in Figure 7.1.

```
plt.figure(figsize = (12,7))
R1 = dendrogram(Z, orientation = 'top', leaf_rotation = 90,
            leaf_font_size = 7, color_threshold = Z[1-n_clusters, 2])
plt.show()
```

The dendrogram illustrates the steps by which the clusters are constructed, with the horizontal bars drawn at the height of the corresponding distance. For example, from the contents of Z above, we know that the first step is to combine 59 and 62, for a distance of 0.36. Indeed, we can find the lowest horizontal bar connecting 59 and 62 in the purple cluster. The second grouping, between 13 and 21, for a distance of 0.54 is shown in the brown cluster, etc.

An interesting side result of the dendrogram calculation dictionary is the `"leaves_color_list"` item. It contains the color codes associated with each cluster as a distinct string. We can now use the `cluster_stats` function from our helper module to create a table with the cluster cardinality (the only argument is the list of labels). Note that unlike what is the case in scikit-learn, cluster labels are not explicitly provided by the `scipy.cluster.hierarchy` functionality.

The result again shows the five clusters, but now in a slightly different order.

```
c_stats = cluster_stats(R1["leaves_color_list"])
```

```
Labels Cardinality
    C1          13
    C2          15
    C3          15
    C4          13
    C5          21
```

7.2.2.1 `plot_dendrogram` helper function

The helper function `plot_dendrogram` provides a one-line way to create a dendrogram plot. The first required argument is either the result of a `linkage` function as input (a numpy array), or a standardized data matrix. The default is to have the linkage result. If a standardized data matrix is the input, then the argument `package` must be set to `"scikit"` (the default is `"scipy"`, for a linkage result). The second required argument is the number of clusters, `n_clusters`.

Other arguments include `labels` (default `None`) for any labels other than sequence numbers to be assigned to the leaves of the graph, a linkage method (default `"ward"`, only required when a standardized array is passed, otherwise ignored), and a couple of customizations of the plot. These consist of `figsize` (default `(12,7)`), and `title` (default "Dendrogram").

Note that this function only works well for smallish data sets. Large data sets require further customization, which is currently not implemented.

In the example given in the code block below, we pass `X`, keep the number of clusters to `n_clusters`, set the `package = "scikit"`, use the `community` variable from the data frame as the labels, and customize the title to `"Ward Dendrogram"`. The result

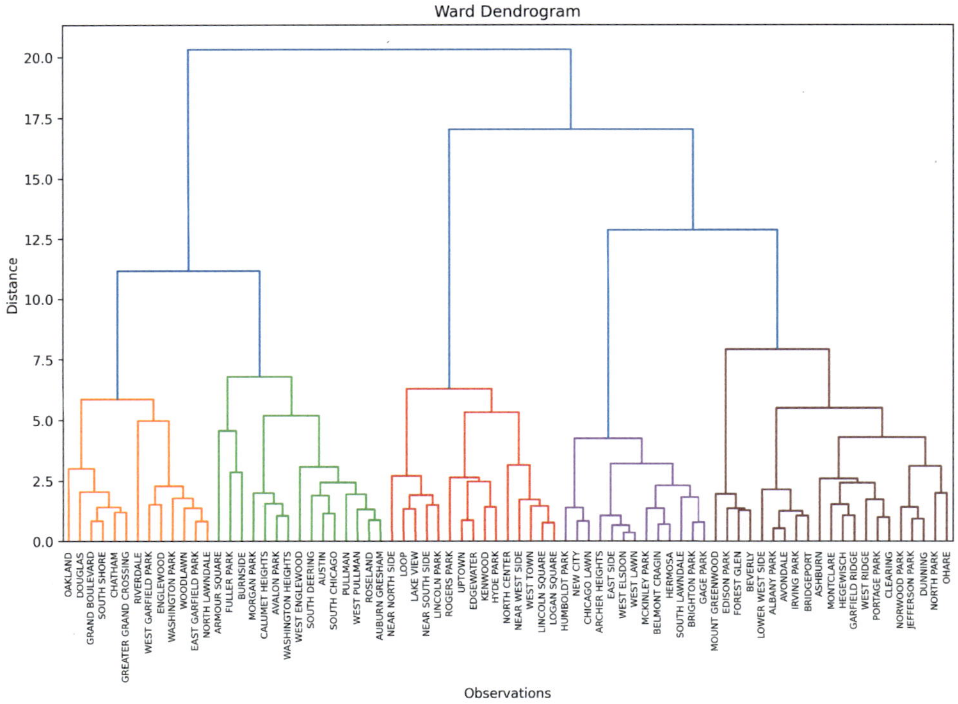

Figure 7.2: Dendrogram graph obtained from helper function

dictionary is passed to R2, which is then used to summarize the cluster labels. The dendrogram in Figure 7.2 is identical to the one in Figure 7.1 on page 98, except that now the community area names are used as labels for the observations.

```
R2 = plot_dendrogram(X, n_clusters = n_clusters, package = "scikit",
                     labels = dfs['community'].values,
                     title = "Ward Dendrogram")
```

We obtain the same cluster statistics as before with cluster_stats, but now pass R2["leaves_color_list"] from the result dictionary (R2).

```
c_stats = cluster_stats(R2["leaves_color_list"])
```

```
Labels Cardinality
    C1          13
    C2          15
    C3          15
    C4          13
    C5          21
```

7.2.3 Cluster Centers

A useful property of each cluster is its *center*, i.e., the mean or median of the variables for those observations included in the cluster.

We accomplish this by means of a **groupby** computation on the cluster labels. These are first added to the DataFrame with the original observations (not the standardized values). The resulting centers can be visualized in a number of different ways, for example in a parallel coordinate plot or as a conditional box plot . This is not further pursued here.

```
dt_clust = data_cluster.copy().assign(cluster = cluster_labels)
clust_means = dt_clust.groupby('cluster').mean()
clust_medians = dt_clust.groupby('cluster').median()
print("Cluster Means:\n", np.round(clust_means, 2))
print("\nCluster Medians:\n", np.round(clust_medians, 2))
```

```
Cluster Means:
         INCPERCAP  Und20   Ov65  Minrty  Unemprt  Noveh  Lt_high  Rentocc
cluster
0         34837.81  24.17  14.66   50.99     5.46   5.66    13.66    33.37
1         22405.93  23.39  19.44   94.75    16.61  13.73    16.41    40.44
2         62399.07  16.61  10.79   42.53     4.29  18.05     5.73    54.33
3         18938.69  30.29  10.61   89.55    10.88   6.69    30.92    41.98
4         19440.38  29.99  11.92   96.43    18.75  22.93    16.20    62.47

        Rntburd  Noeng
cluster
0         19.05  45.71
1         28.29  12.52
2         21.55  25.26
3         25.13  73.03
4         38.88   7.23

Cluster Medians:
         INCPERCAP  Und20   Ov65  Minrty  Unemprt  Noveh  Lt_high  Rentocc
cluster
0          31267.0  23.60  15.63   57.22     5.21   5.80    14.69    30.76
1          21723.0  24.65  18.23   98.39    16.13  11.99    15.41    41.20
2          57167.0  17.34   9.62   43.40     4.02  19.41     5.77    56.28
3          19446.0  30.50  10.43   87.37    11.35   6.12    29.41    44.43
4          18641.0  29.41  11.94   97.45    17.07  22.14    13.45    61.76

        Rntburd  Noeng
cluster
0         19.55  49.63
1         27.92   7.29
```

```
2            21.52  24.57
3            24.81  77.56
4            38.31   5.06
```

The helper function `cluster_center` computes the cluster means and medians in a single command. The required arguments are a DataFrame with the variables used in the clustering exercise and an array of cluster labels. The function returns a tuple with DataFrames of the means and medians.

To illustrate this, we pass the `data_cluster` DataFrame and the set of labels from `R2["leaves_color_list"]`, and print out the means.

```
c_means,c_medians = cluster_center(data_cluster, R2["leaves_color_list"])
print("Cluster Means:\n", np.round(c_means, 2))
```

```
Cluster Means:
           INCPERCAP  Und20   Ov65  Minrty  Unemprt  Noveh  Lt_high  Rentocc
cluster
C1          32349.54  24.53  14.64   70.26    11.19  18.16    10.97    55.98
C2          29496.73  25.42  11.35   69.98     7.73   9.53    19.70    47.75
C3          40604.53  20.07  14.86   72.58     9.56  17.65    15.36    50.04
C4          30449.69  26.57  13.76   77.16    12.43  10.43    16.15    38.07
C5          30223.24  25.93  13.90   71.09    11.75   9.57    16.82    37.65

         Rntburd  Noeng
cluster
C1         28.84  23.32
C2         26.47  46.41
C3         26.31  28.09
C4         23.28  31.36
C5         24.31  35.32
```

7.2.4 Cluster Fit

The main objective of a clustering exercise is to decompose the total sum of squared differences from the mean (TSS) indexTSS into a within cluster (WSS) and between cluster (BSS) part. The more similar the members of a cluster are, the smaller WSS will be. As a consequence, BSS will be larger, since the two are complements: TSS = WSS + BSS. The higher the ratio of BSS to TSS, the *better* the fit.

Since we typically standardize the variables before the clustering exercise, the mean is zero and the variance for each variable equals 1, hence the TSS will equal $p \times n$, where p is the number of variables and n is the number of observations. In our example, this would be

770. This is a direct result of how `StandardScaler` carries out the standardization, i.e., it uses n as the denominator in the computation of the variance/standard deviation.

In contrast, `GeoDa` uses $n-1$ as the denominator (for an *unbiased* estimate). As a result, `GeoDa` will report 760 as the TSS. We address this in our helper function (`cluster_fit`), by rescaling `X` with $\sqrt{(n-1)/n}$.

First, we illustrate the steps using the `StandardScaler` approach. Note that the ratio BSS/TSS is not affected by the choice of the standardization, but the individual WSS and the TSS measures are.

In order to compute the WSS by cluster, we need to compute the cluster means. In contrast to what we just carried out, now the calculation must be done for the standardized variables, but otherwise the approach is the same, using `groupby` for the cluster labels.

In each cluster, the WSS is the sum of squared deviations from the mean. The sum of all the cluster-specific WSS is the total WSS. The BSS is obtained as TSS - WSS. The final ratio is BSS/TSS.

First, the TSS.

```
tss = np.sum(np.square(X))
print("TSS:", tss)
```

```
TSS: 770.0
```

We compute the WSS for each cluster by first calculating the cluster mean using the same `groupby` approach as above, but now applied to the standardized variables. We then square the difference between each cluster member observation and the mean and sum the result.

```
data_tmp = data_cluster.copy().assign(cluster = cluster_labels)
wss_per_cluster = []
for cluster in set(cluster_labels):
    cluster_data = X[data_tmp['cluster'] == cluster]
    cluster_mean = cluster_data.mean(axis = 0)
    wss = np.sum(np.square(cluster_data - cluster_mean))
    wss_per_cluster.append(wss)
wss_per_cluster = [float(wss) for wss in wss_per_cluster]
print("Cluster WSS:\n", np.round(wss_per_cluster, 3))
```

```
Cluster WSS:
 [81.496 68.007 57.317 22.29  44.942]
```

The total WSS is simply the sum of the cluster-specific WSS.

```
wss = np.sum(wss_per_cluster)
print("WSS:", np.round(wss, 3))
```

```
WSS: 274.052
```

Finally, the BSS is the complement of WSS, or TSS - WSS and the ratio BSS/TSS can be computed.

```
bss = tss - wss
btratio = bss/tss
print("BSS:", np.round(bss, 3), "\nBSS/TSS:", np.round(btratio, 3))
```

```
BSS: 495.948
BSS/TSS: 0.644
```

The helper function `cluster_fit` carries out these calculations and returns them as a dictionary, optionally listing the result. Its required arguments are `data` for the original cluster variable observations, `clustlabels` for the cluster labels (to carry out the `groupby`), and `n_clusters`, the number of clusters. Optional arguments are `correct` (default is `False`) and `printopt` (default is `True`).

Computing the standardized values with n-1 as the denominator is achieved by setting `correct = True`, and avoiding a listing of the results is set with `printopt = False`.

We first illustrate this for the standard options. The results are identical to those shown above.

```
clusfit = cluster_fit(data = data_cluster, clustlabels = cluster_labels,
                n_clusters = n_clusters)
```

```
Total Sum of Squares (TSS): 770.0
Within-cluster Sum of Squares (WSS) for each cluster: [81.496 68.007
                                                        57.317  22.29  44.942]
Total Within-cluster Sum of Squares (WSS): 274.052
Between-cluster Sum of Squares (BSS): 495.948
Ratio of BSS to TSS: 0.644
```

With `correct = True`, the standardization is different. The results now replicate those given by `GeoDa`. Note how the BSS/TSS ratio is unaffected.

```
clusfit = cluster_fit(data = data_cluster, clustlabels = cluster_labels,
                n_clusters = n_clusters, correct = True)
```

```
Total Sum of Squares (TSS): 760.0
Within-cluster Sum of Squares (WSS) for each cluster: [80.437 67.124
                                                    56.572  22.    44.358]
Total Within-cluster Sum of Squares (WSS): 270.493
Between-cluster Sum of Squares (BSS): 489.507
Ratio of BSS to TSS: 0.644
```

7.2.5 Cluster Map

A final summary of the cluster results is a cluster map , a simple categorical thematic map that highlights the membership of clusters.

The cluster map is implemented in the helper function `cluster_map`, with some very simple defaults. It takes as required arguments the GeoDataFrame and the cluster labels. Other arguments are `figsize` (default `(5,5)`), `title` (default `"Clusters"`), and `cmap` for the color map (default `"Set2"`). The result is shown in Figure 7.3 on page 106.

In our example:

```
cluster_map(dfs, cluster_labels, figsize = (5,5),
            title="", cmap='Set2', legend_fontsize=8)
```

7.3 Other Linkage Functions

The other linkage functions are invoked with methods `"single"`, `"complete"` and `"average"`. In the code block below, we create a loop over the linkage functions and use our helper functions to list the cluster results, centers, measures of fit and the cluster map. The corresponding dendrograms and cluster maps are given in Figures 7.4 to 7.6.

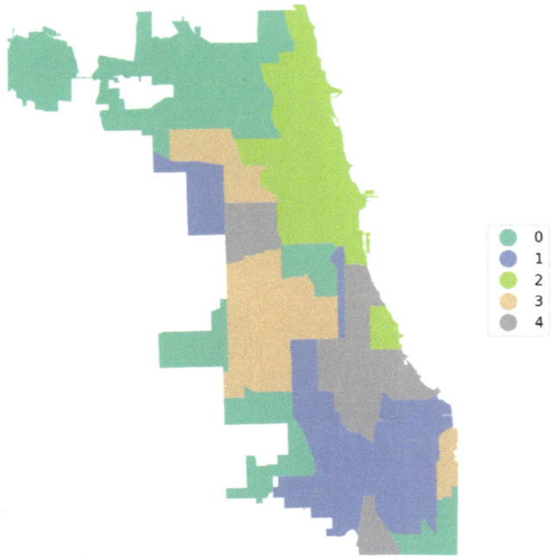

Figure 7.3: Cluster map for Ward linkage clustering

```
clustmethods = ['single', 'complete', 'average']
for cl in clustmethods:
    clust = AgglomerativeClustering(n_clusters = n_clusters,
                    linkage = cl, compute_distances = True)
    clust.fit(X)
    cluster_labels = clust.labels_
    print("---------------------------------\n")
    print("Clusters", cl, "linkage")
    c_stats = cluster_stats(cluster_labels)
    plot_dendrogram(X, n_clusters = n_clusters, package = "scikit",
                    method = cl,labels = dfs['community'].values)
    c_means,c_medians = cluster_center(data_cluster, cluster_labels)
    print("Cluster Means:\n", np.round(c_means, 2))
    print("Cluster Medians:\n", np.round(c_medians, 2))
    clusfit = cluster_fit(data = data_cluster,
                 clustlabels = cluster_labels,
                 n_clusters = n_clusters)
    cluster_map(dfs, cluster_labels, title="",
                cmap='Set2', legend_fontsize=8)
```

```
---------------------------------

Clusters single linkage
 Labels  Cardinality
      0           73
```

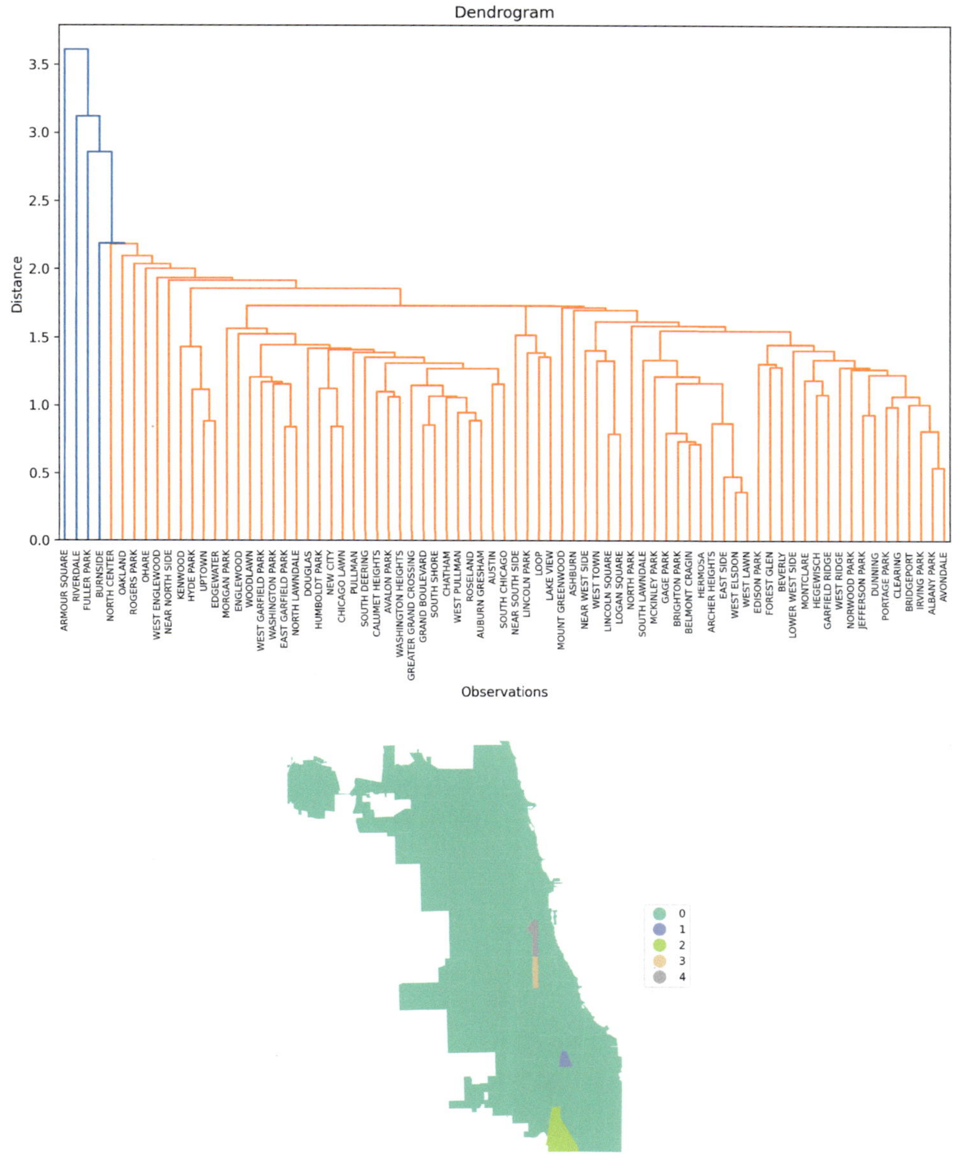

Figure 7.4: Single Linkage Clustering

```
1            1
2            1
3            1
4            1

Cluster Means:
```

```
         INCPERCAP  Und20   Ov65   Minrty  Unemprt  Noveh  Lt_high  Rentocc
cluster
0         33320.42  24.59  13.31   70.78    10.01  12.04    15.64    44.51
1         19972.00  13.31  26.52   99.50    20.14  16.95    15.41    36.60
2         11857.00  44.28   4.80   98.79    30.42  30.33    15.69    76.92
3         16519.00  19.88  26.44   96.37    23.62  34.31    21.40    56.20
4         21858.00  18.54  24.82   86.05     8.21  19.92    37.18    61.19

         Rntburd  Noeng
cluster
0          25.49  34.05
1          29.95   4.41
2          30.71   3.09
3          31.26   7.38
4          27.29  69.47
Cluster Medians:
         INCPERCAP  Und20   Ov65   Minrty  Unemprt  Noveh  Lt_high  Rentocc
cluster
0          26943.0  25.14  12.73   82.70     8.34  10.01    14.41    48.32
1          19972.0  13.31  26.52   99.50    20.14  16.95    15.41    36.60
2          11857.0  44.28   4.80   98.79    30.42  30.33    15.69    76.92
3          16519.0  19.88  26.44   96.37    23.62  34.31    21.40    56.20
4          21858.0  18.54  24.82   86.05     8.21  19.92    37.18    61.19

         Rntburd  Noeng
cluster
0          23.62  28.02
1          29.95   4.41
2          30.71   3.09
3          31.26   7.38
4          27.29  69.47

Total Sum of Squares (TSS): 770.0
Within-cluster Sum of Squares (WSS) for each cluster: [677.299   0.
                                                        0.      0.      0.]
Total Within-cluster Sum of Squares (WSS): 677.299
Between-cluster Sum of Squares (BSS): 92.701
Ratio of BSS to TSS: 0.12


---------------------------------

Clusters complete linkage
 Labels  Cardinality
      0           21
      1           29
```

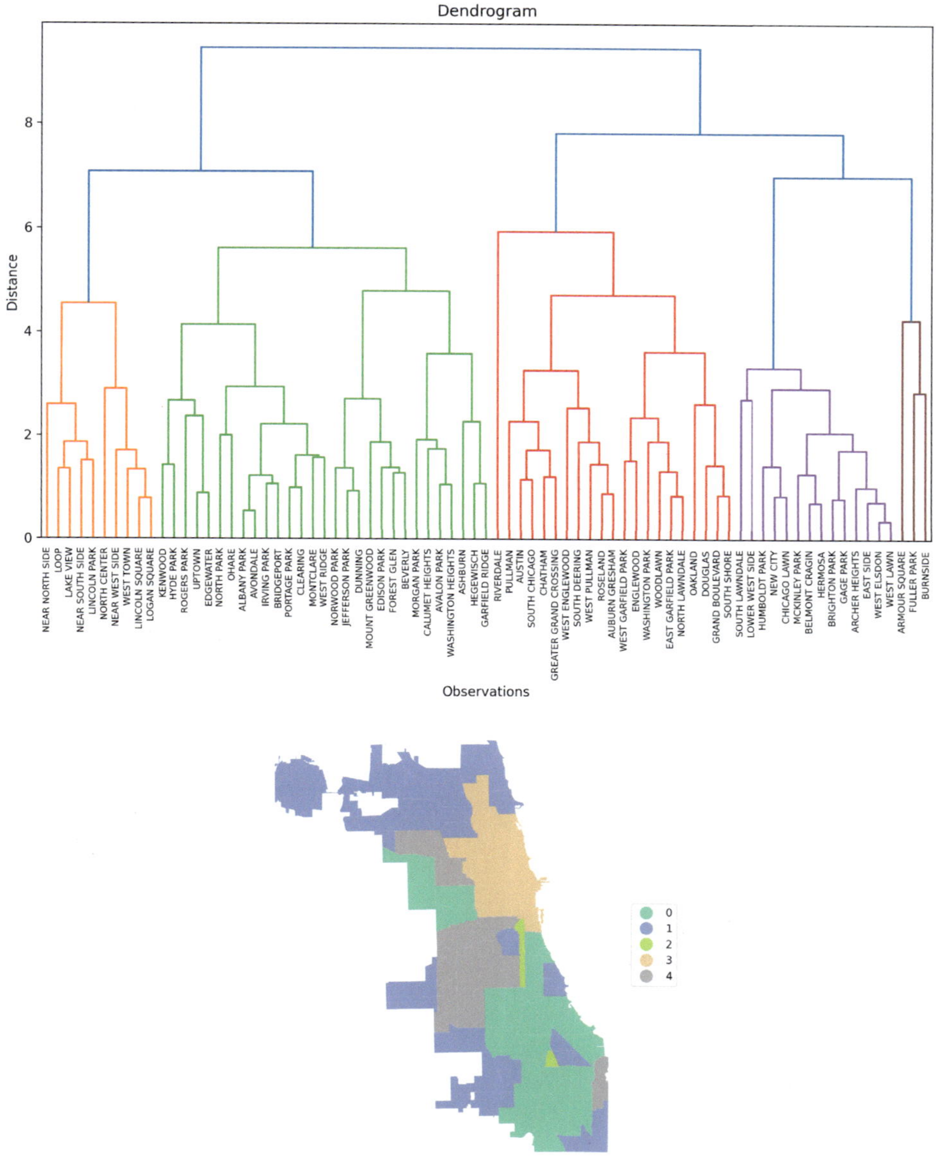

Figure 7.5: Complete Linkage Clustering

2	3
3	10
4	14

```
Cluster Means:
         INCPERCAP  Und20   Ov65  Minrty  Unemprt  Noveh  Lt_high  Rentocc
cluster
0         19837.71  28.62  13.65   96.50    18.62  19.02    16.47    54.96
1         35389.38  22.82  15.51   56.44     6.54   8.46    11.63    36.30
2         19449.67  17.24  25.93   93.97    17.32  23.73    24.67    51.33
3         72820.90  16.13   9.23   35.95     3.33  16.38     4.45    51.17
4         19511.07  29.66  10.55   88.80    10.52   7.20    30.73    43.41

        Rntburd  Noeng
cluster
0         35.69   8.86
1         20.52  36.37
2         29.50  27.09
3         19.69  23.27
4         24.97  72.51
Cluster Medians:
         INCPERCAP  Und20   Ov65  Minrty  Unemprt  Noveh  Lt_high  Rentocc
cluster
0          19493.0  26.77  14.36   97.45    17.07  20.12    15.69    53.08
1          31866.0  22.95  15.71   57.22     5.39   6.05    10.82    31.36
2          19972.0  18.54  26.44   96.37    20.14  19.92    21.40    56.20
3          73295.0  15.91   8.75   35.95     2.89  15.92     4.24    54.05
4          19699.0  30.39  10.31   87.36    10.42   6.16    29.23    45.87

        Rntburd  Noeng
cluster
0         34.59   6.04
1         21.07  37.18
2         29.95   7.38
3         19.38  23.52
4         24.37  76.95

Total Sum of Squares (TSS): 770.0
Within-cluster Sum of Squares (WSS) for each cluster: [ 86.209 149.571
                                                       14.489  29.811  27.436]
Total Within-cluster Sum of Squares (WSS): 307.515
Between-cluster Sum of Squares (BSS): 462.485
Ratio of BSS to TSS: 0.601


-----------------------------------

Clusters average linkage
 Labels  Cardinality
      0           18
```

```
1        30
2        27
3         1
4         1


Cluster Means:
         INCPERCAP  Und20  Ov65  Minrty  Unemprt  Noveh  Lt_high  Rentocc
cluster
0         60754.28  18.41  11.65  36.84     3.74  14.52     5.42    45.22
1         25780.70  26.63  12.71  70.96     8.09   6.53    22.38    39.64
2         22292.00  25.85  16.07  95.23    17.21  17.52    15.17    49.59
3         21858.00  18.54  24.82  86.05     8.21  19.92    37.18    61.19
4         11857.00  44.28   4.80  98.79    30.42  30.33    15.69    76.92

        Rntburd  Noeng
cluster
0         19.30  23.58
1         22.54  61.68
2         33.26   8.24
3         27.29  69.47
4         30.71   3.09
Cluster Medians:
         INCPERCAP  Und20  Ov65  Minrty  Unemprt  Noveh  Lt_high  Rentocc
cluster
0          55224.5  18.07  10.34  37.36     3.73  15.92     4.63    54.05
1          26443.5  26.32  11.92  73.81     7.19   6.04    19.62    42.87
2          20439.0  25.46  15.64  97.45    16.17  18.84    14.41    50.28
3          21858.0  18.54  24.82  86.05     8.21  19.92    37.18    61.19
4          11857.0  44.28   4.80  98.79    30.42  30.33    15.69    76.92

        Rntburd  Noeng
cluster
0         19.38  24.43
1         21.91  58.43
2         30.28   5.11
3         27.29  69.47
4         30.71   3.09


Total Sum of Squares (TSS): 770.0
Within-cluster Sum of Squares (WSS) for each cluster: [103.805 124.272
                                                 139.236   0.      0. ]
Total Within-cluster Sum of Squares (WSS): 367.312
Between-cluster Sum of Squares (BSS): 402.688
Ratio of BSS to TSS: 0.523
```

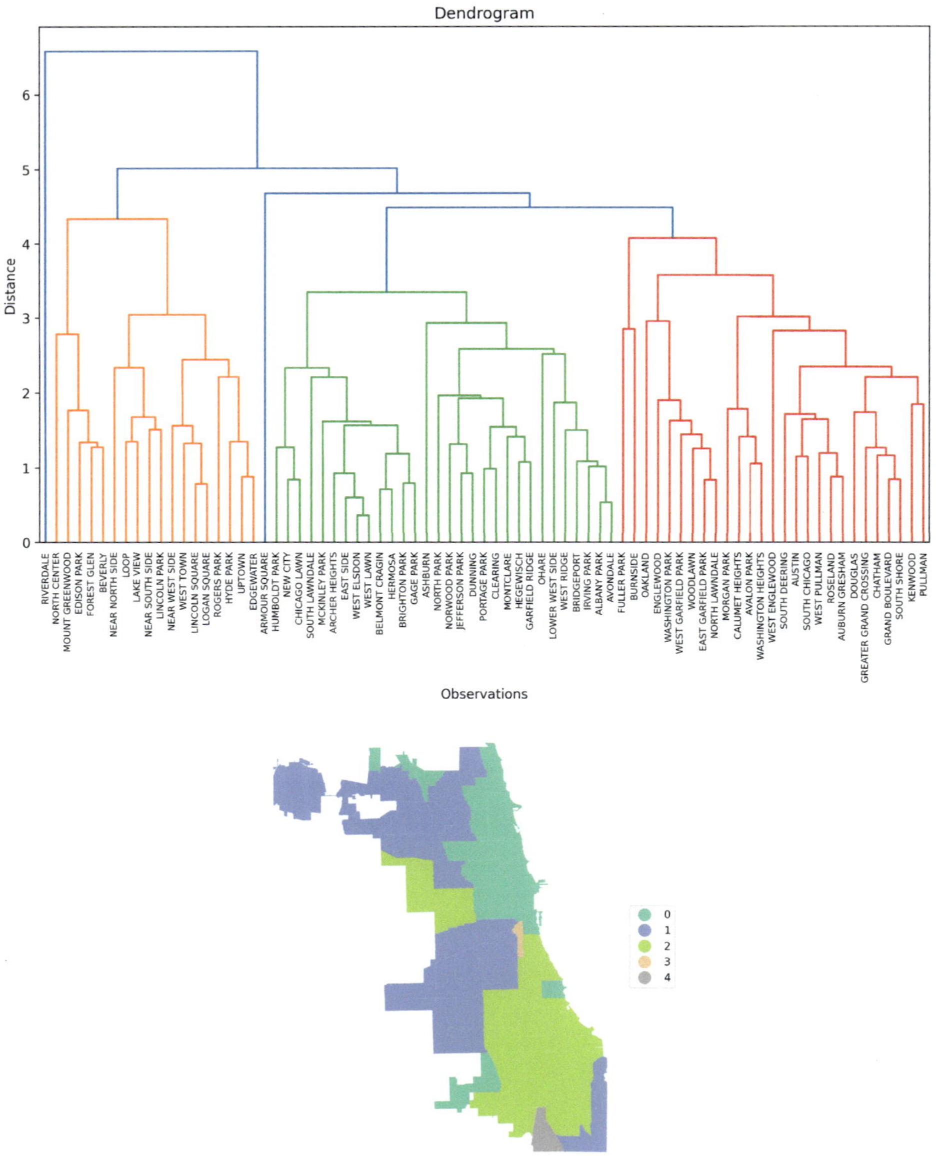

Figure 7.6: Average Linkage Clustering

The results show the superiority of Ward's method, with only Complete Linkage coming close (BSS/TSS ratio of 0.60 to 0.64 for Ward's). Single linkage typically results in one or two very large clusters and several singletons. Average linkage is somewhere in-between.

7.4 Practice

Select a different subset of variables or use your own data set to carry out an in-depth comparison of the results of the four different linkage methods. Assess how the findings change with a different cut point.

8 Partitioning Clustering Methods

This Chapter considers *partitioning clustering* methods as the second broad category of techniques, with a particular focus on *K-Means*. K-Means is a partitioning clustering method that starts with an initial solution and moves forward by means of *iterative relocation* to find a better solution. The objective function is to find an allocation (an *encoding*) of each observation to one of the k clusters that minimizes the within cluster dissimilarity (or, maximizes the between cluster dissimilarity). This corresponds to the sum of squared deviations from the mean in each cluster, i.e., the within sum of squared errors. The material is discussed in detail in Chapter 6 of the *GeoDa Cluster Book*.

The K-Means algorithm is implemented in the `KMeans` class of `sklearn.cluster`. As before, to carry out variable standardization we will use `StandardScaler` from `sklearn.preprocessing`. To characterize the solution in K-Means, we also apply `silhouette_samples` and `silhouette_score` from `sklearn.metrics`. The specific illustration will implement K-Means clustering on principal components, for which we will again use `PCA` from `sklearn.decomposition`, as in Chapter 5. We will require `numpy`, `geopandas` and `matplotlib.pyplot` as well.

Finally, to implement some of the *spatialization* of these methods, we import several functions from the `spatial-cluster-helper` package:

- `ensure_datasets`
- `cluster_stats`
- `cluster_map`
- `cluster_center`
- `cluster_fit`
- `elbow_plot`
- `plot_silhouette`

To illustrate K-Means clustering, we will use the same **Chi-SDOH** sample data set as in Chapter 3.

> Required Packages
>
> numpy, geopandas, matplotlib.pyplot, sklearn.cluster, sklearn.preprocessing, sklearn.decomposition, sklearn.metrics, spatial-cluster-helper

Required Data Sets

Chi-SDOH

8.1 Preliminaries

8.1.1 Import Required Modules

```
import pandas as pd
import geopandas as gpd
import numpy as np
import matplotlib.pyplot as plt
from sklearn.cluster import KMeans
from sklearn.preprocessing import StandardScaler
from sklearn.metrics import silhouette_samples, silhouette_score
from sklearn.decomposition import PCA
from spatial_cluster_helper import ensure_datasets, cluster_stats, \
                cluster_map, cluster_center, \
                cluster_fit, elbow_plot, plot_silhouette
```

8.1.2 Load Data

The data are read from the `Chi-SDOH.shp` shape file. As usual, we carry out a quick check of the contents. A partial listing of the top three lines is given in Table 8.1.

```
# Setting working folder:
#path = "/your/path/to/data/"
path = "./datasets/"
# Select the Chicago census tract data:
shpfile = "Chi-SDOH/Chi-SDOH.shp"
# Load the data:
ensure_datasets(shpfile, folder_path = path)
dfs = gpd.read_file(path + shpfile)
print(dfs.shape)
dfs.head(3)
```

```
(791, 56)
```

Table 8.1: Partial Contents of Chi-SDOH

	OBJECTID	Shape_Leng	Shape_Area	TRACTCE10	geoid10	commarea	ChldPvt14	EP_CROWD
0	1	22777.477721	2.119089e+07	842400.0	1.703184e+10	44.0	30.2	2.0
1	2	16035.054986	8.947394e+06	840300.0	1.703184e+10	59.0	38.9	4.8
2	3	15186.400644	1.230614e+07	841100.0	1.703184e+10	34.0	40.4	4.9

Table 8.2: K-Means Variables

Column Name	Variable Description
EP_MINRTY	Minority population share
Ovr6514P	Population share aged > 65
EP_AGE17	Population share aged < 18
EP_DISABL	Disabled population share
EP_HOHSDP	No high school
EP_LIMENG	Limited English proficiency
EP_SNGPNT	Percentage of single parent households
Pov14	Poverty rate
EP_PCI	Per capita income
Unemp14	Unemployment rate
EP_UNINSUR	Percent without health insurance
EP_CROWD	Percent crowded housing
EP_NOVEH	Percent without a car
ChldPvt14	Child poverty rate
HealthLit	Health literacy index
FORCLRISK	Foreclosure risk

8.1.3 Variables

As in Chapter 6 of the *GeoDa Cluster Book*, we select variables that are a close match to the variables identified in Kolak et al. (2020) for an analysis that includes all U.S. census tracts. However, unlike what is the case in Chapter 7, the observations here are for census tracts and not for Community Areas. We select 16 variables, listed in Table 8.2.

As in in Chapter 7, we start by creating a list with the respective variables names, `varlist`, and obtain a subset of the full data set for just these variables, as `data_cluster`.

```
varlist = ['EP_MINRTY', 'Ovr6514P', 'EP_AGE17', 'EP_DISABL',
           'EP_NOHSDP', 'EP_LIMENG', 'EP_SNGPNT', 'Pov14',
           'EP_PCI', 'Unemp14', 'EP_UNINSUR', 'EP_CROWD',
           'EP_NOVEH', 'ChldPvt14', 'HealthLit', 'FORCLRISK']
data_cluster = dfs[varlist]
```

8.1.4 Standardization

Before proceeding further, we extract the number of observations and compute the scaling factor $\sqrt{(n-1)/n}$ needed to replicate the results from GeoDa (see Chapter 7).

```
n = data_cluster.shape[0]
nn = np.sqrt((n-1.0)/n)
```

8.2 Clustering with Dimension Reduction

In practice, when many variables are involved, it is often more efficient to carry out the clustering exercise after a dimension reduction. More specifically, the clustering is applied to the main principal components of the original variables.

We first transform the variables using `StandardScaler`. In order to retain compatibility with the results for GeoDa, we rescale those results by $\sqrt{(n-1)/n}$ (the `nn` variable just created) and then apply the `PCA().fit()` method to create `pca_res` as the result object. The factor loadings are in the resulting `components_` attribute of `pca_res`.

```
X0 = StandardScaler().fit_transform(data_cluster)
X1 = X0 * nn
pca_res = PCA().fit(X1)
pca_res.components_
```

```
array([[ 0.33824863, -0.02767885,  0.29159216,  0.19532335,  0.28473044,
         0.10177461,  0.3168122 ,  0.32666508, -0.32245438,  0.28719305,
         0.25713029,  0.22366353,  0.11580138,  0.31762617, -0.01704885,
         0.21435943],
       [-0.06920095, -0.32122211,  0.10745714, -0.36333146,  0.28673661,
         0.49749526, -0.07628474, -0.10662782, -0.04344009, -0.25805376,
         0.2914494 ,  0.33241983, -0.29503893, -0.09891616, -0.0204966 ,
        -0.20096159],
       [ 0.12996788,  0.60193803, -0.07823625,  0.30737561,  0.1736577 ,
         0.23359596, -0.21902106, -0.2687673 , -0.18572297, -0.05220259,
         0.10643154, -0.03100825, -0.36802528, -0.20257751,  0.06986895,
         0.29048044],
       [-0.06484105,  0.19858591, -0.27120191,  0.19752884,  0.12097044,
         0.1780976 , -0.16748035,  0.11172722,  0.06180415, -0.08390976,
         0.16760664,  0.17480623,  0.49277773,  0.08114224,  0.54731901,
        -0.37205383],
```

```
[-0.01771277, -0.15430746,  0.27237767, -0.12234097, -0.07065488,
 -0.13099058,  0.10975812, -0.05803475,  0.02937634,  0.08607726,
 -0.17815627,  0.01667127, -0.30711122, -0.01610845,  0.81831768,
  0.21128788],
[ 0.15756767, -0.27192672, -0.49211235, -0.2640276 , -0.08233546,
 -0.00680378, -0.24531422, -0.08693787,  0.04371917,  0.21192293,
  0.39138329, -0.07029299,  0.15546542,  0.00915944,  0.07987495,
  0.52839605],
[ 0.01710768,  0.14042738,  0.08052682, -0.06484484,  0.05513617,
 -0.09825969,  0.05014743, -0.13348896,  0.32292809, -0.04858752,
 -0.25859919,  0.71569002,  0.27523261, -0.22636103, -0.10216948,
  0.33631691],
[-0.16928011,  0.27475708, -0.02465148, -0.25609387,  0.18292454,
  0.24739228, -0.10725098,  0.32512576,  0.42180632, -0.07999192,
 -0.19287099, -0.13646173, -0.12495858,  0.55518004, -0.0303803 ,
  0.22996604],
[-0.00366352, -0.17391089, -0.1757881 ,  0.33651032, -0.25661352,
 -0.31037813, -0.28562529,  0.11156684, -0.10007061, -0.31050183,
  0.06369376,  0.40983189, -0.35046234,  0.40884423, -0.03103305,
 -0.0013363 ],
[-0.28616948,  0.30497287,  0.04181145, -0.25696408, -0.20205869,
 -0.11617441, -0.16391205,  0.04675566, -0.04089465,  0.66793167,
  0.20014968,  0.27524592, -0.20015627,  0.02827778, -0.05035372,
 -0.25868787],
[-0.14025286, -0.39449529, -0.00575086,  0.3928861 ,  0.46309684,
  0.04619709, -0.40271685, -0.0020914 ,  0.13575911,  0.40899255,
 -0.30225178, -0.03112526, -0.06129094, -0.08418149, -0.04981699,
 -0.0132952 ],
[ 0.11945958, -0.02109346, -0.07423843,  0.27807943,  0.07746011,
 -0.11638656,  0.3777289 , -0.12652341,  0.68040839,  0.0816599 ,
  0.41594474, -0.03565666, -0.24529279, -0.02160758, -0.0047099 ,
 -0.14017415],
[ 0.65392971,  0.02857446, -0.41314791, -0.19960292,  0.03019588,
  0.07188768,  0.09233702,  0.00192229, -0.01145205,  0.16188207,
 -0.4171966 ,  0.11025993, -0.20233042,  0.04403266,  0.02200409,
 -0.30084813],
[ 0.49377496,  0.01040831,  0.53729337, -0.0248907 , -0.24908989,
  0.05908971, -0.51860949, -0.10202386,  0.25115871, -0.00255258,
  0.11041623, -0.09225063,  0.14637002,  0.07289198, -0.01903675,
 -0.10480098],
[-0.10246771, -0.14452211, -0.04574585,  0.29993213, -0.58534793,
  0.65843969,  0.16817894, -0.02235705,  0.06151077,  0.17480916,
```

```
 -0.14577086,  0.07255365,  0.00221709,  0.02588026, -0.01670772,
  0.09896415],
[ 0.08847644,  0.01348562, -0.02523972,  0.02229942, -0.10450118,
  0.00886041, -0.11167941,  0.78815678,  0.10381648, -0.08261031,
  0.06746452, -0.00240211, -0.14912046, -0.54632534,  0.01832656,
  0.05467755]])
```

The results match the values in Figure 6.12 of the *GeoDa Cluster Book*, except that the loadings on each principal component are represented by a row. The share of the explained variance is given by the `explained_variance_ratio_` attribute. The cumulative share is then easily computed by means of `numpy cumsum`. The result reveals how the first four components explain 77.4% of the total variance.

```
np.cumsum(pca_res.explained_variance_ratio_)
```

```
array([0.44343332, 0.61996478, 0.70615391, 0.77350516, 0.8348708 ,
       0.8680793 , 0.894729  , 0.91510188, 0.9331911 , 0.94876398,
       0.96125779, 0.97276386, 0.98239453, 0.98997297, 0.99598198,
       1.        ])
```

The variance of each component is included in the `explained_variance_` attribute. These are also the eigenvalues of $X'X$. We use the Kaiser criterion and select the four principal components with an eigenvalue larger than one.

```
pca_res.explained_variance_
```

```
array([7.09493309, 2.82450339, 1.37902613, 1.07761989, 0.98185035,
       0.531336  , 0.42639517, 0.32596605, 0.28942756, 0.24916599,
       0.19990103, 0.18409716, 0.15409062, 0.12125515, 0.09614416,
       0.06428826])
```

We will replicate the example in the *GeoDa Cluster Book* and carry out the clustering exercise on these four principal components. These are obtained by the `transform` method of `pca_res`, from which we extract the first four columns and turn them into a DataFrame. For the cluster analysis, we first need to standardize the principal components with `StandardScaler`. We also rescale them by `nn` to conform to the `GeoDa` results.

```
pca_vars = pca_res.transform(X1)[:, 0:4]
pca_df = pd.DataFrame(pca_vars, columns=["PC1", "PC2", "PC3", "PC4"])

XX = StandardScaler().fit_transform(pca_df)
X = XX * nn
```

8.3 K-Means Principle

The iterative relocation principle that underlies K-Means computes a new set of cluster centers after each move and then allocates observations to their nearest center. This is the classic *Lloyds* algorithm, a special case of EM (expectation, maximization). It stops when no further improvement is possible, but this does *not* guarantee that a global optimum is reached. In fact, the algorithm can easily get stuck in *local* optima. For mathematical details, see Chapter 6 of the *GeoDa Cluster Book*.

A critical aspect of this process is the initial starting solution. Since all further moves proceed from this initial assignment, the end result critically depends on it. To address this sensitivity, typically several different starting points are compared, each randomly generated.

We use `sklearn.cluster.KMeans` to illustrate this method. It works in the same way as the other scikit-learn methods: first an instance of the class is created, to which then a `fit` method is applied for the given data set (`X`). The default arguments for a KMeans instance are `n_clusters = 8`, for the number of clusters, `init = "k-means++"` for the KMeans++ initialization method, and `random_state`, a random number seed. Whereas the default for this argument is `None`, it should be set to an integer value to obtain reproducible results.

It should also be kept in mind that the initial starting solution will depend on the random number seed and it should be varied to assess the sensitivity of the results. Finally, we also set `n_init = 150` to retain compatibility with `GeoDa` (the number of initial solutions that are evaluated).

The final cluster allocation is contained in the usual `labels_` attribute, which can be summarized and visualized using the helper functions `cluster_stats`, `cluster_center`, `cluster_fit` and `cluster_map`, as illustrated in Chapter 7.

In addition to the types of analyses of cluster results employed so far, we also try to find the best value for k by means of an *elbow plot* and assess the solution by means of a *silhouette plot*.

8.4 K-Means Solution

8.4.1 K-means++

In scikit-learn, the default starting solution is obtained with KMeans++, which is an adjusted random allocation. The equal probabilities from a pure random allocation are adjusted in function of the distance to the remaining points, so as to obtain a more even coverage over all observations.

We illustrate this method for our principal components with 8 clusters. The only argument that needs to be set is the random number seed. We list the result by means of our cluster_stats helper function.

```
n_clusters = 8
kmeans1 = KMeans(n_clusters = n_clusters, n_init = 150,
                 random_state = 123456789).fit(X)
cluster_labels1 = kmeans1.labels_
c_stats = cluster_stats(cluster_labels1)
```

Labels	Cardinality
0	89
1	116
2	154
3	115
4	128
5	60
6	85
7	44

The cluster centers are given by the cluster_center helper function. This is not as useful as before since it is expressed in terms of the principal components. However, it can still be used in visualizations by means of a PCP or conditional box plot.

```
c_means, c_medians = cluster_center(pca_df, cluster_labels1)
print("Mean Centers:\n", np.round(c_means, 2))
print("\nMedian Centers:\n", np.round(c_medians, 2))
```

```
Mean Centers:
          PC1   PC2   PC3   PC4
cluster
0        1.24 -1.98  1.41 -0.63
```

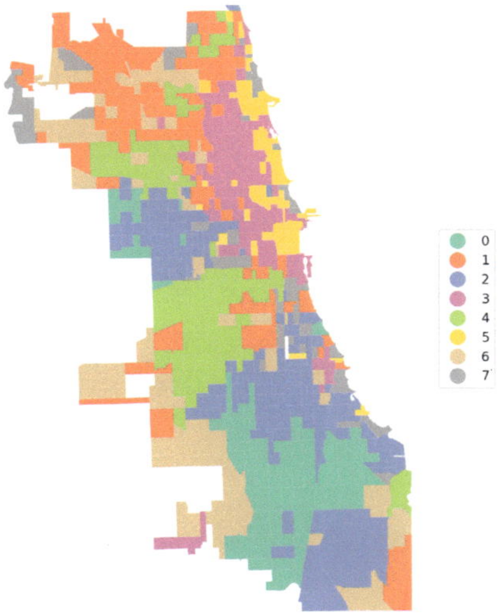

Figure 8.1: K-Means++ cluster map

```
1       -1.13  0.67  0.49  0.29
2        2.99 -1.26 -1.09 -0.05
3       -3.51  0.21 -0.98 -0.40
4        2.06  2.72  0.38  0.28
5       -2.55 -0.45 -0.98  1.30
6       -1.15  0.38  0.57 -1.39
7       -1.10 -1.95  1.35  1.81

Median Centers:
           PC1   PC2   PC3   PC4
cluster
0         1.21 -2.01  1.42 -0.56
1        -1.03  0.65  0.46  0.25
2         3.11 -1.31 -0.99 -0.06
3        -3.67  0.27 -1.05 -0.39
4         1.98  2.65  0.44  0.33
5        -3.14 -0.40 -0.91  1.15
6        -1.32  0.31  0.63 -1.22
7        -1.08 -1.89  1.11  1.84
```

The fit is given by `cluster_fit`. There are minor differences with the example in `GeoDa`, due to slightly different random initialization. However, the BSS/TSS ratio is the same, at 0.685.

```
clusfit = cluster_fit(data = pca_df, clustlabels = cluster_labels1,
                n_clusters = n_clusters)
```

```
Total Sum of Squares (TSS): 3164.0000000000005
Within-cluster Sum of Squares (WSS) for each cluster: [103.375 104.333
                       241.471  91.07  169.104  69.919 116.038 101.08 ]
Total Within-cluster Sum of Squares (WSS): 996.39
Between-cluster Sum of Squares (BSS): 2167.61
Ratio of BSS to TSS: 0.685
```

Finally, `cluster_map` provides a view of the spatial pattern of the solution, shown in Figure 8.1 on page 123.

```
cluster_map(dfs, cluster_labels1, figsize = (6,6),
            title="", cmap='Set2', legend_fontsize=8)
```

8.4.2 Random Initial Allocation

We also illustrate random initial allocation by setting the argument `init = "random"`. We only summarize the results with the cluster allocation and measures of fit. The resulting clusters are slightly different, but the overall BSS/TSS ratio is the same as before. Further experimenting with random seeds is recommended, but not further considered here.

```
kmeans2 = KMeans(n_clusters = n_clusters, init = 'random',
                n_init = 150, random_state = 123456789).fit(X)
cluster_labels2 = kmeans2.labels_
c_stats = cluster_stats(cluster_labels2)
```

Labels	Cardinality
0	61
1	83
2	44
3	154
4	117
5	89
6	129
7	114

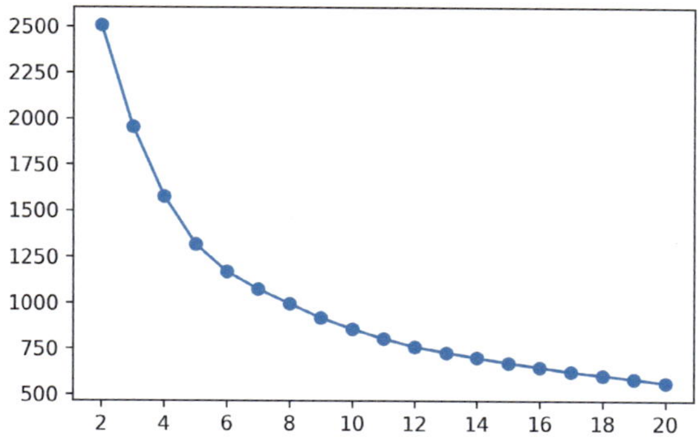

Figure 8.2: Elbow plot

```
clusfit = cluster_fit(data = pca_df, clustlabels = cluster_labels2,
                      n_clusters = n_clusters)
```

```
Total Sum of Squares (TSS): 3164.0000000000005
Within-cluster Sum of Squares (WSS) for each cluster: [ 71.038 114.852
                                101.08   241.471 105.99   103.375 168.654  89.956]
Total Within-cluster Sum of Squares (WSS): 996.416
Between-cluster Sum of Squares (BSS): 2167.584
Ratio of BSS to TSS: 0.685
```

8.5 Elbow Plot

So far, we have taken the number of clusters as a given. However, unless a specific policy issue dictates the number, this is typically a variable that needs to be chosen. As the number of clusters goes up, the WSS will necessarily decline.

A *best* number of clusters can be chosen based on the pattern in this decline, by means of the so-called *elbow plot.* This plot visualizes the decline in WSS (or, alternativatively, the increase in BSS) with an increase in k. A *kink* in the elbow plot would suggest a point at which increasing k is not worth the decline in WSS. In practice, this is not always that straightforward. The k-means object contains the total WSS in the `inertia_` attribute.

We illustrate an elbow plot by running K-Means in a loop for values of n_clusters going from 2 to 20 in a simple line plot. This functionality is also encapsulated in the helper function `elbow_plot`.

```
inertia = []
for k in range(2, 21):
    kmeans = KMeans(n_clusters = k, n_init = 150,
                    random_state=123456789).fit(X)
    inertia.append(kmeans.inertia_)
plt.plot(range(2, 21), inertia, marker = 'o')
plt.xticks(range(2, 21, 2))
plt.show()
```

As evidenced by Figure 8.2 on page 125, the elbow plot does not show much of a *kink* in this application. This is actually (unfortunately) the case in many empirical instances. In our illustration, the improvement in WSS seems to decline starting at $k = 6$.

The helper function `elbow_plot` takes as arguments the standardized data and the maximum number of clusters, `max_clusters` (default 20), as well as some arguments to customize the K-Means algorithm (e.g., `init`, `n_init`, `random_state`). We illustrate this below.

With `X` as the standardized data and all the other arguments set to their default values, the elbow plot is invoked as `elbow_plot(X)`. The result, shown in Figure 8.3, is identical to the graph in Figure 8.2.

```
elbow_plot(X,title="")
```

8.6 Silhouette Score

A measure of the degree of effective separation between clusters is given by the so-called *silhouette* coefficient. For each observation assigned to a cluster, this is based on the average distance to the other cluster members (say, nn_i) as well as the average distance to the nearest member in a different cluster (say, nn_j).

The silhouette score is then the ratio $(nn_j - nn_i)/max(nn_i, nn_j)$. It varies between +1 (densest) and -1 (least dense). The average of this score over all observations is an overall measure of separation, i.e., the closer this value is to +1, the better the cluster separation.

Scikit-learn computes the observation-specific silhouette values in `silhouette_samples`, a class of `sklearn.metrics`. This takes as arguments the standardized data set (`X`) and the cluster labels. In our example, this yields an array with 791 values. The mean of this array is the same value as obtained with `sklearn.metrics.silhouette_score`.

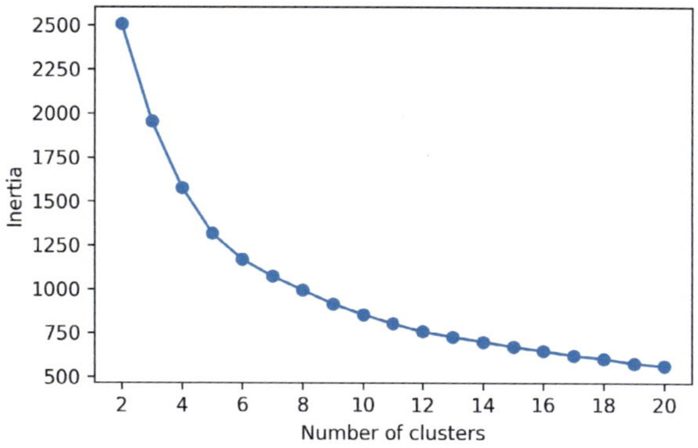

Figure 8.3: Elbow plot from helper function

```
sample_silhouette_values = silhouette_samples(X, cluster_labels1)
print(sample_silhouette_values.shape)
print("Mean silhouette value:", np.round(
                      sample_silhouette_values.mean(), 4))
print("Silhouette Score:", np.round(
                      silhouette_score(X, cluster_labels1), 4))
```

```
(791,)
Mean silhouette value: 0.2725
Silhouette Score: 0.2725
```

The typical application for silhouette scores is to plot them as a horizontal bar chart for each cluster, showing the score for each individual observation. For 791 observations, this is not going to be too practical.

We illustrate the general idea for cluster with label 5, which has only 44 observations. To this effect, we extract the observation label from the initial DataFrame, then create an array with the silhouette values, ID and cluster label and extract only those observations with cluster label = 5. Finally, we sort on the silhouette values and create two arrays with respectively the observation IDs and the silhouette values in sorted order.

These arrays are passed to the `barh` plot with `y` as the sequence of IDs and `width` as the actual value of the silhouette score, in a bare bones graph.

```
id = np.array(dfs['OBJECTID'])
sil = np.stack((sample_silhouette_values, id, cluster_labels1), axis = 1)
silclus = (sil[:,2] == 5)
clus = sil[silclus, :]
```

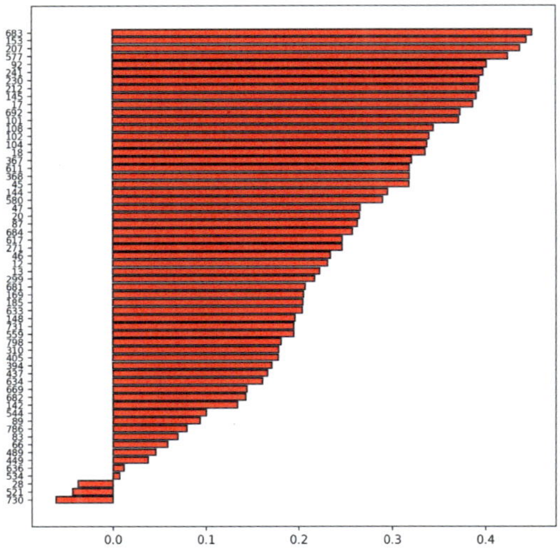

Figure 8.4: Silhouette score

```
sorted_indices = np.argsort(clus[:, 0])
sortclus = clus[sorted_indices, :]
silvals = clus[sorted_indices, 0]
sil_labels = clus[sorted_indices, 1]
sil_labels = sil_labels.astype(int)

fig, ax = plt.subplots(figsize = (8, 8))
ax.barh(
    np.arange(len(silvals)), silvals,
    color = "red",
    edgecolor = "black"
)
ax.set_yticks(np.arange(len(sil_labels)))
ax.set_yticklabels(sil_labels, fontsize = 8)
plt.show()
```

The bar plot in Figure 8.4 shows the evolution of the silhouette scores from a maximum of 0.438 to a minimum of -0.128. The labels on the left-hand side correspond with the ID numbers of the census tracts. The negative values for the tracts at the bottom of the graph indicate tracts that do not fit the given cluster very well. These may be candidates to be moved over to a different cluster.

The `plot_silhouette` helper function does all the sorting and labeling for a complete silhouette plot. As mentioned, this is only practical for smaller data sets. For our 791 observations, it is a bit of a stretch, but can still be accomplished be setting the `figsize`

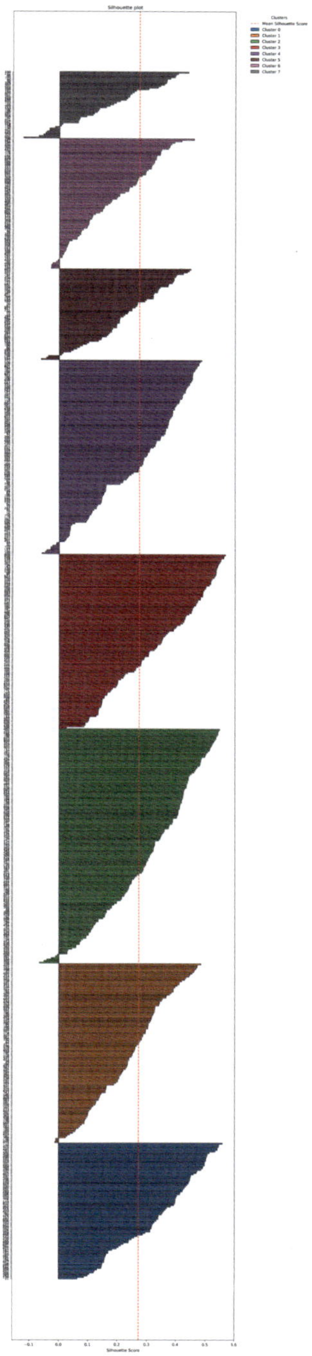

Figure 8.5: Silhouette score helper plot

large enough, as in Figure 8.5. For larger data sets such as these, a better approach would be to create a silhouette plot for each cluster separately, as illustrated above.

```
plot_silhouette(sample_silhouette_values, dfs['OBJECTID'],
                cluster_labels1,
                title = "Silhouette plot",
                figsize = (10, 60))
```

8.7 Practice

The K-Means algorithm is very sensitive to the starting value. Assess the effect of using different random seeds, number of initial clusters and starting point (K-Means++ vs. random) on the solution.

9 Advanced Clustering Methods

Chapter 7 of the *GeoDa Cluster Book* considers two more advanced partitioning clustering techniques . The first, K-Medians, is a straightforward variant on K-Means. It operates in exactly the same manner, except that the representative center of each cluster is the median instead of the mean.

The second method is similar to K-Medians and is often confused with it. *K-Medoids* is a method where the center of each cluster is an actual cluster member, in contrast to what holds for both K-Means and K-Medians.

Both methods operate in largely the same manner as K-Means, but they differ in the way the central point of each cluster is defined and the manner in which the nearest points are assigned.

Scikit-learn currently does not have a built-in class for either K-Medians or K-Medoids. However, a separate `kmedoids` package is available that implements a range of algorithms for K-Medoids, but not for K-Medians (https://python-kmedoids.readthedocs.io/en/latest/). We therefore only consider K-Medoids.

In addition to `kmedoids`, we again use `StandardScaler` from `sklearn.preprocessing` to standardize the variables. In addition, we will also need `pairwise_distances` from `sklearn.metrics`. Finally, we use `ensure_datasets`, `cluster_stats`, `cluster_fit` and `cluster_map` from the `spatial-cluster-helper` package. We only rely on `geopandas` and `numpy` for other manipulations. All the other required functionality is covered by the various utility functions.

We continue to illustrate the clustering methods with the **Chi-SDOH** data set for Chicago census tracts. However, to highlight the special nature of K-Medoids, we carry out the clustering on the centroids of the census tracts.

> Required Packages
>
> geopandas, numpy, kmedoids, sklearn.preprocessing, sklearn.metrics, spatial-cluster-helper

Required Data Sets

Chi-SDOH

9.1 Preliminaries

9.1.1 Import Required Modules

```
import geopandas as gpd
import numpy as np

import kmedoids

from sklearn.preprocessing import StandardScaler
from sklearn.metrics import pairwise_distances

from spatial_cluster_helper import ensure_datasets, cluster_stats, \
                cluster_fit, cluster_map
```

9.1.2 Load Data

We read the data from the `Chi-SDOH.shp` shape file and carry out a quick check of its contents. Details are given in Table 8.1 on page 117.

```
# Setting working folder:
#path = "/your/path/to/data/"
path = "./datasets/"
# Select the Chicago census tract data:
shpfile = "Chi-SDOH/Chi-SDOH.shp"
# Load the data:
ensure_datasets(shpfile, folder_path = path)
dfs = gpd.read_file(path + shpfile)
print(dfs.shape)
dfs.head(3)
```

```
(791, 56)
```

Table 9.1: Census Tract Centroid Coordinates

	X	Y
count	791.000000	791.000000
mean	1163.015429	1891.993831
std	15.921978	32.441766
min	1116.485166	1815.974666
25%	1152.687269	1864.475054
50%	1163.879674	1896.433233
75%	1173.499461	1919.530711
max	1203.419742	1951.021208

```
# the full set of variables
print(list(dfs.columns))
```

```
['OBJECTID', 'Shape_Leng', 'Shape_Area', 'TRACTCE10', 'geoid10',
'commarea', 'ChldPvt14', 'EP_CROWD', 'EP_UNINSUR', 'EP_MINRTY',
'Ovr6514P', 'EP_AGE17', 'EP_DISABL', 'EP_NOHSDP',
 ...
  'EP_GROUPQ', 'SchHP_Mi', 'BrownF_Mi', 'card',
 'cpval', 'COORD_X', 'COORD_Y', 'geometry']
```

9.1.3 Variables - Census Tract Centroids

We follow the illustration in Chapter 7 of the *GeoDa Cluster Book* and use the centroids of the census tracts for our example. This illustrates the similarity of K-Medoids to the solution of an (unweighted) facility location-allocation problem.

We use the geopandas `centroid` attribute applied to our GeoDataFrame (`dfs`), then extract the x and y coordinates and add them as new variables. We rescale them by 1000 to keep the distance units manageable.

Finally, we create the DataFrame `data_cluster` that contains just the centroids and compute some descriptive statistics, listed in Table 9.1.

```
cent = dfs.centroid
dfs['X'] = cent.x / 1000
dfs['Y'] = cent.y / 1000
data_cluster = dfs[['X','Y']]
data_cluster.describe()
```

9.1.4 Standardization

As in the previous Chapters, we compute the rescaling factor to retain compatibility with the results provided by GeoDa.

```
n = data_cluster.shape[0]
nn = np.sqrt((n-1.0)/n)
```

9.2 K-Medoids

K-Medoids attempts to minimize the sum of distances from the observations in each cluster to a representative center for that cluster. In contrast to what is the case for K-Means, this center is one of the observations.

K-Medoids works with any dissimilarity matrix, especially with a distance matrix based on a Manhattan distance metric, which is less affected by outliers.

The kmedoids package implements several algorithms to find the cluster solution, all refinements of the original PAM method (*partitioning around medoids*) of Kaufman and Rousseeuw (2005).

We compare the results of pam, fastpam1 and fasterpam. We first use the coordinates in standardized form, rescaled for compatibility with GeoDa. There are two ways in which these algorithms can be invoked. One way is directly as one of the methods supported by kmedoids, the other uses an interface like scikit-learn, which is a little more cumbersome (see details in the documentation). We illustrate the former.

9.2.1 Data Preparation

We start by transforming the coordinates with StandardScaler and rescaling them for compatibility with GeoDa. We also set the number of clusters (n_clusters) to 8.

As a final initialization, we set up the distance matrix using Manhattan distances with pairwise_distances from sklearn.metrics, to which we pass metric = 'manhattan' (the default is Euclidean distance, which is less appropriate for K-Medoids).

```
X0 = StandardScaler().fit_transform(data_cluster)
X = X0 * nn

n_clusters = 8

dist_X = pairwise_distances(X, metric = 'manhattan')
```

9.2.2 PAM

All the PAM methods take as argument a distance matrix, `diss`, the number of clusters, `medoids`, and, optionally, the maximum number of iterations (`iter`), the initialization method (`init` equal to `'build'` as the default), and a `random_state`, i.e., a seed for the random number generator. The default is `None`, but we recommend setting a seed to ensure reproducibility.

The original PAM algorithm is invoked as `kmedoids.pam`. We pass the distance matrix, the number of clusters and the random seed.

Several results are provides as attributes of the K-Medoids solution:

- the cluster labels as `labels`
- the observation numbers of the medoid centers as `medoids`
- the number of iterations as `n_iter`
- the number of swaps as `n_swap`

We also summarize the cluster membership using our `cluster_stats` helper function.

```
kmedoids_instance = kmedoids.pam(dist_X, n_clusters,
                                 random_state = 123456789)
cluster_labels = kmedoids_instance.labels
print("Medoids:", kmedoids_instance.medoids)
print("Iterations:", kmedoids_instance.n_iter)
print("Swaps:", kmedoids_instance.n_swap)
c_stats = cluster_stats(cluster_labels)
```

```
Medoids: [513 148 413 549 753 386 305 464]
Iterations: 10
Swaps: 9
 Labels  Cardinality
    0.0        113.0
    1.0         76.0
    2.0        146.0
    3.0        111.0
    4.0        109.0
    5.0         89.0
    6.0         88.0
    7.0         59.0
```

9.2.2.1 Silhouette scores

Whereas we can (and will) compute the usual cluster fit measures with the `cluster_fit` helper function, the squared Euclidean distance metric is not the one used in the objective function for the PAM algorithms. A more appropriate indicator is the silhouette coefficient, based on the distance metric used in the algorithm (whatever is passed as the distance matrix). This is given by `kmedoids.silhouette` method. It takes the distance matrix and cluster labels as arguments and returns a tuple. This may be a bit confusing, since the default setting for the third argument, `samples` is `False`, which does not return the distances for each observation. However, the returned object remains a tuple, with an empty second item. The first element is the average silhouette score. In `GeoDa`, this is called the ratio of total within to total sum of distances. A *smaller* value indicates a closer fit.

```
sil = kmedoids.silhouette(dist_X, cluster_labels, samples = False)
print("Average silhouette score:", np.round(sil[0], 4))
```

```
Average silhouette score: 0.3538
```

9.2.2.2 Cluster fit

For comparison purposes, we summarize the classic BSS/TSS measures of fit with our `cluster_fit` helper function.

```
clusfit = cluster_fit(data = data_cluster, clustlabels = cluster_labels,
                 correct = True, n_clusters = n_clusters)
```

```
Total Sum of Squares (TSS): 1579.9999999999995
Within-cluster Sum of Squares (WSS) for each cluster: [23.144 18.348
                          34.334 17.362 46.75  13.519 30.243 15.738]
Total Within-cluster Sum of Squares (WSS): 199.438
Between-cluster Sum of Squares (BSS): 1380.562
Ratio of BSS to TSS: 0.874
```

9.2.2.3 Cluster map

Finally, we create the cluster map with `cluster_map`, yielding Figure 9.1.

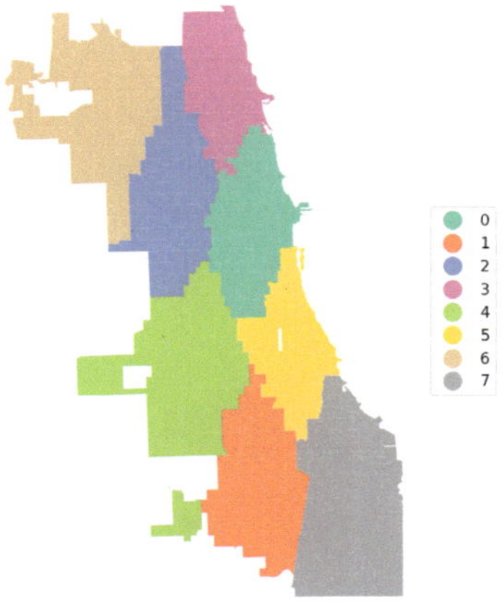

Figure 9.1: Cluster map for K-Medoids PAM

```
cluster_map(dfs, cluster_labels, figsize = (5, 5),
            title="", cmap='Set2', legend_fontsize=8)
```

The results of the various PAM algorithms are very sensitive to initial conditions as well as the implementation of the algorithm. We cannot illustrate all the permutations of starting values and algorithms, but just repeat the process with the same settings as before for `fastpam1` and `fasterpam`. We report the cluster makeup, silhouette score , measures of fit and show the cluster map for each option.

9.2.3 FASTPAM1

```
kmedoids_instance2 = kmedoids.fastpam1(dist_X, n_clusters,
                            random_state = 123456789)
cluster_labels2 = kmedoids_instance2.labels
print("Medoids:", kmedoids_instance2.medoids)
print("Iterations:", kmedoids_instance2.n_iter)
print("Swaps:", kmedoids_instance2.n_swap)
c_stats = cluster_stats(cluster_labels2)

sil = kmedoids.silhouette(dist_X, cluster_labels2, samples = False)
print("Average silhouette score:", np.round(sil[0], 4))

clusfit = cluster_fit(data = data_cluster, clustlabels = cluster_labels2,
                correct = True, n_clusters = n_clusters)
```

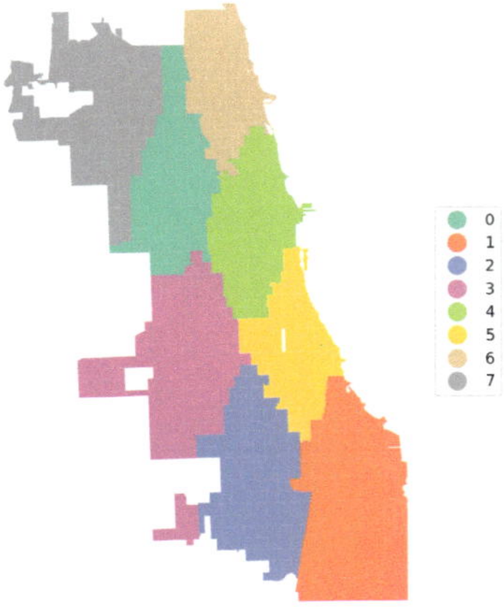

Figure 9.2: Cluster map for K-Medoids FASTPAM

```
Medoids: [344 464 524 765 513 386 549 305]
Iterations: 28
Swaps: 27
 Labels  Cardinality
    0.0        131.0
    1.0         61.0
    2.0         86.0
    3.0        110.0
    4.0        116.0
    5.0         90.0
    6.0        111.0
    7.0         86.0
Average silhouette score: 0.3501

Total Sum of Squares (TSS): 1579.9999999999995
Within-cluster Sum of Squares (WSS) for each cluster: [27.192 16.667
                           23.181 43.82  24.358 14.155 17.362 29.302]
Total Within-cluster Sum of Squares (WSS): 196.038
Between-cluster Sum of Squares (BSS): 1383.962
Ratio of BSS to TSS: 0.876
```

```
cluster_map(dfs, cluster_labels2, figsize = (5, 5),
            title="", cmap='Set2', legend_fontsize=8)
```

The results differ slightly, with a marginally better (smaller) silhouette score (0.350 vs 0.354), different medoid centers and a slightly altered cluster map in Figure 9.2.

9.2.4 FASTERPAM

```
kmedoids_instance3 = kmedoids.fasterpam(dist_X, n_clusters,
                              random_state = 123456789)
cluster_labels3 = kmedoids_instance3.labels
print("Medoids:", kmedoids_instance3.medoids)
print("Iterations:", kmedoids_instance3.n_iter)
print("Swaps:", kmedoids_instance3.n_swap)
c_stats = cluster_stats(cluster_labels3)

sil = kmedoids.silhouette(dist_X, cluster_labels3, samples = False)
print("Average silhouette score:", np.round(sil[0], 4))

clusfit = cluster_fit(data = data_cluster, clustlabels = cluster_labels3,
                 correct = True, n_clusters = n_clusters)
```

```
Medoids: [353 386 423 482 607 295 600 781]
Iterations: 3
Swaps: 34
 Labels  Cardinality
    0.0        109.0
    1.0         80.0
    2.0         99.0
    3.0         80.0
    4.0         93.0
    5.0        128.0
    6.0        115.0
    7.0         87.0
Average silhouette score: 0.3476

Total Sum of Squares (TSS): 1579.9999999999995
Within-cluster Sum of Squares (WSS) for each cluster: [41.116 10.472
                           27.344 29.534 16.387 22.832 20.861 31.432]
Total Within-cluster Sum of Squares (WSS): 199.978
Between-cluster Sum of Squares (BSS): 1380.022
Ratio of BSS to TSS: 0.873
```

```
cluster_map(dfs, cluster_labels3, figsize = (5, 5),
          title="", cmap='Set2', legend_fontsize=8)
```

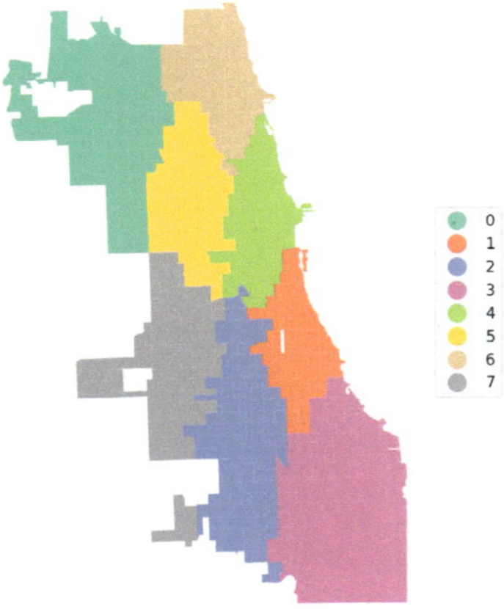

Figure 9.3: Cluster map for K-Medoids FASTERPAM

For FASTERPAM, the outcome is marginally the best of the three, with an average silhouette score of 0.348 and again a slightly different assignment of medoids. The associated cluster map is shown in Figure 9.3.

9.2.5 Using Actual Coordinates

The standardization of the x-y coordinates induces a compression of the distances in the largest direction. Since both standardized variables have a variance of 1, this will yield a different transformation of actual distances when the horizontal and vertical dimension of the map are not the same. This is clearly not the case in Chicago, with a much longer vertical than horizontal dimension. Therefore, it is recommended to *not* standardize coordinates when the goal is to use actual geographical distances. This is further illustrated in our discussion of spatialized cluster methods in Chapter 11.

To illustrate the effect of this, we re-run the analysis for untransformed coordinates. All the steps are the same as before, except for the use of different x-y coordinates.

```
dist_X = pairwise_distances(data_cluster, metric = 'manhattan')

kmedoids_instance4 = kmedoids.pam(dist_X, n_clusters,
                                  random_state = 123456789)
cluster_labels4 = kmedoids_instance4.labels
print("Medoids:", kmedoids_instance4.medoids)
print("Iterations:", kmedoids_instance4.n_iter)
print("Swaps:", kmedoids_instance4.n_swap)
c_stats = cluster_stats(cluster_labels4)
```

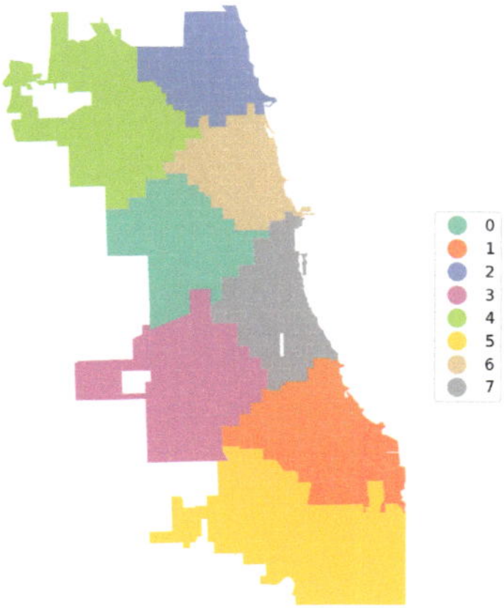

Figure 9.4: Cluster map for K-Medoids on actual coordinates

```
sil = kmedoids.silhouette(dist_X, cluster_labels4, samples = False)
print("Average silhouette score:", np.round(sil[0], 4))

clusfit = cluster_fit(data = data_cluster, clustlabels = cluster_labels4,
                correct = True, n_clusters = n_clusters)
```

```
Medoids: [772 488 654 753 353 516 205 437]
Iterations: 10
Swaps: 9
 Labels  Cardinality
    0.0        114.0
    1.0         97.0
    2.0         88.0
    3.0        105.0
    4.0        105.0
    5.0         64.0
    6.0        133.0
    7.0         85.0
Average silhouette score: 0.3565

Total Sum of Squares (TSS): 1579.9999999999995
Within-cluster Sum of Squares (WSS) for each cluster: [30.176 35.784
                            16.016 45.859 41.827 40.086 29.556 16.952]
Total Within-cluster Sum of Squares (WSS): 256.256
Between-cluster Sum of Squares (BSS): 1323.744
```

```
Ratio of BSS to TSS: 0.838
```

```
cluster_map(dfs, cluster_labels4, figsize = (5, 5),
            title="", cmap='Set2', legend_fontsize=8)
```

In the cluster map depicted in Figure 9.4 on page 141, note how the resulting regions are less elongated in the vertical direction. This is a direct result of using actual distances instead of the transformed values.

9.3 Practice

The different variants of PAM are very sensitive to the various tuning parameters. Assess the effect of changing these on the resulting clusters.

10 Spectral Clustering

Spectral Clustering is a graph partitioning method that can be interpreted as simultaneously implementing dimension reduction with cluster identification. It is designed to identify potentially non-convex groupings in the multi-attribute space , something the cluster methods reviewed so far are not able to do. It has become one of the go-to methods in modern machine learning.

While a partitioning method like K-Means, spectral clustering is a totally different approach as it is aimed at discovering cluster shapes that are *not convex*. In machine learning, there are several famous such examples, such as the *spirals* data set (used in this Chapter) and the Swiss roll data set. Spectral clustering approaches the problem by reprojecting the observations onto a new set of axes, based on eigenvalues and eigenvectors (hence, *spectral* clustering). Mathematical details are provided in Chapter 8 of the *GeoDa Cluster Book*.

The method is implemented as the `SpectralClustering` class from `sklearn.cluster`. For comparison purposes, we also use `KMeans` from `sklearn.cluster`. As before, variable standardization is carried out by means of `StandardScaler` from `sklearn.preprocessing`. To load the data and summarize the results, we import the helper functions `ensure_datasets`, `cluster_stats`, `cluster_fit` and `cluster_map` from the `spatial-cluster-helper` package. Finally, as usual, we need `numpy` and `geopandas`. Optionally, we also rely on `warnings` to suppress some warning messages by means of `filterwarnings`.

To illustrate spectral clustering, we use the **spirals** point data set. Note that the spirals data have no projection, they are just points in two-dimensional space. We use them as a GeoDataFrame to facilitate visualization.

> Required Packages
>
> numpy, geopandas, warnings, sklearn.cluster, sklearn.preprocessing, spatial-cluster-helper

> Required Data Sets
>
> spirals

Table 10.1: Contents of Spirals Data Set

	x	y	cl	geometry
0	0.812357	-0.987127	1.0	POINT (0.81236 -0.98713)
1	-0.267589	-0.325520	1.0	POINT (-0.26759 -0.32552)
2	0.373975	-0.012937	2.0	POINT (0.37397 -0.01294)

10.1 Preliminaries

10.1.1 Import Required Modules

```
import numpy as np
import geopandas as gpd
from sklearn.cluster import KMeans, SpectralClustering
from sklearn.preprocessing import StandardScaler
from spatial_cluster_helper import ensure_datasets, cluster_stats, \
            cluster_fit, cluster_map
import warnings
warnings.filterwarnings("ignore")
```

10.1.2 Load Data

We read the 300 point coordinates from the `spirals.shp` shape file and do a quick check of the data set, listed in Table 10.1.

```
# Setting working folder:
#path = "/your/path/to/data/"
path = "./datasets/"
# Select the spirals data set:
shpfile = "spirals/spirals.shp"
# Load the data:
ensure_datasets(shpfile, folder_path = path)
dfs = gpd.read_file(path + shpfile)
print(dfs.shape)
dfs.head(3)
```

```
(300, 4)
```

Figure 10.1: Spirals data set

10.1.3 Spirals Plot

To illustrate the non-convex nature of the clusters, we use the `cluster_map` helper function for the variable `cl`, which contains the actual cluster membership. This yields the two-color spiral rings shown in Figure 10.1.

```
cluster_map(dfs, dfs["cl"], figsize = (4,4), title = "",
            legend_fontsize=8)
```

10.1.4 Standardization

As before, we compute the `nn` scaling factor to retain compatibility with the results in `GeoDa`.

```
n = dfs.shape[0]
nn = np.sqrt((n - 1.0)/n)
```

10.1.5 Data Preparation

Finally, we specify the number of clusters as 2, create a subset with just the coordinates (`data_cluster`) and compute the scaled input array as `X` after applying the scaling factor to the result of `StandardScaler().fit_transform`.

```
n_clusters = 2
data_cluster = dfs[['x', 'y']]
X0 = StandardScaler().fit_transform(data_cluster)
X = X0 * nn
```

10.2 K-Means Clustering of Spirals

Before tackling the spectral clustering, we illustrate the poor performance of K-Means on non-convex clusters like the **spirals** data. As covered in Chapter 8, we use the class `KMeans` from `sklearn.cluster`. As arguments, we pass the number of clusters (`n_clusters = 2`), `k-means++` as the initialization method and a `random_state` for reproducibility.

We summarize the results with our usual helper functions `cluster_stats`, `cluster_fit` and `cluster_map`, shown in Figure 10.2.

```
kmeans = KMeans(n_clusters = n_clusters, init = 'k-means++',
                random_state = 123456789).fit(X)
cluster_labels = kmeans.labels_
c_stat = cluster_stats(cluster_labels)
clusfit = cluster_fit(data = data_cluster, clustlabels = cluster_labels,
                      correct = True, n_clusters = n_clusters)
```

```
 Labels  Cardinality
      0          151
      1          149

Total Sum of Squares (TSS): 597.9999999999999
Within-cluster Sum of Squares (WSS) for each cluster: [183.227 180.93 ]
Total Within-cluster Sum of Squares (WSS): 364.157
Between-cluster Sum of Squares (BSS): 233.843
Ratio of BSS to TSS: 0.391
```

```
cluster_map(dfs, cluster_labels, figsize = (4,4), title = "",
            legend_fontsize=8)
```

The results reveal a fairly balanced cluster, but it completely misses the separation between the two spirals. The BSS/TSS ratio is pretty dismal as well.

10.3 Spectral Clustering

We now apply the spectral clustering method as `SpectralClustering` from `sklearn.cluster` (for details, see https://scikit-learn.org/stable/modules/generated/sklearn.cluster.SpectralClustering.html). Besides the usual number of clusters

Figure 10.2: Cluster map for K-Means on spirals data set

(`n_clusters`) and `random_state`, this also takes several other arguments to fine tune the approach.

An important argument is the affinity matrix, `affinity`, typically based on an adjacency matrix or kernel function. The default in `SpectralClustering` is to use a radial basis kernel function (`rbf`). A commonly used alternative is an affinity matrix based on k-nearest neighbors, which is also the approach taken here. This requires `affinity = "nearest_neighbors"` as well as the number of neighbors as `n_neighbors`. To replicate the results in Chapter 8 of the *GeoDa Cluster Book*, we use `nearest_neighbors` to construct the affinity matrix and start by setting `n_neighbors = 3`.

In addition to `rbf` and `nearest_neighbors`, several other options to construct the affinity matrix are available as well. This is not further considered here (see the detailed documentation).

Finally, `n_init` determines the number of times the K-Means stage of the analysis will be rerun with different starting points. The default is `n_init = 10`.

In the usual manner, we apply the `fit` method to the cluster instance. The main result are the cluster labels, again contained in the `labels_` attribute. We apply our helper functions to summarize the results (if `filterwarnings` was not used, there will be a warning that can safely be ignored).

```
spectral = SpectralClustering(n_clusters = n_clusters,
                    random_state = 123456789,
                    affinity = 'nearest_neighbors',
                    n_neighbors = 3).fit(X)
cluster_labels = spectral.labels_
c_stat = cluster_stats(cluster_labels)
clusfit = cluster_fit(data = data_cluster,
                      clustlabels = cluster_labels,
                      correct = True, n_clusters = n_clusters)
```

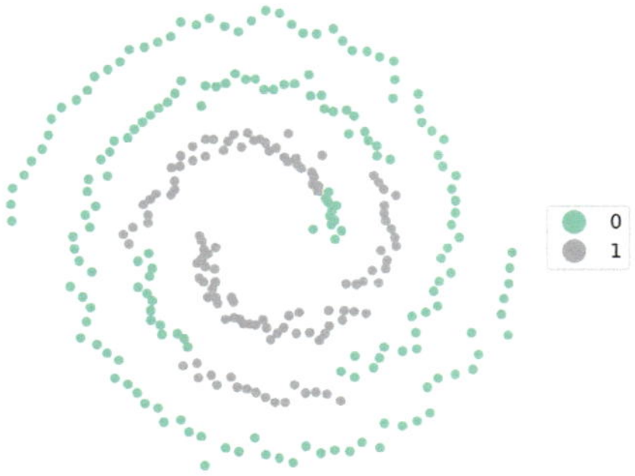

Figure 10.3: Spectral clustering result for knn=3

```
 Labels  Cardinality
      0          183
      1          117

Total Sum of Squares (TSS): 597.9999999999999
Within-cluster Sum of Squares (WSS) for each cluster: [489.101 102.65 ]
Total Within-cluster Sum of Squares (WSS): 591.751
Between-cluster Sum of Squares (BSS): 6.249
Ratio of BSS to TSS: 0.01
```

```
cluster_map(dfs, cluster_labels, figsize = (4,4), title = "",
            legend_fontsize=8)
```

The result, visualized in the cluster map in Figure 10.3, is an unbalanced set of clusters that does better than K-Means at following the spirals, but is by no means satisfactory. The BSS/TSS ratio is also pretty dismal, but this is not surprising since it is the wrong criterion to assess a clustering of non-convex data.

We fine tune the approach by setting `n_neighbors = 4` and summarize the result.

```
spectral = SpectralClustering(n_clusters = n_clusters,
                     random_state = 123456789,
                     affinity = 'nearest_neighbors',
                     n_neighbors = 4).fit(X)
cluster_labels = spectral.labels_
c_stat = cluster_stats(cluster_labels)
clusfit = cluster_fit(data = data_cluster, clustlabels = cluster_labels,
                       correct = True, n_clusters = n_clusters)
```

Figure 10.4: Spectral clustering result for knn=4

```
 Labels  Cardinality
      0          150
      1          150

Total Sum of Squares (TSS): 597.9999999999999
Within-cluster Sum of Squares (WSS) for each cluster: [287.864 285.729]
Total Within-cluster Sum of Squares (WSS): 573.594
Between-cluster Sum of Squares (BSS): 24.406
Ratio of BSS to TSS: 0.041
```

```
cluster_map(dfs, cluster_labels, figsize = (4,4), title = "",
            legend_fontsize=8)
```

In contrast to the previous results, these settings yield a perfectly balanced set of clusters that is able to identify the two spirals exactly, as illustrated in Figure 10.4.

In practice, it may take some experimenting to find a satisfactory solution. Also, one typically does not know beforehand whether the data is highly non-convex of not. Nevertheless, spectral clustering has become one of the most commonly used methods.

10.4 Practice

Spectral clustering is very sensitive to the various tuning parameters. The result of changes can be readily seen with the **spectral** example. In addition, spectral clustering could be applied to the Chicago census tract data as an alternative to K-Means or Hierarchical Clustering. Major discrepancies of the results might suggest the presence of non-convexity in the multi-attribute data distribution.

11 Spatializing Classic Clustering Methods

As such, the results of a classic clustering method like K-Means typically do not form spatially connected clusters, i.e., clusters for which the elements are spatially contiguous. In Chapter 12 and Chapter 13, we cover methods to impose *hard* spatial constraints to a clustering method. Here, we illustrate a way to impose *soft* spatial constraints, in the sense that the solution is *nudged* towards a spatially contiguous set, but this is not necessarily satisfied.

First, we show a simple *regionalization* method by applying a classic clustering method to the centroid coordinates of spatial units. We already illustrated an example of this for K-Medoids in Chapter 9. Here, we will apply K-Means to the centroid coordinates.

A second approach adds the centroid coordinates as additional features to the clustering procedure. This pushes the solution to a more spatially contiguous one, but it is only a soft constraint. In addition, the degree to which the nudging is effective depends on the number of other variables in the clustering exercise.

Further details are provided in Chapter 9 of the *GeoDa Cluster Book*. That Chapter also includes two additional methods that are primarily for pedagogical purposes to illustate the trade-offs involved in imposing spatial constraints. Since they are non-standard, they are not considered here.

To implement the *spatialization*, no new packages are required, since the methods are the same as before. The only changing element is the inclusion of coordinates among the features. Therefore, we again use `StandardScaler` from `sklearn.preprocessing` for variable standardization, as well as `KMeans` from `sklearn.cluster` to illustrate the effect on the cluster results. We also import the helper functions `ensure_datasets`, `cluster_stats`, `cluster_fit` and `cluster_map` from the `spatial-cluster-helper` package. Furthermore, we use `numpy` and `geopandas`.

The empirical illustration replicates the examples in Chapter 9 of the *GeoDa Cluster Book* with the **ceara** sample data set.

> Required Packages
>
> numpy, geopandas, sklearn.cluster, sklearn.preprocessing, spatial-cluster-helper

Required Data Sets

ceara

11.1 Preliminaries

11.1.1 Import Required Modules

```
import numpy as np
import geopandas as gpd

from sklearn.cluster import KMeans
from sklearn.preprocessing import StandardScaler

from spatial_cluster_helper import ensure_datasets, cluster_stats, \
            cluster_fit, cluster_map
```

11.1.2 Load Data

We read the data from the `ceara.shp` shape file and carry out a quick check of its contents, shown in Table 11.1.[1]

```
# Setting working folder:
#path = "/your/path/to/data/"
path = "./datasets/"
# Select the Ceará data:
shpfile = "ceara/ceara.shp"

# Load the data:
ensure_datasets(shpfile, folder_path = path)
dfs = gpd.read_file(path + shpfile, encoding = 'utf-8')
print(dfs.shape)
dfs.head(3)
```

```
(184, 36)
```

[1]For this sample data, we use the argument `encoding = 'utf-8'` in the `read_file` function to account for the special characters in Brazilian Portuguese.

Table 11.1: Partial Contents of Ceará Data Set

	code7	mun_name	state_init	area_km2	state_code	micro_code	micro_name
0	2300101.0	Abaiara	CE	180.833	23	23019	19ª Região Brejo Santo
1	2300150.0	Acarape	CE	130.002	23	23003	3ª Região Maracanaú
2	2300200.0	Acaraú	CE	842.471	23	23012	12ª Região Acaraú

```
# the full set of variables
print(list(dfs.columns))
```

```
['code7', 'mun_name', 'state_init', 'area_km2', 'state_code',
 ...
 'zika_d', 'mic_d', 'geometry']
```

11.1.3 Município Centroids

The locational coordinates are obtained as the centroids of the municípios. As illustrated for K-Medoids in Chapter 9, we use the geopandas `centroid` attribute applied to our GeoDataFrame (`dfs`), then extract the `x` and `y` coordinates and add them as new variables. We rescale them by 1000 to keep the distance units manageable. Since the original coordinates are projected, it is appropriate to apply Euclidean distance.

```
cent = dfs.centroid
dfs['X'] = cent.x / 1000
dfs['Y'] = cent.y / 1000
```

11.1.4 Data Preparation

As customary, we compute the scaling factor `nn` for `GeoDa` compatibility. We also set the number of clusters to 12.

```
n = dfs.shape[0]
nn = np.sqrt((n - 1.0)/n)
n_clusters = 12
```

11.2 K-Means on Centroid Coordinates

We first illustrate a straightforward application of K-Means to the centroids of the municípios. We define `data_cluster` as a subset of the GeoDataFrame with just the coordinates and apply `StandardScaler` and the `nn` rescaling to create the input array X. Note that this runs counter to our earlier recommendation *not* to standardize coordinates. However, we use it here to keep the results comparable with the other clustering methods.

```
data_cluster = dfs[['X', 'Y']]
X0 = StandardScaler().fit_transform(data_cluster)
X = X0 * nn
```

We now apply KMeans with the usual arguments (see Chapter 8 for details) and obtain the cluster labels as labels_. We then apply cluster_stats, cluster_fit and cluster_map to characterize the results.

```
kmeans = KMeans(n_clusters = n_clusters, n_init = 150,
                init = 'k-means++', random_state = 123456789).fit(X)
cluster_labels = kmeans.labels_
c_stats = cluster_stats(cluster_labels)
clusfit = cluster_fit(data = data_cluster, clustlabels = cluster_labels,
                      correct = True, n_clusters = n_clusters)
```

Labels	Cardinality
0	20
1	12
2	21
3	10
4	16
5	7
6	16
7	11
8	12
9	29
10	13
11	17

```
Total Sum of Squares (TSS): 366.0
Within-cluster Sum of Squares (WSS) for each cluster: [2.075 1.514
                           2.613 1.915 1.847 1.115 1.272 1.033 1.614
                           2.798 1.523 2.391]
Total Within-cluster Sum of Squares (WSS): 21.709
Between-cluster Sum of Squares (BSS): 344.291
Ratio of BSS to TSS: 0.941
```

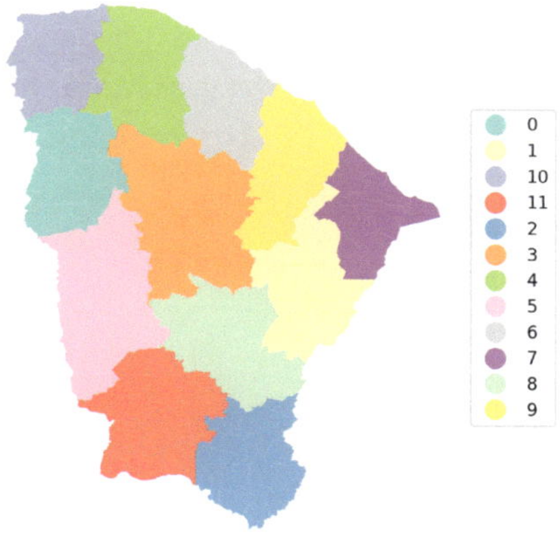

Figure 11.1: Cluster map for K-Means on município centroids

```
cluster_map(dfs, cluster_labels, figsize = (4,4),
            cmap = 'Set3', title = "", legend_fontsize=8)
```

The results, illustrated in Figure 11.1, show a very nice regionalization, with good separation for BSS/TSS of 0.941.

The resulting regions can then be used for data aggregation or as fixed effects variables in a spatial regression, among several other possibilities.

Similar results can be obtained by applying other classic clustering methods to the coordinates. This is not pursued further.

11.3 K-Means with Coordinates as Additional Features

A *soft* spatial constraint is introduced by adding the X-Y coordinates to the regular features. We illustrate this for K-Means.

We create two lists with cluster variables from the Ceará data set, following the example in Section 9.3.1. of the *GeoDa Cluster Book*. In the first list (`clust_vars1`), we include six socio-economic indicators: mobility, environ, housing, sanitation, infra, and gdpcap. The second list (`clust_vars2`) also contains X and Y.

```
clust_vars1 = ["mobility", "environ", "housing", "sanitation",
               "infra","gdpcap"]
clust_vars2 = clust_vars1 + ["X", "Y"]
```

11.3.1 K-Means with Features Only

We proceed in the by now familiar manner to create `data_cluster1` as a subset of the GeoDataFrame, and apply the `StandardScaler` and the `nn` scaling factor to obtain the input matrix `X`. We then carry out `KMeans` with the usual arguments and summarize the results by means of our helper functions. The cluster map is shown in Figure 11.2.

```
data_cluster1 = dfs[clust_vars1]
X0 = StandardScaler().fit_transform(data_cluster1)
X = X0 * nn

kmeans = KMeans(n_clusters = n_clusters, n_init = 150,
                init = 'k-means++', random_state=123456789).fit(X)
cluster_labels1 = kmeans.labels_
c_stats = cluster_stats(cluster_labels1)
clusfit = cluster_fit(data = data_cluster1,
                      clustlabels = cluster_labels1,
                      correct = True, n_clusters = n_clusters)
```

```
 Labels  Cardinality
      0           21
      1           30
      2            3
      3           22
      4            4
      5           10
      6            7
      7            1
      8           23
      9           26
     10           26
     11           11

Total Sum of Squares (TSS): 1098.0
Within-cluster Sum of Squares (WSS) for each cluster: [35.969 37.901
                     5.341 43.958 11.088 27.469 27.094  0.     38.359
                    46.621 51.678 22.647]
Total Within-cluster Sum of Squares (WSS): 348.125
Between-cluster Sum of Squares (BSS): 749.875
Ratio of BSS to TSS: 0.683
```

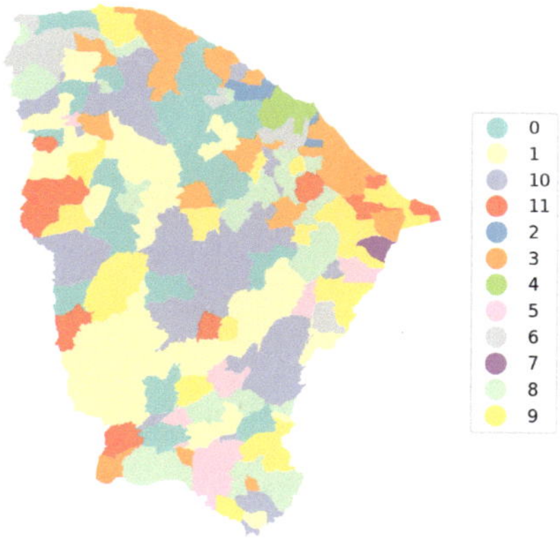

Figure 11.2: K-Means for Ceará variables

```
cluster_map(dfs, cluster_labels1, figsize = (4,4),
            cmap = 'Set3', title = "", legend_fontsize=8)
```

The clusters are not identical to the solution obtained with `GeoDa`, but the results are close. The fit is quite good, with a BSS/TSS ratio of 0.683. However, there is very little *spatial* clustering. Cluster 4 is the only one that turns out to be spatially contiguous, consisting of 4 municípios surrounding the main city of Fortaleza. However, in contrast, for cluster 7, which also consists of 4 units, the four entities are totally disconnected in space.

11.3.2 K-Means with X-Y Included as Features

We now include the X and Y coordinates among the features using `clust_vars2` as the input, but otherwise we proceed in exactly the same way as before.

```
data_cluster2 = dfs[clust_vars2]
X0 = StandardScaler().fit_transform(data_cluster2)
X = X0 * nn

kmeans = KMeans(n_clusters = n_clusters, n_init = 150,
                init = 'k-means++', random_state = 123456789).fit(X)
cluster_labels2 = kmeans.labels_
c_stats = cluster_stats(cluster_labels2)
clusfit = cluster_fit(data = data_cluster2,
                      clustlabels = cluster_labels2,
                      correct = True, n_clusters = n_clusters)
```

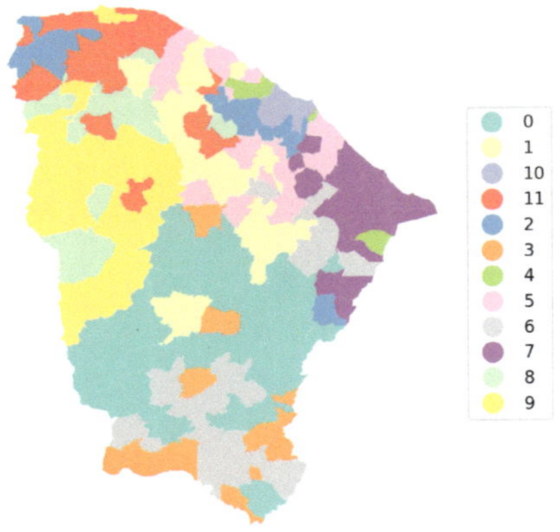

Figure 11.3: K-Means augmented with município centroids

```
Labels  Cardinality
     0           30
     1           15
     2            9
     3           15
     4            3
     5           17
     6           19
     7           15
     8           13
     9           24
    10            4
    11           20

Total Sum of Squares (TSS): 1464.0
Within-cluster Sum of Squares (WSS) for each cluster: [93.898 28.392
                     51.527 57.266 14.62  38.063 49.986 49.473 45.144
                     64.804 11.152 52.565]
Total Within-cluster Sum of Squares (WSS): 556.891
Between-cluster Sum of Squares (BSS): 907.109
Ratio of BSS to TSS: 0.62
```

```
cluster_map(dfs, cluster_labels2, figsize = (4,4),
            cmap = 'Set3', title = "", legend_fontsize=8)
```

The cluster map in Figure 11.3 shows more of a spatial grouping, although the solution is by no means fully contiguous. The price we pay for the inclusion of the coordinates is a decline of BSS/TSS to 0.62.

11.4 Practice

It is straightforward to include X-Y coordinates into the cluster analyses carried out in the previous Chapters. Assess the extent to which this creates more spatially contiguous cluster results.

12 Spatially Constrained Clustering - Hierarchical Methods

In this Chapter, we introduce methods to impose *hard* spatial constraints in a clustering procedure. We consider three approaches that use a hierarchical clustering logic: spatially constrained hierarchical clustering (SCHC), SKATER (Spatial Kluster Analysis by Tree Edge Removal), Assunçao et al. (2006), and REDCAP (REgionalization with Dynamically Constrained Agglomerative clustering and Partitioning), Guo (2008), Guo and Wang (2011). These methods are covered in Chapter 10 of the *GeoDa Cluster Book*.

Other than a form of spatially constrained hierarchical clustering, spatially constrained clustering methods are not (yet) part of scikit-learn. The corresponding functionality from `GeoDa` is included in the `pygeoda` package. In addition, we also employ `AgglomerativeClustering` from `sklearn.cluster`, `StandardScaler` from `sklearn.preprocessing`, and the helper functions `ensure_datasets`, `cluster_stats`, `cluster_center`, `cluster_fit` and `cluster_map` from the `spatial-cluster-helper` package. We rely on `geopandas` and `numpy` for the basics, and use `libpysal.weights` to construct a contiguity matrix from a GeoDataFrame.

We also import `time` to compare the relative performance of the different implementations, as well as `warnings` to avoid some warning messages (suppressed by means of `filterwarnings`).

We continue with the **ceara** sample data set for the empirical illustration.

> Required Packages
>
> geopandas, numpy, time, warnings, sklearn.cluster, sklearn.preprocessing, pygeoda, libpysal.weights, spatial-cluster-helper

> Required Data Sets
>
> ceara

12.1 Preliminaries

12.1.1 Import Required Modules

```
import geopandas as gpd
import numpy as np
import time

from sklearn.cluster import AgglomerativeClustering
from sklearn.preprocessing import StandardScaler

from spatial_cluster_helper import ensure_datasets, cluster_stats, \
              cluster_fit, cluster_center, cluster_map

import pygeoda
import libpysal.weights as weights

import warnings
warnings.filterwarnings("ignore")
```

12.1.2 Load Data

We read the data from the `ceara.shp` shape file and carry out a quick check of its size. Its contents are the same as listed in Table 11.1 on page 153 and are not further detailed here.

```
# Setting working folder:
#path = "/your/path/to/data/"
path = "./datasets/"

# Select the Ceará data:
shpfile = "ceara/ceara.shp"

# Load the data:
ensure_datasets(shpfile, folder_path = path)
dfs = gpd.read_file(path + shpfile, encoding = 'utf-8')
print(dfs.shape)
```

```
(184, 36)
```

Table 12.1: Spatial Clustering Variables

Column Name	Variable Description
mobility	Mobility index
environ	Environment index
housing	Housing index
sanitation	Sanitation index
infra	Infrastructure index
gdpcap	GDP per capita

12.1.3 Variables

We follow the empirical illustration in Chapter 10 of the *GeoDa Cluster Book* and select six variables from the **ceara** sample data set, listed in Table 12.1.

As before, we specify the variables in a list for later use.

```
varlist = ['mobility', 'environ', 'housing', 'sanitation', 'infra',
           'gdpcap']
```

12.1.4 Pygeoda Data Preparation

`pygeoda` uses its own internal data format. It requires a few extra steps to convert a GeoDataFrame to this format. This is accomplished by means of the `open` command to which the GeoDataFrame (`dfs`) is passed.

In addition, we create queen contiguity weights using `queen_weights` and briefly check their characteristics. These weights are critical to obtain spatially constrained cluster results.

```
ceara_g = pygeoda.open(dfs)
queen_w = pygeoda.queen_weights(ceara_g)
queen_w
```

```
Weights Meta-data:
 number of observations:                 184
           is symmetric:                True
               sparsity:  0.02953686200378072
        # min neighbors:                   1
        # max neighbors:                  13
       # mean neighbors:   5.434782608695652
     # median neighbors:                 5.0
```

```
has isolates:                  False
```

We need the relevant variables in a `pygeoda` data format. This is accomplished in the same way as for a standard DataFrame, by selecting a subset with a list of variables (`varlist`). This yields the data object `data_g` that we will use in the `pygeoda` functions. However, because we will also use the various helper functions from the `spatial_cluster_helper` module, we will need the usual GeoDataFrame subset as well. We extract the variables as `data` for future use.

```
data_g = ceara_g[varlist]
data = dfs[varlist]
```

12.1.5 PySAL Spatial Weights

The implementation of SCHC by means of scikit-learn requires a sparse array as an argument. The spatial weights created in `pygeoda` do not have such a property. Instead, we must rely on the `sparse` attribute that is part of a `PySAL` spatial weights object.

We use `libpysal.weights` to obtain a queen contiguity matrix from the GeoDataFrame `dfs`. Since only the contiguity information is used, we do not need to row-standardize the weights. If the `warningsfilter` was not set to `ignore`, this will yield some warnings. They can safely be ignored, but can also be suppressed with the code as shown in the import statements.

```
wq = weights.Queen.from_dataframe(dfs)
```

12.1.6 Miscellaneous Arguments

We set the number of clusters to 12.

```
n_clusters = 12
```

Finally, we also compute the usual scaling factor as `nn`.

```
n = data.shape[0]
nn = np.sqrt((n-1.0)/n)
```

12.2 SCHC

The first method we consider is *spatially constrained hierarchical clustering*, or SCHC. This method proceeds in the same manner as hierarchical clustering (see Chapter 7), but the closest units are only merged when they are also contiguous, as defined by the spatial weights. This requires a continuous updating of the spatial weights information, carried out under the hood. The specific `pygeoda` method is `schc`. It takes the number of clusters (`n_clusters`), the spatial weights object (`queen_w`, from `pygeoda`), the variables in `pygeoda` format (`data_g`), and the linkage method, here set to `"ward"`.

The result is a *dictionary* that contains various measures of fit, as well as a cluster label for each observation. In contrast to what is the case for cluster computations in scikit-learn, the labels start at 1, not at 0.

We apply this for 12 clusters for the **ceara** variables and list the `keys` of the return object.

```
t0 = time.time()
ceara_clusters1 = pygeoda.schc(n_clusters, queen_w, data_g, "ward")
t1 = time.time()
tpygeoda = t1 - t0
print("Time for pygeoda schc",tpygeoda)
print(ceara_clusters1.keys())
```

```
Time for pygeoda schc 0.007730245590209961
dict_keys(['Total sum of squares', 'Within-cluster sum of squares',
                'Total within-cluster sum of squares',
                'Total between-cluster sum of squares',
                'The ratio of between to total sum of squares',
                'Clusters'])
```

The cluster labels are contained in the `'Clusters'` item in the dictionary. We can extract them as `cluster_labels1` for use in our helper functions.

For example, the helper function `cluster_stats` will return the cardinality of each cluster. To accomplish this, we need to make sure that `cluster_labels1` is a `numpy` array (hence, the application of `np.array`).

```
cluster_labels1 = np.array(ceara_clusters1['Clusters'])
c_stats1 = cluster_stats(cluster_labels1)
```

```
 Labels  Cardinality
      1           79
      2           48
      3           21
      4           17
      5            5
      6            4
      7            3
      8            2
      9            2
     10            1
     11            1
     12            1
```

The remaining keys contain measures of fit. We can print them in a simple loop, excluding the last item (the cluster labels).

```
for key in list(ceara_clusters1.keys())[:-1]:
    print(f"{key}: {np.round(ceara_clusters1[key],4)}")
```

```
Total sum of squares: 1098.0
Within-cluster sum of squares: [225.7318 168.248   93.8421  46.7944
                                  18.098   11.0881   5.5954  16.9901
                                   2.0036   0.       0.       0.    ]
Total within-cluster sum of squares: 588.3915
Total between-cluster sum of squares: 509.6085
The ratio of between to total sum of squares: 0.4641
```

Alternatively, we can also apply our `cluster_fit` helper function. The results are identical, as long as we set the `correct` argument to `True`. This ensures that the same standardization is used as in `GeoDa` (the default in scikit-learn is a variance computation without degrees of freedom correction).

```
fit1 = cluster_fit(data, cluster_labels1, n_clusters,
                   correct = True, printopt = True)
```

```
Total Sum of Squares (TSS): 1098.0
Within-cluster Sum of Squares (WSS) for each cluster: [225.732 168.248
               93.842  46.794  18.098  11.088   5.595  16.99    2.004
```

```
                 0.        0.        0.    ]
Total Within-cluster Sum of Squares (WSS): 588.391
Between-cluster Sum of Squares (BSS): 509.609
Ratio of BSS to TSS: 0.464
```

The `cluster_center` helper function will list the cluster mean and median for each variable.

```
clust_means1, clust_medians1 = cluster_center(data, cluster_labels1)
print("Cluster Means:\n", np.round(clust_means1, 3))
print("Cluster Medians:\n", np.round(clust_medians1, 3))
```

```
Cluster Means:
          mobility  environ  housing  sanitation  infra  gdpcap
cluster
1            0.965    0.891    0.846       0.672  0.524   4.508
2            0.952    0.844    0.795       0.597  0.504   4.483
3            0.950    0.879    0.844       0.576  0.441   6.834
4            0.951    0.758    0.844       0.649  0.588   4.821
5            0.968    0.815    0.792       0.581  0.438   4.246
6            0.833    0.766    0.818       0.792  0.574  12.600
7            0.992    0.942    0.824       0.870  0.625   6.823
8            0.974    0.657    0.781       0.823  0.693   5.432
9            0.859    0.687    0.722       0.584  0.417   4.644
10           0.957    0.966    0.857       0.593  0.357  40.018
11           0.936    0.789    0.794       0.545  0.425  27.625
12           0.951    0.824    0.771       0.573  0.443  25.464
Cluster Medians:
          mobility  environ  housing  sanitation  infra  gdpcap
cluster
1            0.968    0.895    0.848       0.669  0.523   4.319
2            0.953    0.871    0.794       0.572  0.498   4.120
3            0.954    0.896    0.836       0.575  0.427   5.837
4            0.950    0.758    0.845       0.636  0.590   4.214
5            0.967    0.805    0.804       0.594  0.477   4.285
6            0.835    0.766    0.824       0.799  0.583  11.557
7            0.993    0.932    0.829       0.885  0.606   4.488
8            0.974    0.657    0.781       0.823  0.693   5.432
9            0.859    0.687    0.722       0.584  0.417   4.644
10           0.957    0.966    0.857       0.593  0.357  40.018
11           0.936    0.789    0.794       0.545  0.425  27.625
12           0.951    0.824    0.771       0.573  0.443  25.464
```

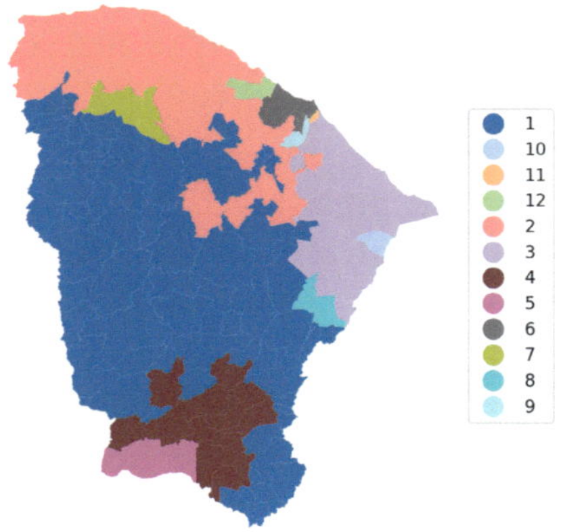

Figure 12.1: Spatially constrained hierarchical clustering

Finally, as before, we can use `cluster_map` to create a unique values map for the clusters. This is shown in Figure 12.1.

```
cluster_map(dfs, cluster_labels1, figsize=(4, 4),
            title="", cmap='tab20', legend_fontsize=8)
```

12.2.1 SCHC with Scikit-Learn

The `AgglomerativeClustering` functionality in `sklearn.cluster` includes an option for a so-called *structured* approach. It imposes prior constraints through a `connectivity` argument, which takes a sparse CSR array. In practice, this can yield a spatially constrained clustering solution, although it is not directly referred to as such (the constraints are generic). For spatial constraints, we can readily obtain an array in the proper sparse format by applying the `sparse` method to a `PySAL` spatial weights object. In our application, this is `wq.sparse`. Note that the `sparse` method does **not** work for the spatial weights object created by `pygeoda` (i.e., `queen_w` in our example).

The call to `AgglomerativeClustering` is structured in the same way as in Chapter 7. First, `StandardScaler` is used to `fit_transform` the cluster variables, followed by a scaling for compatibility. An instance of the `AgglomerativeClustering` class is created as `agg_clust`, which has all the standard arguments, with the addition of `connectivity = wq.sparse`. After the `fit` method is applied, the cluster labels (`cluster_labels1a`) are extracted from `agg_clust.labels_`. We then apply the `cluster_stats` helper function. Whereas the ordering of the cluster cardinalities is different from that provided by `pygeoda`, the values are identical.

```
method = 'ward'
t0 = time.time()
X0 = StandardScaler().fit_transform(data)
X = X0 * nn

agg_clust = AgglomerativeClustering(n_clusters=n_clusters,
                                    connectivity = wq.sparse,
                                    linkage=method,
                                    compute_distances=True)
agg_clust.fit(X)
cluster_labels1a = agg_clust.labels_
cl1a = cluster_stats(cluster_labels1a)
t1 = time.time()
tsklearn = t1 - t0
print("\nTime for scikit-learn schc ",tsklearn)
```

```
 Labels  Cardinality
      0           48
      1           21
      2            2
      3           17
      4           79
      5            3
      6            4
      7            1
      8            1
      9            2
     10            5
     11            1

Time for scikit-learn schc  0.004796028137207031
```

The cluster fit properties are the same as well, as is the resulting cluster map, shown in Figure 12.2 on page 170.

```
fit1a = cluster_fit(data,cluster_labels1a,n_clusters,
                    correct=True,printopt=True)
```

```
Total Sum of Squares (TSS): 1098.0
```

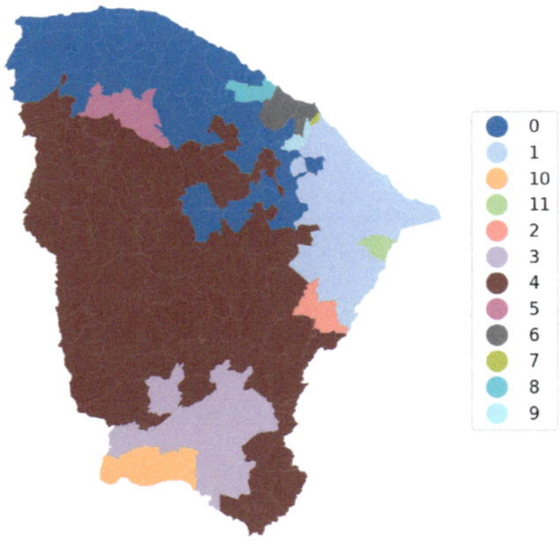

Figure 12.2: Spatially constrained hierarchical cluster (scikit-learn)

```
Within-cluster Sum of Squares (WSS) for each cluster: [168.248  93.842
                16.99   46.794 225.732   5.595  11.088   0.       0.
                 2.004  18.098   0.    ]
Total Within-cluster Sum of Squares (WSS): 588.391
Between-cluster Sum of Squares (BSS): 509.609
Ratio of BSS to TSS: 0.464
```

```
cluster_map(dfs, cluster_labels1a, figsize=(4,4),
            title="", cmap='tab20', legend_fontsize=8)
```

12.3 SKATER

In contrast to the agglomerative SCHC, SKATER is a *divisive* hierarchical approach. It is based on a reduction of the graph structure implied by the spatial weights to a *minimum spanning tree*, based on the inter-observation dissimilarity. The original graph is essentially a weighted form of the spatial weights matrix, where the existence of a contiguity between two observations is weighted by their dissimilarity. From the initial minimum spanning tree, the SKATER algorithm proceeds by finding optimal *cuts* in the tree, which each form a subcluster. This process continues until the desired number of clusters is found.

One downside of this approach is that observations are trapped in subclusters and cannot further be swapped. Technical details are provided in Chapter 10 of the *GeoDa Cluster Book*.

The algorithm is invoked with the `skater` method of `pygeoda`. This again requires the number of clusters (`n_clusters`), the spatial weights (`queen_w`) and the `pygeoda` variables (`data_g`) as arguments. The return object is a dictionary with the same structure as before.

We use the helper functions to generate the cluster cardinality, cluster fit, cluster centers and cluster map.

For simplicity, all commands are combined.

```
t0 = time.time()
ceara_clusters2 = pygeoda.skater(n_clusters, queen_w, data_g)
t1 = time.time()
tskater = t1 - t0
print("Time for pygeoda skater ",tskater)
cluster_labels2 = np.array(ceara_clusters2['Clusters'])
cl2 = cluster_stats(cluster_labels2)
fit2 = cluster_fit(data, cluster_labels2, n_clusters,
                   correct = True, printopt = True)
clust_means2, clust_medians2 = cluster_center(data, cluster_labels2)

print("Cluster Means:\n", np.round(clust_medians2, 3))
print("Cluster Medians:\n", np.round(clust_medians2, 3))
```

```
Time for pygeoda skater  0.027920246124267578
 Labels  Cardinality
      1          107
      2           41
      3           15
      4            4
      5            4
      6            3
      7            3
      8            3
      9            1
     10            1
     11            1
     12            1

Total Sum of Squares (TSS): 1098.0
Within-cluster Sum of Squares (WSS) for each cluster: [398.019 135.799
                48.297  11.088   9.206   9.127   5.956   5.595   0.
                 0.      0.      0.    ]
```

```
Total Within-cluster Sum of Squares (WSS): 623.089
Between-cluster Sum of Squares (BSS): 474.911
Ratio of BSS to TSS: 0.433
Cluster Means:
         mobility  environ  housing  sanitation  infra  gdpcap
cluster
1           0.966    0.880    0.844       0.638  0.537   4.152
2           0.954    0.879    0.807       0.594  0.490   4.598
3           0.948    0.882    0.835       0.544  0.414   6.760
4           0.835    0.766    0.824       0.799  0.583  11.557
5           0.963    0.708    0.751       0.544  0.471   4.263
6           0.966    0.957    0.906       0.671  0.566   5.837
7           0.885    0.687    0.730       0.622  0.427   5.110
8           0.993    0.932    0.829       0.885  0.606   4.488
9           0.936    0.789    0.794       0.545  0.425  27.625
10          0.983    0.644    0.865       0.858  0.859   5.578
11          0.957    0.966    0.857       0.593  0.357  40.018
12          0.951    0.824    0.771       0.573  0.443  25.464
Cluster Medians:
         mobility  environ  housing  sanitation  infra  gdpcap
cluster
1           0.966    0.880    0.844       0.638  0.537   4.152
2           0.954    0.879    0.807       0.594  0.490   4.598
3           0.948    0.882    0.835       0.544  0.414   6.760
4           0.835    0.766    0.824       0.799  0.583  11.557
5           0.963    0.708    0.751       0.544  0.471   4.263
6           0.966    0.957    0.906       0.671  0.566   5.837
7           0.885    0.687    0.730       0.622  0.427   5.110
8           0.993    0.932    0.829       0.885  0.606   4.488
9           0.936    0.789    0.794       0.545  0.425  27.625
10          0.983    0.644    0.865       0.858  0.859   5.578
11          0.957    0.966    0.857       0.593  0.357  40.018
12          0.951    0.824    0.771       0.573  0.443  25.464
```

The corresponding cluster map is shown in Figure 12.3.

```
cluster_map(dfs, cluster_labels2, figsize = (4, 4),
            title="", cmap='tab20', legend_fontsize=8)
```

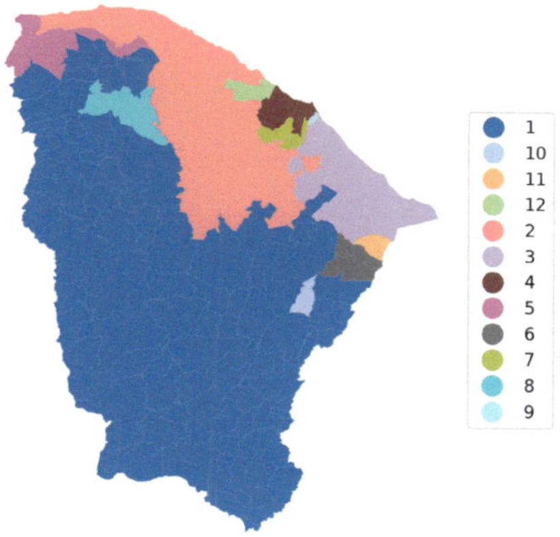

Figure 12.3: SKATER spatially constrained clustering

12.3.1 Additional Constraints in the Clustering

`GeoDa` offers the option to provide a constraint on the cluster size. This is typically expressed as a function of a spatially extensive variable, such as population in the Ceará example. This additional constraint ensures that no cluster contains less than the set limit. In practice, this is often needed when building regions to report rates on rare diseases to protect privacy. Note that the specified constraints may sometimes conflict with the desired number of clusters, in the sense that there is no solution that satisfies both the number of clusters and the minimum size constraint. In that case, the largest number of possible clusters that satisfy the constraint is given as the solution.

Even though there is no explicit option to provide the *number* of cluster elements as the constraint, this can readily be accomplished by creating an additional *constant* variable equal to 1 for all observations. The constraint can then be expressed by selecting this constant variable and setting the number of observations as the value for the constraint (the sum of all the `1` values).

A contraint is implemented in `pygeoda` by means of the `bound_variable` and `min_bound` arguments. Similar to the example in Chapter 10 of the *GeoDa Cluster Book*, we use population (`pop`) to set the bound at a minimum of 10% of the overall population. In all other respects, the approach remains the same as the unconstrained solution.

We again group all commands.

```
t0 = time.time()
ceara_clusters3 = pygeoda.skater(n_clusters, queen_w, data_g,
                          bound_variable = dfs['pop'],
                          min_bound = dfs['pop'].sum()/10)
```

```
t1 = time.time()
tskaterc = t1 - t0
print("Time for pygeoda constrained skater ",tskaterc)
cluster_labels3 = np.array(ceara_clusters3['Clusters'])
cl3 = cluster_stats(cluster_labels3)
fit3 = cluster_fit(data, cluster_labels3, n_clusters,
                   correct = True, printopt = True)
clust_means3, clust_medians3 = cluster_center(data, cluster_labels3)
print("Cluster Means:\n", np.round(clust_means3, 3))
print("Cluster Medians:\n", np.round(clust_medians3, 3))
```

```
Time for pygeoda constrained skater  0.016527891159057617
 Labels  Cardinality
      1           43
      2           40
      3           36
      4           32
      5           26
      6            7

Total Sum of Squares (TSS): 1098.0
Within-cluster Sum of Squares (WSS) for each cluster: [156.507 172.008
                                           158.72  113.536 208.516  43.745]
Total Within-cluster Sum of Squares (WSS): 853.033
Between-cluster Sum of Squares (BSS): 244.967
Ratio of BSS to TSS: 0.223
Cluster Means:
         mobility  environ  housing  sanitation  infra  gdpcap
cluster
1          0.964    0.884    0.841       0.644  0.532   4.562
2          0.956    0.857    0.797       0.617  0.495   5.292
3          0.961    0.817    0.836       0.645  0.535   4.485
4          0.964    0.880    0.844       0.711  0.544   4.601
5          0.946    0.861    0.830       0.566  0.451   8.434
6          0.851    0.742    0.785       0.715  0.508   9.475
Cluster Medians:
         mobility  environ  housing  sanitation  infra  gdpcap
cluster
1          0.970    0.896    0.845       0.607  0.537   4.097
2          0.954    0.878    0.803       0.591  0.488   4.635
3          0.963    0.828    0.836       0.625  0.547   4.120
```

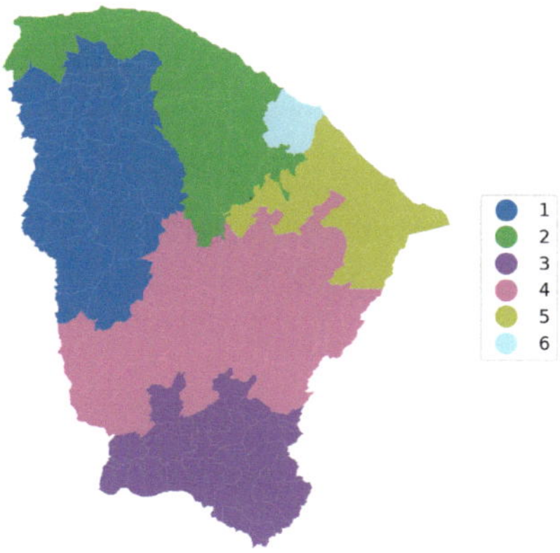

Figure 12.4: SKATER with minimum population bounds

4	0.968	0.892	0.849	0.711	0.535	4.417
5	0.949	0.870	0.831	0.545	0.450	5.300
6	0.845	0.741	0.795	0.710	0.497	7.675

The cluster map is shown in Figure 12.4.

```
cluster_map(dfs, cluster_labels3, figsize=(4, 4),
            title="", cmap='tab20', legend_fontsize=8)
```

Note how even though we set the number of clusters to 12, only a solution with six clusters could be obtained such that the minimum population requirement is satisfied. Also, the overall fit of the solution is seriously deteriorated, to a BSS/TSS ratio of 0.223, compared to the original 0.433.

12.4 REDCAP

The final hierarchical method covered in Chapter 10 of the *GeoDa Cluster Book* is REDCAP, which is a combination of an agglomerative approach with the use of a minimum spanning tree. Several variants of the method are available, combining a type of hierarchical clustering linkage with the way the neighbor structure is updated (for full details, see the *GeoDa Cluster Book* and the detailed `pygeoda` documentation). Of all the combinations, five are supported by `pygeoda`:

- `firstorder-singlelinkage`
- `fullorder-singlelinkage`

- fullorder-averagelinkage
- fullorder-completelinkage
- fullorder-wardlinkage

Here, as in Chapter 10 of the *GeoDa Cluster Book*, we will illustrate the **fullorder-wardlinkage** method, which is passed as the **method** argument to the **redcap** function. Everything else operates as before. Again, we combine all commands, with the cluster map in Figure 12.5.

```
t0 = time.time()
ceara_clusters4 = pygeoda.redcap(n_clusters, queen_w, data_g,
                                  method = 'fullorder-wardlinkage')
t1 = time.time()
print("Time for pygeoda redcap ",t1 - t0)
cluster_labels4 = np.array(ceara_clusters4['Clusters'])
cl4 = cluster_stats(cluster_labels4)
fit4 = cluster_fit(data, cluster_labels4, n_clusters,
                   correct = True, printopt = True)
clust_means4, clust_medians4 = cluster_center(data, cluster_labels4)
print("Cluster Means:\n", np.round(clust_means4, 3))
print("Cluster Medians:\n", np.round(clust_medians4, 3))
```

```
Time for pygeoda redcap  0.03205990791320801
 Labels  Cardinality
      1           77
      2           52
      3           21
      4           16
      5            5
      6            3
      7            3
      8            2
      9            2
     10            1
     11            1
     12            1

Total Sum of Squares (TSS): 1098.0
Within-cluster Sum of Squares (WSS) for each cluster: [214.614 173.74
                63.005  66.063  38.299   9.602   5.595  16.99    2.004
                 0.      0.      0.   ]
Total Within-cluster Sum of Squares (WSS): 589.912
```

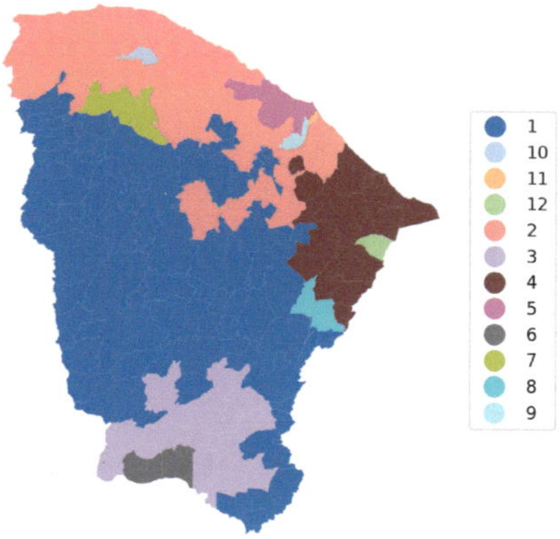

Figure 12.5: REDCAP spatially constrained clustering

```
Between-cluster Sum of Squares (BSS): 508.088
Ratio of BSS to TSS: 0.463
Cluster Means:
         mobility  environ  housing  sanitation  infra  gdpcap
cluster
1           0.966    0.894    0.847       0.675  0.526   4.527
2           0.951    0.842    0.793       0.583  0.495   4.974
3           0.952    0.762    0.839       0.626  0.571   4.646
4           0.950    0.887    0.858       0.603  0.440   6.011
5           0.857    0.777    0.809       0.749  0.548  15.173
6           0.969    0.829    0.777       0.632  0.387   4.390
7           0.992    0.942    0.824       0.870  0.625   6.823
8           0.974    0.657    0.781       0.823  0.693   5.432
9           0.859    0.687    0.722       0.584  0.417   4.644
10          0.958    0.973    0.928       0.798  0.647   3.884
11          0.936    0.789    0.794       0.545  0.425  27.625
12          0.957    0.966    0.857       0.593  0.357  40.018


Cluster Medians:
         mobility  environ  housing  sanitation  infra  gdpcap
cluster
1           0.969    0.896    0.848       0.672  0.523   4.369
2           0.952    0.864    0.793       0.564  0.495   4.243
3           0.956    0.758    0.842       0.609  0.569   4.127
4           0.956    0.906    0.856       0.594  0.425   5.300
5           0.845    0.791    0.823       0.784  0.561  15.132
```

6	0.968	0.805	0.763	0.642	0.400	4.313
7	0.993	0.932	0.829	0.885	0.606	4.488
8	0.974	0.657	0.781	0.823	0.693	5.432
9	0.859	0.687	0.722	0.584	0.417	4.644
10	0.958	0.973	0.928	0.798	0.647	3.884
11	0.936	0.789	0.794	0.545	0.425	27.625
12	0.957	0.966	0.857	0.593	0.357	40.018

```
cluster_map(dfs, cluster_labels4, figsize=(4, 4),
            title="", cmap='tab20', legend_fontsize=8)
```

12.5 Practice

The three spatially constrained hierarchical clustering methods can be applied to any of the data sets used in the previous Chapters to assess the effect of the constraint. In particular, it provides a way to quantify the trade-off between the non-spatial and spatial perspective.

13 Spatially Constrained Clustering - Partitioning Methods

.In this Chapter, we continue with methods that impose *hard* spatial constraints in a clustering procedure. We consider two methods that use a partitioning clustering logic: *AZP* (automatic zoning procedure), Openshaw (1977) ,Openshaw and Rao (1995), and *max-p*, Duque, Anselin, and Rey (2012). Both are covered in Chapter 11 of the *GeoDa Cluster Book*.

As in Chapter 12, we need to rely on the functionality from `GeoDa` that is included in the `pygeoda` package. We again use the helper functions `ensure_datasets`, `cluster_stats`, `cluster_center`, `cluster_fit` and `cluster_map` from the `spatial-cluster-helper` package. We rely on `geopandas` and `numpy` for the basics. As in the previous chapter, we import `time` to get insight into the performance of the different algorithms. We also continue with the **ceara** sample data set for the empirical illustration.

> Required Packages
>
> geopandas, numpy, pygeoda, spatial-cluster-helper

> Required Data Sets
>
> ceara

13.1 Preliminaries

13.1.1 Import Required Modules

```
import geopandas as gpd
import numpy as np
import time
from spatial_cluster_helper import ensure_datasets, cluster_stats, \
            cluster_fit, cluster_center, cluster_map
import pygeoda
```

13.1.2 Load Data

As in Chapter 12, we load the **ceara.shp** shape file. The code block is the same as before and is listed here for completeness. The results are skipped.

```
# Setting working folder:
#path = "/your/path/to/data/"
path = "./datasets/"
# Select the Ceará data:
shpfile = "ceara/ceara.shp"
# Load the data:
ensure_datasets(shpfile, folder_path = path)
dfs = gpd.read_file(path + shpfile, encoding = 'utf-8')
print(dfs.shape)
dfs.head(3)
```

13.1.3 Variables

We continue to use the same set of variables to replicate the empirical illustration in Chapter 11 of the *GeoDa Cluster Book*. The variable names and descriptions are given in Table 12.1 on page 163. As before, we specify the variables in the `varlist` list for later use.

```
varlist = ['mobility', 'environ', 'housing', 'sanitation', 'infra',
           'gdpcap']
```

13.1.4 Pygeoda Data Preparation

We follow the same steps as in Chapter 12 to set up a data set in the `pygeoda` internal format as `ceara_g` and to create queen contiguity spatial weights (`queen_w`).

```
ceara_g = pygeoda.open(dfs)
queen_w = pygeoda.queen_weights(ceara_g)
queen_w
```

```
Weights Meta-data:
 number of observations:                 184
          is symmetric:                 True
              sparsity:  0.029536862003780 72
        # min neighbors:                    1
```

```
    # max neighbors:                    13
   # mean neighbors:     5.434782608695652
 # median neighbors:                   5.0
       has isolates:                 False
```

As in the previous Chapter, we create subsets with the relevant variables in both the `pygeoda` format (`data_g`) and as a GeoDataFrame (`data`).

```
data_g = ceara_g[varlist]
data = dfs[varlist]
```

We set the number of clusters to 12.

```
n_clusters = 12
```

13.2 AZP

The first spatially constrained partitioning method we consider is AZP. It is contained in `pygeoda`, which uses the same underlying code as `GeoDa`, except for some technical implementations related to memory management. Even though these differences are very low-level, they can influence the way the heuristic proceeds, since it moves sequentially through alternative configurations. The order in which these sequences are considered matters, and slight differences in the memory allocation can produce different results.

As a consequence, it is not possible to completely replicate the results from Chapter 11 in the *GeoDa Cluster Book*, given the differences between the low-level implementations in C++ and in Python. This is a general feature of any heuristic, where not only the algorithms matter, but also seemingly unrelated issues such as starting points, random numbers and the particular ordering of moves.

AZP is implemented as three different functions, corresponding to the *greedy*, *tabu* and *simulated annealing* optimization approaches (see Chapter 11 in the *GeoDa Cluster Book* for technical details). The matching functions are `azp_greedy`, `azp_tabu`, and `azp_sa`. Required arguments are the number of clusters, the spatial weights and the `pygeoda` data object.

13.2.1 AZP-Greedy

The first example uses greedy search, implemented in **azp_greedy**. We use the same approach as in the previous Chapter and employ the helper functions **cluster_stats**, **cluster_fit**, **cluster_center** and **cluster_map** (in Figure 13.1) to list the properties of the clusters (see Chapter 12 for technical details).

```
t0 = time.time()
ceara_clusters1 = pygeoda.azp_greedy(n_clusters, queen_w, data_g)
t1 = time.time()
tazp1 = t1 - t0
print("AZP Greedy Clustering Time: ", tazp1)
cluster_labels1 = np.array(ceara_clusters1['Clusters'])

c_stats = cluster_stats(cluster_labels1)
fit = cluster_fit(data, cluster_labels1, n_clusters,
                  correct = True, printopt = True)

clust_means, clust_medians = cluster_center(data, cluster_labels1)
print("Cluster Means:\n", np.round(clust_means, 3))
print("\nCluster Medians:\n", np.round(clust_medians, 3))

cluster_map(dfs, cluster_labels1, figsize = (4, 4),
            title = "", cmap = 'tab20',legend_fontsize=8)
```

```
AZP Greedy Clustering Time:  0.030981779098510742
 Labels  Cardinality
      1           46
      2           37
      3           29
      4           25
      5           21
      6            7
      7            5
      8            5
      9            4
     10            2
     11            2
     12            1

Total Sum of Squares (TSS): 1098.0
Within-cluster Sum of Squares (WSS) for each cluster: [124.036 115.162
```

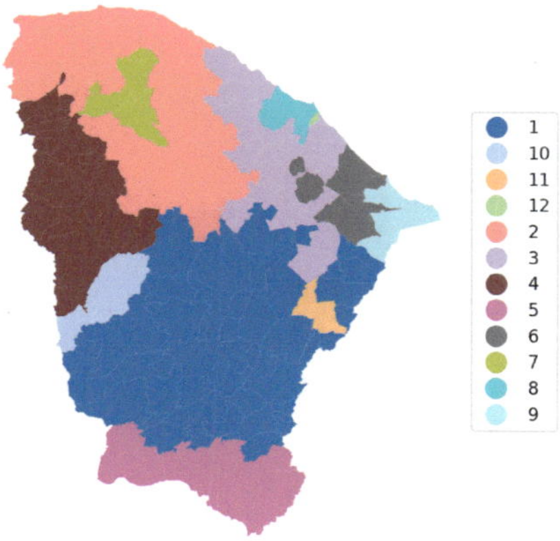

Figure 13.1: AZP Greedy cluster map

```
             139.302  71.455 105.922  16.194  16.279  26.967  53.98
               2.921  16.99    0.    ]
Total Within-cluster Sum of Squares (WSS): 689.208
Between-cluster Sum of Squares (BSS): 408.792
Ratio of BSS to TSS: 0.372

Cluster Means:
         mobility  environ  housing  sanitation  infra  gdpcap
cluster
1           0.965    0.883    0.852       0.686  0.552   4.524
2           0.959    0.864    0.800       0.603  0.513   4.490
3           0.946    0.814    0.798       0.592  0.469   6.265
4           0.960    0.883    0.852       0.629  0.528   4.591
5           0.960    0.797    0.826       0.646  0.512   4.679
6           0.942    0.924    0.846       0.573  0.391   5.208
7           0.982    0.939    0.839       0.833  0.612   5.691
8           0.833    0.750    0.800       0.743  0.537  11.102
9           0.944    0.897    0.841       0.593  0.405  16.482
10          0.960    0.930    0.900       0.641  0.424   4.170
11          0.974    0.657    0.781       0.823  0.693   5.432
12          0.936    0.789    0.794       0.545  0.425  27.625


Cluster Medians:
         mobility  environ  housing  sanitation  infra  gdpcap
cluster
1           0.968    0.888    0.849       0.677  0.560   4.220
```

2	0.959	0.885	0.801	0.581	0.505	4.140
3	0.948	0.824	0.807	0.573	0.470	4.742
4	0.968	0.896	0.851	0.602	0.534	4.395
5	0.963	0.805	0.831	0.636	0.514	4.140
6	0.935	0.943	0.842	0.575	0.377	5.114
7	0.983	0.932	0.829	0.798	0.606	4.099
8	0.834	0.741	0.823	0.784	0.561	7.982
9	0.957	0.882	0.846	0.590	0.419	9.262
10	0.960	0.930	0.900	0.641	0.424	4.170
11	0.974	0.657	0.781	0.823	0.693	5.432
12	0.936	0.789	0.794	0.545	0.425	27.625

13.2.2 AZP-Tabu

The Tabu algorithm for AZP is invoked with **azp_tabu**. In addition to the same arguments as for the basic AZP function, a **tabu_length** is required (the size of the tabu list of observations for which a swap is not possible), as well as the maximum number of non-improving moves, **conv_tabu**. In our illustration, these are set to respectively 50 and 25, as in Chapter 11 of the *GeoDa Cluster Book*. We use the same set of commands as before. The cluster map is shown in Figure 13.2.

```
t0 = time.time()
ceara_clusters2 = pygeoda.azp_tabu(n_clusters, queen_w, data_g,
                                    tabu_length = 50, conv_tabu = 25)
t1 = time.time()
tazp2 = t1 - t0
print("AZP Tabu Clustering Time: ", tazp2)
cluster_labels2 = np.array(ceara_clusters2['Clusters'])
c_stats = cluster_stats(cluster_labels2)
fit = cluster_fit(data, cluster_labels2, n_clusters,
                  correct = True, printopt = True)
clust_means, clust_medians = cluster_center(data, cluster_labels2)
print("Cluster Means:\n", np.round(clust_means, 3))
print("\nCluster Medians:\n", np.round(clust_medians, 3))
cluster_map(dfs, cluster_labels2, figsize=(4, 4),
            title = "", cmap = 'tab20',legend_fontsize=8)
```

```
AZP Tabu Clustering Time:  0.36793017387390137
 Labels  Cardinality
      1           50
      2           41
```

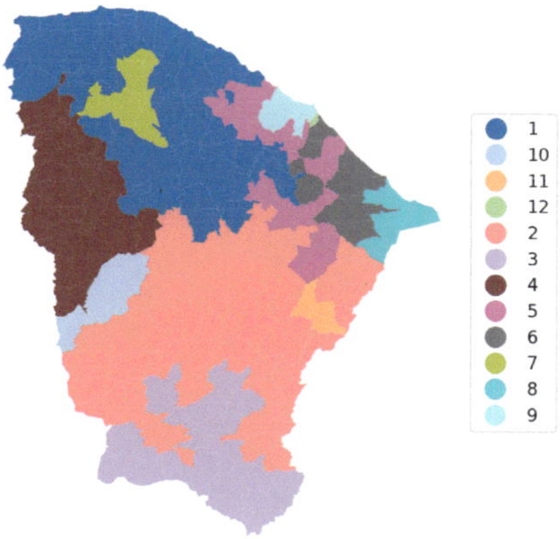

Figure 13.2: AZP Tabu cluster map

3	26
4	25
5	14
6	10
7	5
8	4
9	4
10	2
11	2
12	1

```
Total Sum of Squares (TSS): 1098.0
Within-cluster Sum of Squares (WSS) for each cluster: [155.14  119.919
                97.683  71.455  78.79   34.08   16.279  53.98   11.088
                 2.921  16.99    0.    ]
Total Within-cluster Sum of Squares (WSS): 658.326
Between-cluster Sum of Squares (BSS): 439.674
Ratio of BSS to TSS: 0.4
```

```
Cluster Means:
          mobility  environ  housing  sanitation  infra  gdpcap
cluster
1            0.959    0.860    0.803       0.608  0.502   4.575
2            0.968    0.904    0.849       0.693  0.538   4.533
3            0.956    0.780    0.835       0.644  0.542   4.636
4            0.960    0.883    0.852       0.629  0.528   4.591
```

```
5          0.922     0.759     0.779        0.580  0.465   6.315
6          0.947     0.909     0.834        0.550  0.409   7.222
7          0.982     0.939     0.839        0.833  0.612   5.691
8          0.944     0.897     0.841        0.593  0.405  16.482
9          0.833     0.766     0.818        0.792  0.574  12.600
10         0.960     0.930     0.900        0.641  0.424   4.170
11         0.974     0.657     0.781        0.823  0.693   5.432
12         0.936     0.789     0.794        0.545  0.425  27.625

Cluster Medians:
        mobility  environ  housing  sanitation  infra  gdpcap
cluster
1          0.957     0.878     0.808        0.581  0.495   4.322
2          0.970     0.902     0.844        0.680  0.542   4.242
3          0.960     0.774     0.838        0.630  0.564   4.134
4          0.968     0.896     0.851        0.602  0.534   4.395
5          0.933     0.763     0.785        0.581  0.458   4.802
6          0.949     0.911     0.836        0.535  0.382   5.281
7          0.983     0.932     0.829        0.798  0.606   4.099
8          0.957     0.882     0.846        0.590  0.419   9.262
9          0.835     0.766     0.824        0.799  0.583  11.557
10         0.960     0.930     0.900        0.641  0.424   4.170
11         0.974     0.657     0.781        0.823  0.693   5.432
12         0.936     0.789     0.794        0.545  0.425  27.625
```

13.2.3 AZP-Simulated Annealing

The simulated annealing algorithm for AZP is invoked with `azp_sa`. In addition to the same arguments as for the basic AZP function, a `cooling_rate` is required (the rate at which the simulated annealing temperature is allowed to decrease), as well as the maximum number of iterations allowed for each swap, `sa_maxit`. In our illustration, these are set to, respectively, 0.8 and 5. We use the same set of functions as before. The cluster map is in Figure 13.3.

Note that the results differ slightly from the ones reported in Chapter 11 of the *GeoDa Cluster Book* even though the parameters are the same.

```
t0 = time.time()
ceara_clusters3 = pygeoda.azp_sa(n_clusters, queen_w, data_g,
                                 cooling_rate = 0.8, sa_maxit = 5)
t1 = time.time()
tazp3 = t1 - t0
```

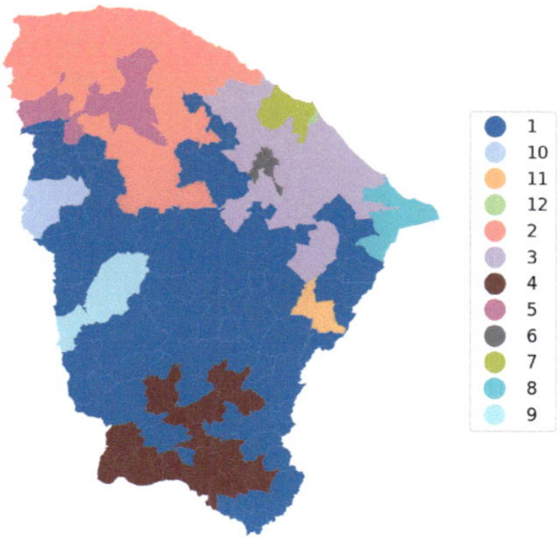

Figure 13.3: AZP Simulated Annealing cluster map

```
print("AZP SA Clustering Time: ", tazp3)
cluster_labels3 = np.array(ceara_clusters3['Clusters'])
c_stats = cluster_stats(cluster_labels3)
fit = cluster_fit(data, cluster_labels3, n_clusters,
                  correct = True, printopt = True)
clust_means, clust_medians = cluster_center(data, cluster_labels3)
print("Cluster Means:\n", np.round(clust_means, 3))
print("\nCluster Medians:\n", np.round(clust_medians, 3))
cluster_map(dfs, cluster_labels3, figsize = (4, 4),
            title = "", cmap = 'tab20',legend_fontsize=8)
```

```
AZP SA Clustering Time:  3.2580177783966064
 Labels  Cardinality
      1           71
      2           33
      3           28
      4           19
      5           12
      6            5
      7            5
      8            4
      9            2
     10            2
     11            2
     12            1
```

```
Total Sum of Squares (TSS): 1098.0
Within-cluster Sum of Squares (WSS) for each cluster: [204.08  101.845
              129.825  50.521  41.189   7.637  26.967  53.98    2.921
                1.109  16.99    0.    ]

Total Within-cluster Sum of Squares (WSS): 637.065
Between-cluster Sum of Squares (BSS): 460.935
Ratio of BSS to TSS: 0.42
Cluster Means:
         mobility  environ  housing  sanitation  infra  gdpcap
cluster
1           0.965    0.903    0.847       0.674  0.533   4.621
2           0.958    0.860    0.795       0.586  0.505   4.473
3           0.938    0.816    0.802       0.565  0.453   6.141
4           0.953    0.732    0.834       0.615  0.545   4.734
5           0.981    0.879    0.848       0.748  0.594   5.154
6           0.974    0.896    0.831       0.746  0.452   5.363
7           0.833    0.750    0.800       0.743  0.537  11.102
8           0.944    0.897    0.841       0.593  0.405  16.482
9           0.960    0.930    0.900       0.641  0.424   4.170
10          0.917    0.921    0.829       0.562  0.369   3.810
11          0.974    0.657    0.781       0.823  0.693   5.432
12          0.936    0.789    0.794       0.545  0.425  27.625

Cluster Medians:
         mobility  environ  housing  sanitation  infra  gdpcap
cluster
1           0.968    0.905    0.846       0.671  0.526   4.319
2           0.959    0.883    0.800       0.571  0.498   4.140
3           0.940    0.811    0.808       0.567  0.464   4.738
4           0.958    0.720    0.833       0.608  0.563   4.140
5           0.984    0.909    0.851       0.752  0.584   4.234
6           0.983    0.906    0.836       0.775  0.409   4.985
7           0.834    0.741    0.823       0.784  0.561   7.982
8           0.957    0.882    0.846       0.590  0.419   9.262
9           0.960    0.930    0.900       0.641  0.424   4.170
10          0.917    0.921    0.829       0.562  0.369   3.810
11          0.974    0.657    0.781       0.823  0.693   5.432
12          0.936    0.789    0.794       0.545  0.425  27.625
```

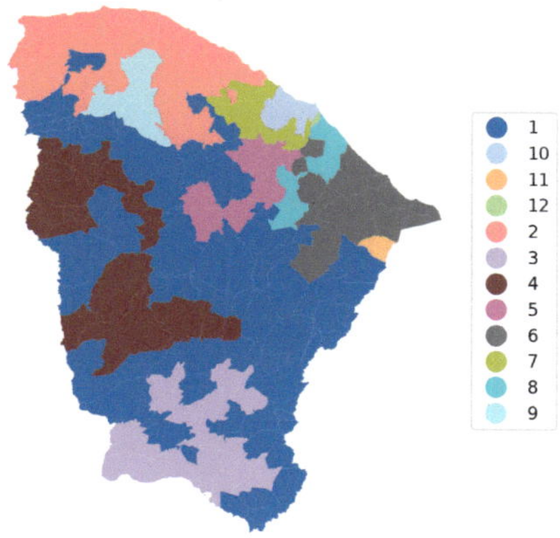

Figure 13.4: AZP ARiSel cluster map

13.2.4 ARiSel

As in K-Means, an alternative to a random initial feasible solution is to use a K-Means++ like logic. This is implemented in the ARiSel approach, through the additional `inits` argument to any azp function. In the example below, we set `inits = 50`. We use `azp_sa` with a `cooling_rate` of 0.8 and `sa_maxit` as 5.

The commands are the same as in the previous examples. The cluster map is in Figure 13.4.

```
t0 = time.time()
ceara_clusters4 = pygeoda.azp_sa(n_clusters, queen_w, data_g,
                                  cooling_rate = 0.8, sa_maxit = 5, inits = 50)
t1 = time.time()
tazp4 = t1 - t0
print("AZP ARiSel Clustering Time: ", tazp4)
cluster_labels4 = np.array(ceara_clusters4['Clusters'])
c_stats = cluster_stats(cluster_labels4)
fit = cluster_fit(data, cluster_labels4, n_clusters,
                  correct = True, printopt = True)
clust_means, clust_medians = cluster_center(data, cluster_labels4)
print("Cluster Means:\n", np.round(clust_means, 3))
print("\nCluster Medians:\n", np.round(clust_medians, 3))
cluster_map(dfs, cluster_labels4, figsize=(4, 4),
            title = "", cmap = 'tab20',legend_fontsize=8)
```

```
AZP ARiSel Clustering Time:  5.389322996139526
 Labels  Cardinality
      1           67
      2           29
      3           19
      4           19
      5           14
      6           13
      7            6
      8            6
      9            5
     10            4
     11            1
     12            1


Total Sum of Squares (TSS): 1098.0
Within-cluster Sum of Squares (WSS) for each cluster: [224.399  88.688
                 50.521  51.732  48.429  44.554  39.958   8.893  16.279
                 11.088  0.       0.    ]
Total Within-cluster Sum of Squares (WSS): 584.54
Between-cluster Sum of Squares (BSS): 513.46
Ratio of BSS to TSS: 0.468
Cluster Means:
          mobility  environ  housing  sanitation  infra  gdpcap
cluster
1            0.968    0.888    0.844       0.692  0.552   4.663
2            0.954    0.858    0.795       0.586  0.510   4.513
3            0.953    0.732    0.834       0.615  0.545   4.734
4            0.956    0.897    0.855       0.604  0.480   4.272
5            0.960    0.821    0.806       0.644  0.464   4.450
6            0.944    0.883    0.842       0.574  0.416   7.300
7            0.902    0.772    0.748       0.615  0.447   8.392
8            0.939    0.834    0.783       0.486  0.454   5.613
9            0.982    0.939    0.839       0.833  0.612   5.691
10           0.833    0.766    0.818       0.792  0.574  12.600
11           0.957    0.966    0.857       0.593  0.357  40.018
12           0.936    0.789    0.794       0.545  0.425  27.625

Cluster Medians:
          mobility  environ  housing  sanitation  infra  gdpcap
cluster
1            0.970    0.898    0.845       0.678  0.551   4.390
```

2	0.952	0.883	0.792	0.564	0.498	4.183
3	0.958	0.720	0.833	0.608	0.563	4.140
4	0.964	0.896	0.851	0.585	0.491	4.097
5	0.959	0.835	0.812	0.618	0.469	4.355
6	0.951	0.896	0.836	0.579	0.424	6.171
7	0.905	0.779	0.750	0.605	0.444	5.140
8	0.939	0.840	0.790	0.494	0.468	4.802
9	0.983	0.932	0.829	0.798	0.606	4.099
10	0.835	0.766	0.824	0.799	0.583	11.557
11	0.957	0.966	0.857	0.593	0.357	40.018
12	0.936	0.789	0.794	0.545	0.425	27.625

13.2.5 AZP with Initial Clustering Result

As mentioned in the discussion of hierarchical spatially constrained solutions in Chapter 12, one of the drawbacks of those methods is that observations tend to be *trapped* in a branch of the dendrogram or minimum spanning tree. Since AZP implements swapping of observations, we can use the endpoint of one of the hierarchical methods as the feasible initial solution for AZP. In many instances (but not all), this improves on the hierarchical solution and sometimes also obtains better solutions than straight AZP.

In all these illustrations, it is important to keep in mind the sensitivity of the results to the various tuning parameters (which are under the analyst's control) as well as hardware implementations (which are not).

We illustrate this approach by using the end solution of SCHC as the initial solution for AZP, set by means of the `init_regions` argument. The code is the same as for AZP-SA. The associated cluster map is shown in Figure 13.5 on page 193.

```
ceara_clusters = pygeoda.schc(n_clusters, queen_w, data_g, "ward")
schc_cluster_labels = ceara_clusters['Clusters']
t0 = time.time()
ceara_clusters5 = pygeoda.azp_sa(n_clusters, queen_w, data_g,
                                 cooling_rate = 0.8, sa_maxit = 5,
                                 init_regions = schc_cluster_labels)


t1 = time.time()
tazp5 = t1 - t0
print("AZP-SCHC Clustering Time: ", tazp5)
cluster_labels5 = np.array(ceara_clusters5['Clusters'])
```

```
c_stats = cluster_stats(cluster_labels5)
fit = cluster_fit(data, cluster_labels5, n_clusters,
                  correct = True, printopt = True)
clust_means, clust_medians = cluster_center(data, cluster_labels5)
print("Cluster Means:\n", np.round(clust_means, 3))
print("\nCluster Medians:\n", np.round(clust_medians, 3))
cluster_map(dfs, cluster_labels5, figsize=(4, 4),
            title = "", cmap = 'tab20',legend_fontsize=8)
```

```
AZP-SCHC Clustering Time:  3.7134571075439453
 Labels  Cardinality
      1           88
      2           43
      3           15
      4           14
      5            8
      6            4
      7            4
      8            3
      9            2
     10            1
     11            1
     12            1

Total Sum of Squares (TSS): 1098.0
Within-cluster Sum of Squares (WSS) for each cluster: [246.863 134.79
                30.167  49.716  31.033  14.614  11.088   5.956  16.99
                 0.      0.      0.    ]
Total Within-cluster Sum of Squares (WSS): 541.218
Between-cluster Sum of Squares (BSS): 556.782
Ratio of BSS to TSS: 0.507
Cluster Means:
          mobility  environ  housing  sanitation  infra  gdpcap
cluster
1            0.964    0.895    0.847       0.670  0.526   4.600
2            0.950    0.836    0.790       0.578  0.494   4.460
3            0.952    0.719    0.842       0.625  0.575   4.887
4            0.944    0.883    0.837       0.563  0.414   7.450
5            0.984    0.896    0.845       0.786  0.613   5.042
6            0.968    0.835    0.784       0.578  0.413   4.327
7            0.833    0.766    0.818       0.792  0.574  12.600
```

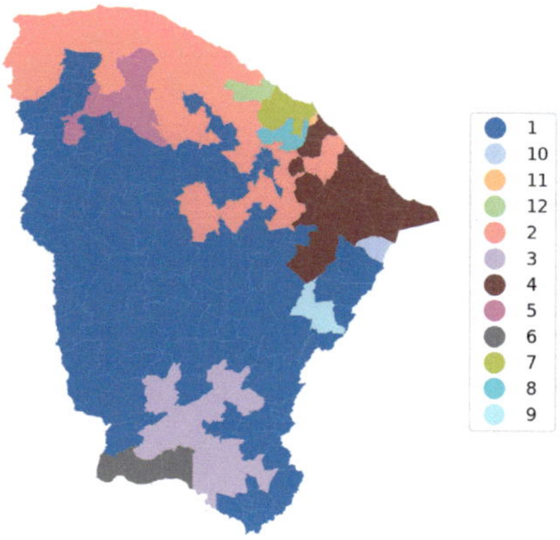

Figure 13.5: AZP with SCHC initialization

8	0.874	0.711	0.742	0.612	0.420	5.307
9	0.974	0.657	0.781	0.823	0.693	5.432
10	0.957	0.966	0.857	0.593	0.357	40.018
11	0.936	0.789	0.794	0.545	0.425	27.625
12	0.951	0.824	0.771	0.573	0.443	25.464

Cluster Medians:

	mobility	environ	housing	sanitation	infra	gdpcap
cluster						
1	0.968	0.896	0.846	0.669	0.523	4.380
2	0.950	0.859	0.791	0.562	0.490	4.229
3	0.950	0.709	0.845	0.608	0.569	3.923
4	0.949	0.889	0.836	0.577	0.419	6.778
5	0.986	0.924	0.844	0.798	0.616	3.992
6	0.966	0.829	0.784	0.604	0.439	4.299
7	0.835	0.766	0.824	0.799	0.583	11.557
8	0.885	0.687	0.730	0.622	0.427	5.110
9	0.974	0.657	0.781	0.823	0.693	5.432
10	0.957	0.966	0.857	0.593	0.357	40.018
11	0.936	0.789	0.794	0.545	0.425	27.625
12	0.951	0.824	0.771	0.573	0.443	25.464

13.2.6 Comparing AZP Implementations

To close the discussion of AZP, we provide a brief summary of the spatial layout and measure of fit for the greedy algorithm, the tabu search, and two simulated annealing

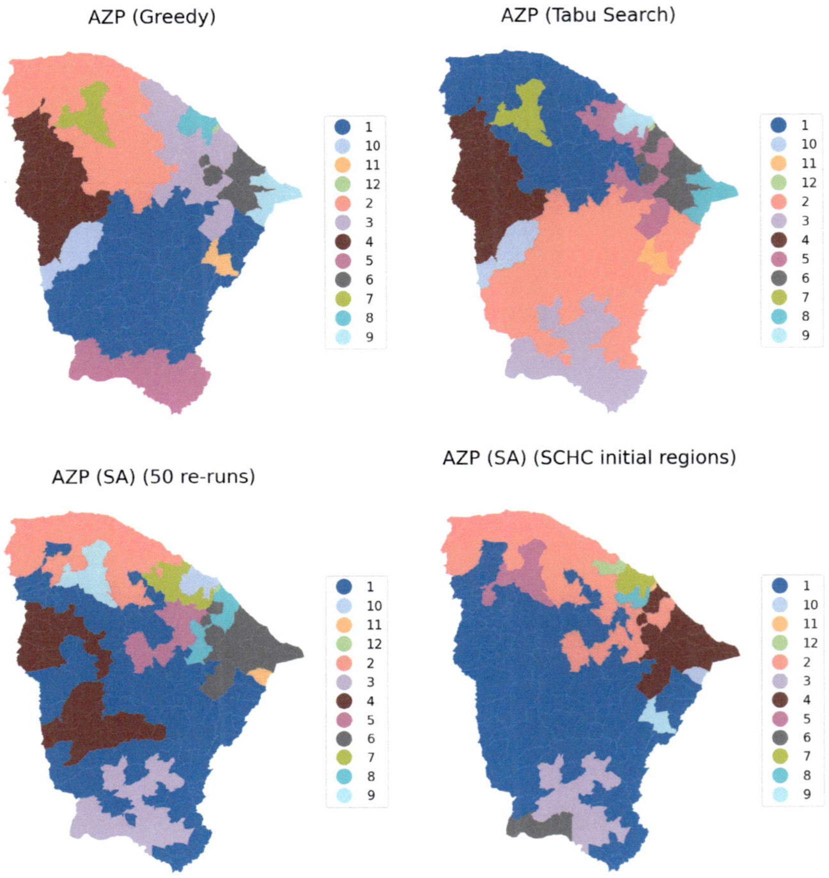

Figure 13.6: AZP solutions

results, one with 50 initial re-runs and one using SCHC as the starting point. The first code block computes the relevant statistics and creates the cluster maps.

The spatial configurations reflected in the respective cluster maps can be compared in Figure 13.6.

```
titles = ["AZP (Greedy)", "AZP (Tabu Search)",
                "AZP (SA) (50 re-runs)",
                "AZP (SA) (SCHC initial regions)"]

cluster_map(dfs, [cluster_labels1, cluster_labels2, cluster_labels4,
            cluster_labels5],
            title = titles, cmap = 'tab20',
            grid_shape = (2, 2), figsize = (8, 8),legend_fontsize=8)
```

A summary of the respective BSS/TSS ratios is computed in the final code block. The AZP-SA solution with SCHC as the starting point clearly achieves the highest BSS/TSS ratio.

```
ceara_clusters = [ceara_clusters1, ceara_clusters2,
                  ceara_clusters4, ceara_clusters5]

print("The ratio of between to total sum of squares:")
for i, cluster in enumerate(ceara_clusters):
    print(titles[i],
        f": {np.round(
             cluster['The ratio of between to total sum of squares'],
                      4)}")
```

```
The ratio of between to total sum of squares:
AZP (Greedy) : 0.3723
AZP (Tabu Search) : 0.4004
AZP (SA) (50 re-runs) : 0.4676
AZP (SA) (SCHC initial regions) : 0.5071
```

13.3 Max-p Regions

Up to this point, we had to specify the number of clusters beforehand as the first argument to be passed to the `pygeoda` clustering routines. The max-p approach takes a different perspective. It attempts to find the largest number of clusters possible (the *max p*) within a given constraint on the cluster size. Without such a constraint, the solution would always equal the number of observations.

The minimum cluster size, or `min_bound` is typically a function of the total for a *spatially extensive* variable, like population or total number of housing units. However, it can be set differently as well. Keep in mind that the larger the minimum bound, the smaller the number of clusters that will be found, and the other way around. When the minimum size is not determined by some fixed policy criterion, it may therefore be good to do some experimentation.

The max-p algorithm is essentially AZP applied to an initial feasible solution that follows a heuristic to maximize the number of regions that satisfy the minimum bounds constraint. As before, several random starting points should be explored as the results are quite sensitive to this initial solution.

We illustrate max-p for the Ceará example using simulated annealing with the `min_bound` set to a percentage of the total population. As for AZP, three functions are available, `maxp_greedy`, `maxp_tabu` and `maxp_sa`.

The AZP-related arguments are the same as for the core AZP functions. The `n_clusters` argument is (obviously) no longer needed. Instead, the `bound_variable` defines the spatially extensive variable for the minimum constraint, and `min_bound` sets its actual value. Here, we take `'pop'` as the variable (from the GeoDataFrame), and compute the percentage for the bound using `sum()` multiplied by a fraction.

In the first example, we use `maxp_greedy` with a population minimum of 10% of the total, or 845,238. This yields a solution with 6 clusters, achieving a miserable BSS/TSS of 0.26.

```
t0 = time.time()
ceara_clusters6 = pygeoda.maxp_greedy(queen_w, data_g,
                                       bound_variable = dfs['pop'],
                                       min_bound = dfs['pop'].sum()*0.1)
t1 = time.time()
tmaxp1 = t1 - t0
print("Max-p (10%) Clustering Time: ", tmaxp1)
cluster_labels6 = np.array(ceara_clusters6['Clusters'])
c_stats = cluster_stats(cluster_labels6)
fit = cluster_fit(data, cluster_labels6, n_clusters,
                  correct = True, printopt = True)
clust_means, clust_medians = cluster_center(data, cluster_labels6)
print("Cluster Means:\n", np.round(clust_means, 3))
print("\nCluster Medians:\n", np.round(clust_medians, 3))
```

```
Max-p (10%) Clustering Time:  0.12141895294189453
 Labels  Cardinality
      1           64
      2           45
      3           35
      4           30
      5            8
      6            2
Total Sum of Squares (TSS): 1098.0
Within-cluster Sum of Squares (WSS) for each cluster: [283.714 150.575
                                        190.247 103.556  69.006  15.465]
Total Within-cluster Sum of Squares (WSS): 812.563
Between-cluster Sum of Squares (BSS): 285.437
Ratio of BSS to TSS: 0.26
```

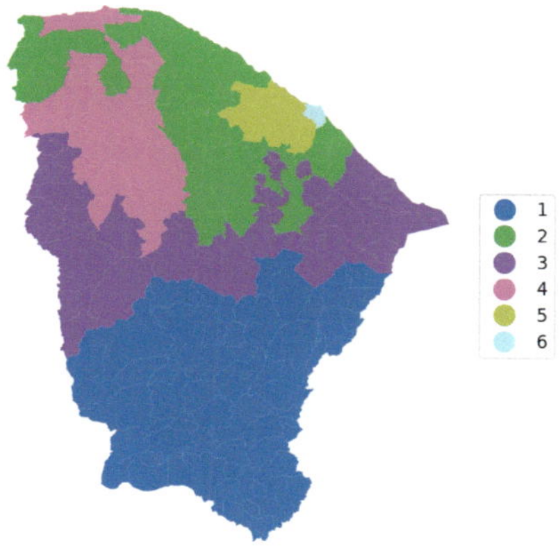

Figure 13.7: Max-p with 10% population bound

```
Cluster Means:
         mobility  environ  housing  sanitation  infra  gdpcap
cluster
1           0.964    0.847    0.841       0.673  0.545   4.521
2           0.951    0.844    0.792       0.577  0.494   5.009
3           0.951    0.892    0.850       0.644  0.456   6.236
4           0.974    0.878    0.841       0.657  0.554   4.818
5           0.871    0.759    0.777       0.682  0.490  10.228
6           0.891    0.806    0.809       0.680  0.515  21.378

Cluster Medians:
         mobility  environ  housing  sanitation  infra  gdpcap
cluster
1           0.965    0.875    0.843       0.661  0.556   4.202
2           0.950    0.862    0.793       0.562  0.490   4.386
3           0.957    0.896    0.850       0.613  0.452   4.985
4           0.978    0.893    0.849       0.620  0.550   4.436
5           0.866    0.750    0.777       0.680  0.471   7.154
6           0.891    0.806    0.809       0.680  0.515  21.378
```

The corresponding cluster map is shown in Figure 13.7.

```
cluster_map(dfs, cluster_labels6, figsize=(4, 4),
            title = "", cmap = 'tab20',legend_fontsize=8)
```

13.3.1 Sensitivity Analysis

The importance of sensitivity analysis for max-p cannot be understated. To illustrate the different outcomes that can be obtained by tuning the various parameters, we give two examples using simulated annealing with a minimum bound of 5% and 3% respectively.

We first consider 5%, i.e., a population minimum of 422,619. We set the number of iterations (`iterations`) to 9999, use a cooling rate of 0.9 and `maxit` of 5. Note that this achieves a p of 13, compared to 12 for `GeoDa` as given in Figure 11.28 of the *GeoDa Cluster Book*, but the BSS/TSS ratio is 0.321, relative to 0.385 for `GeoDa`.

```
t0 = time.time()
ceara_clusters7 = pygeoda.maxp_sa(queen_w, data_g,
                                  bound_variable = dfs['pop'],
                                  min_bound = dfs['pop'].sum()*0.05,
                                  iterations = 9999,
                                  cooling_rate = 0.9,
                                  sa_maxit = 5)
t1 = time.time()
tmaxp2 = t1 - t0
print("Max-p (5%) Clustering Time: ", tmaxp2)
cluster_labels7 = np.array(ceara_clusters7['Clusters'])
c_stats = cluster_stats(cluster_labels7)
fit = cluster_fit(data, cluster_labels7, n_clusters,
                  correct = True, printopt = True)
clust_means, clust_medians = cluster_center(data, cluster_labels7)
print("Cluster Means:\n", np.round(clust_means, 3))
print("\nCluster Medians:\n", np.round(clust_medians, 3))
```

```
Max-p (5%) Clustering Time:  7.919972896575928
 Labels  Cardinality
      1           24
      2           23
      3           20
      4           19
      5           18
      6           18
      7           17
      8           14
      9           11
     10            8
     11            7
```

```
    12          3
    13          2

Total Sum of Squares (TSS): 1098.0
Within-cluster Sum of Squares (WSS) for each cluster: [ 74.807  83.702
               32.777  95.473  65.341  69.935  44.14  103.769  42.53
               36.253  68.153  26.218   2.151]
Total Within-cluster Sum of Squares (WSS): 745.247
Between-cluster Sum of Squares (BSS): 352.753
Ratio of BSS to TSS: 0.321
Cluster Means:
         mobility  environ  housing  sanitation  infra  gdpcap
cluster
1           0.959    0.875    0.845       0.618  0.484   4.593
2           0.963    0.831    0.832       0.614  0.487   4.154
3           0.961    0.907    0.847       0.723  0.548   4.552
4           0.965    0.817    0.846       0.682  0.597   4.648
5           0.941    0.826    0.793       0.616  0.483   4.490
6           0.966    0.811    0.808       0.610  0.540   4.227
7           0.958    0.908    0.809       0.593  0.527   5.050
8           0.946    0.911    0.846       0.580  0.415   9.707
9           0.973    0.908    0.837       0.738  0.570   5.209
10          0.965    0.849    0.839       0.716  0.548   5.356
11          0.906    0.763    0.776       0.568  0.439  10.761
12          0.889    0.764    0.783       0.651  0.456  13.360
13          0.835    0.807    0.826       0.838  0.619  11.404

Cluster Medians:
         mobility  environ  housing  sanitation  infra  gdpcap
cluster
1           0.964    0.870    0.845       0.586  0.495   4.431
2           0.964    0.837    0.827       0.602  0.510   4.058
3           0.965    0.900    0.845       0.708  0.542   4.444
4           0.968    0.855    0.851       0.644  0.590   4.338
5           0.940    0.825    0.793       0.588  0.479   4.342
6           0.972    0.835    0.810       0.579  0.554   3.992
7           0.954    0.900    0.807       0.594  0.505   4.649
8           0.956    0.914    0.839       0.583  0.419   7.266
9           0.976    0.928    0.845       0.756  0.574   4.394
10          0.964    0.931    0.838       0.680  0.578   4.864
11          0.931    0.773    0.788       0.545  0.425   5.110
12          0.903    0.758    0.783       0.669  0.443   7.982
```

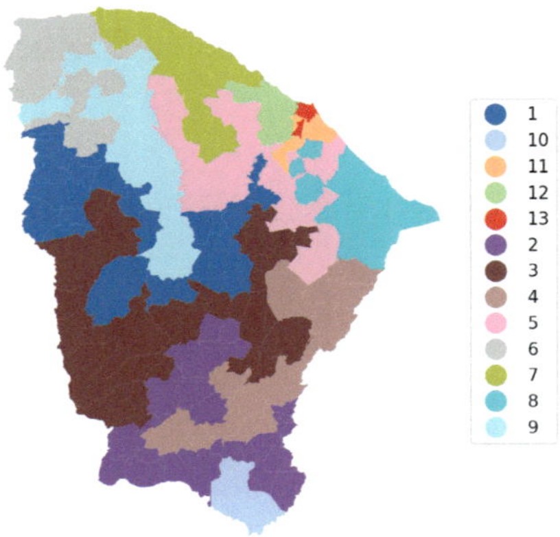

Figure 13.8: Max-p with 5% population bound

```
13          0.835    0.807    0.826       0.838  0.619  11.404
```

The cluster map is in Figure 13.8.

```
cluster_map(dfs, cluster_labels7, figsize=(4, 4),
            title = "", cmap = 'tab20',legend_fontsize=8)
```

In the final example, we set the population minimum to 3%, or 253,571, with the same SA parameters. This yields 19 clusters, with a BSS/TSS ratio of 0.436, similar to the solution obtained with GeoDa (0.439). This again highlights the importance of experimentation with the various parameters.

```
t0 = time.time()
ceara_clusters8 = pygeoda.maxp_sa(queen_w, data_g,
                                  bound_variable = dfs['pop'],
                                  min_bound = dfs['pop'].sum()*0.03,
                                  iterations = 9999,
                                  cooling_rate = 0.9,
                                  sa_maxit = 5)
t1 = time.time()
tmaxp3 = t1 - t0
print("Max-p (3%) Clustering Time: ", tmaxp3)
cluster_labels8 = np.array(ceara_clusters8['Clusters'])
c_stats = cluster_stats(cluster_labels8)
fit = cluster_fit(data, cluster_labels8, n_clusters,
                  correct = True, printopt = True)
```

```
clust_means, clust_medians = cluster_center(data, cluster_labels8)
print("Cluster Means:\n", np.round(clust_means, 3))
print("\nCluster Medians:\n", np.round(clust_medians, 3))
```

```
Max-p (3%) Clustering Time:  10.076975107192993
 Labels  Cardinality
      1           33
      2           16
      3           14
      4           13
      5           12
      6           12
      7           12
      8           10
      9           10
     10           10
     11            8
     12            7
     13            7
     14            6
     15            5
     16            4
     17            2
     18            2
     19            1

Total Sum of Squares (TSS): 1098.0
Within-cluster Sum of Squares (WSS) for each cluster: [71.542 43.964
                    51.354 35.693 57.527 25.585 33.225 20.233 26.853
                    31.334 15.088 84.027 28.591 39.958 16.279  6.894
                    15.465  5.476  0.    ]
Total Within-cluster Sum of Squares (WSS): 609.089
Between-cluster Sum of Squares (BSS): 488.911
Ratio of BSS to TSS: 0.445
Cluster Means:
          mobility  environ  housing  sanitation  infra  gdpcap
cluster
1            0.963    0.904    0.853       0.703  0.543   4.539
2            0.955    0.896    0.853       0.589  0.474   4.279
3            0.972    0.909    0.840       0.675  0.528   4.158
4            0.952    0.825    0.795       0.595  0.458   4.129
```

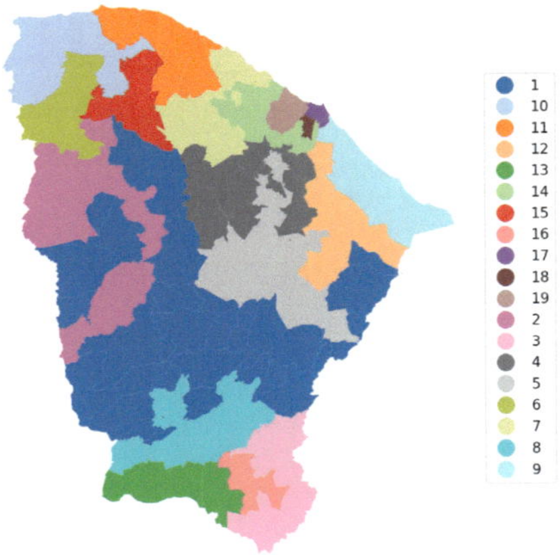

Figure 13.9: Max-p with 3% population bound

5	0.972	0.830	0.826	0.738	0.537	5.244
6	0.974	0.861	0.846	0.653	0.572	4.743
7	0.954	0.887	0.805	0.612	0.550	5.068
8	0.952	0.761	0.849	0.626	0.579	4.278
9	0.938	0.876	0.825	0.526	0.418	6.738
10	0.956	0.784	0.776	0.571	0.509	4.188
11	0.956	0.914	0.810	0.582	0.482	4.655
12	0.949	0.865	0.836	0.576	0.425	12.688
13	0.967	0.783	0.807	0.611	0.471	5.202
14	0.902	0.772	0.748	0.615	0.447	8.392
15	0.982	0.939	0.839	0.833	0.612	5.691
16	0.939	0.666	0.838	0.618	0.567	4.999
17	0.891	0.806	0.809	0.680	0.515	21.378
18	0.836	0.766	0.827	0.822	0.597	13.644
19	0.814	0.709	0.795	0.710	0.497	7.982

Cluster Medians:

	mobility	environ	housing	sanitation	infra	gdpcap
cluster						
1	0.966	0.905	0.856	0.698	0.543	4.390
2	0.964	0.896	0.851	0.577	0.461	4.208
3	0.974	0.918	0.835	0.635	0.518	3.993
4	0.954	0.827	0.810	0.568	0.467	4.229
5	0.971	0.861	0.838	0.777	0.525	5.160
6	0.980	0.878	0.852	0.634	0.562	4.387
7	0.950	0.887	0.804	0.598	0.552	4.635

```
8             0.950    0.774    0.853       0.617  0.580    3.888
9             0.940    0.870    0.827       0.510  0.419    6.024
10            0.963    0.765    0.782       0.554  0.518    3.978
11            0.956    0.928    0.810       0.566  0.483    4.659
12            0.957    0.882    0.836       0.575  0.434    7.957
13            0.965    0.736    0.805       0.638  0.491    4.313
14            0.905    0.779    0.750       0.605  0.444    5.140
15            0.983    0.932    0.829       0.798  0.606    4.099
16            0.939    0.664    0.832       0.595  0.590    4.276
17            0.891    0.806    0.809       0.680  0.515   21.378
18            0.836    0.766    0.827       0.822  0.597   13.644
19            0.814    0.709    0.795       0.710  0.497    7.982
```

The final cluster map is shown in Figure 13.9.

```
cluster_map(dfs, cluster_labels8, figsize = (5, 5),
            title = "", cmap = 'tab20',legend_fontsize=8)
```

13.4 Practice

We can now use the max-p approach to compare the previous solutions with a pre-set number of clusters to what is obtained when this becomes a parameter to be optimized. In each instance, considerable sensitivity analysis is required.

14 Cluster Validation

To close this Companion Book, we consider cluster validation measures. These can be classified as *internal* validation measures, such as the measures of fit we already considered, as well as *external* validation measures, which provide a way to compare cluster solutions to a given (known, or assumed known) reference.

In addition to measures of fit, we also consider indicators of the *balance* of cluster solutions, i.e., the evenness of the number of observations in each cluster. Such measures include *entropy* and *Simpson's index*. Other measures, introduced in the *GeoDa Cluster Book* are based on the *spatial* properties of the clusters. These include the *join count ratio*, an indicator of how many *neighbors* of each observation in a cluster are also members of the cluster. For a spatially compact cluster solution, this measure should equal one (except for boundary effects). For non spatially constrained clusters, it indicates how closely they approximate a spatial solution.

For spatially constrained cluster solutions, *compactness* is a key characteristic. This can be quantified by means of the *isoperimeter quotient (IPQ)*, the ratio of the area of a cluster shape to that of a circle with equal perimeter. A final measure of compactness introduced in the *GeoDa Cluster Book* is the *diameter* of the unweighted graph representation of the spatial weights matrix. To obtain a relative measure, the diameter is rescaled by the number of observations in the cluster. The latter measures are only applicable to spatially constrained clusters.

In addition, we also consider two classic indicators of external validity, i.e., the *Adjusted Rand Index (ARI)* of Hubert and Arabie (1985), based on counting pairs, and the *Normalized Information Distance (NID)*, e.g., Vinh, Epps, and Bailey (2010), derived from measures of entropy.

A detailed coverage of these methods is contained in Chapter 12 of the *GeoDa Cluster Book*.

In addition to the usual `numpy`, `pandas` and `geopandas`, we need several specialized packages from scikit-learn and `pygeoda` to carry out the cluster analysis and implement the validation measures. As before, to carry out variable standardization we import `StandardScaler` from `sklearn.preprocessing`. The specific clustering methods are `AgglomerativeClustering` and `KMeans` from `sklearn.cluster` .

The other clustering solutions are obtained with `pygeoda`. The external validation measures are contained in `sklearn.metrics.adjusted_rand_score` and `sklearn.metrics.adjusted_mutual_info_score`.

The new internal validation measures are based on `pygeoda.spatial_validation`. Several helper functions contained in the `spatial-cluster-helper` module extract the relevant information and present it as a pandas DataFrame: `cluster_fragmentation`, `cluster_joincount`, `cluster_compactness` and `cluster_diameter`. As before, we also use `ensure_datasets`, `cluster_stats` and `cluster_fit`.

We continue the empirical illustration with the Ceará example.

> Required Packages
>
> numpy, pandas, geopandas, sklearn.cluster, sklearn.preprocessing, sklearn.metrics, spatial_cluster_helper, pygeoda

> Required Data Sets
>
> ceara

14.1 Preliminaries

14.1.1 Import Required Modules

```
import geopandas as gpd
import pandas as pd
import numpy as np

from sklearn.cluster import AgglomerativeClustering, KMeans
from sklearn.preprocessing import StandardScaler
from sklearn.metrics import adjusted_rand_score, \
                            adjusted_mutual_info_score

from spatial_cluster_helper import ensure_datasets, cluster_stats, \
         cluster_fit, cluster_fragmentation, cluster_joincount, \
         cluster_compactness, cluster_diameter

import pygeoda
```

14.1.2 Load Data

We continue to use the `ceara.shp` file. The usual commands are given in the code block below, but the output is not considered further.

```
# Setting working folder:
#path = "/your/path/to/data/"
path = "./datasets/"
# Select the Ceará data:
shpfile = "ceara/ceara.shp"
# Load the data:
ensure_datasets(shpfile, folder_path = path)
dfs = gpd.read_file(path + shpfile, encoding = 'utf-8')
print(dfs.shape)
dfs.head(3)
```

14.1.3 Variables

We continue with the same set of variables as in the previous Chapters. The detailed specification is given in Table 12.1 on page 163. As before, they are combined in the list `varlist`.

```
varlist = ['mobility', 'environ', 'housing', 'sanitation', 'infra',
           'gdpcap']
```

14.1.4 Pygeoda Data Preparation

We follow the same steps as in Chapter 12 to set up a data set in the `pygeoda` internal format as `ceara_g` and to create queen contiguity spatial weights as `queen_w`. As in the previous Chapters, we create subsets with the relevant variables in both the `pygeoda` format (`data_g`) and as a GeoDataFrame (`data`).

```
ceara_g = pygeoda.open(dfs)
queen_w = pygeoda.queen_weights(ceara_g)
print(queen_w)
data = dfs[varlist]
data_g = ceara_g[varlist]
```

```
Weights Meta-data:
 number of observations:                    184
```

```
        is symmetric:                True
            sparsity:   0.02953686200378072
     # min neighbors:                   1
     # max neighbors:                  13
    # mean neighbors:    5.434782608695652
  # median neighbors:                 5.0
        has isolates:               False
```

Finally, we set the number of clusters to 13. This differs from the empirical examples in Chapter 12 of the *GeoDa Cluster Book* due to the result for max-p obtained with `pygeoda` in Chapter 13. For consistency, we set the number of clusters for the other methods to that value.

```
n_clusters = 13
```

14.2 Cluster Solutions

Before considering the validation measures, we compute the cluster solutions for hierarchical clustering (using `AgglomerativeClustering`), and K-Means (using `KMeans`), from `sklearn.cluster`. The spatially constrained clustering methods are from `pygeoda`. For details on the arguments and helper functions, see the relevant Chapters.

For each cluster, we extract the `labels` and the `fit` using the respective helper functions.

To illustrate the internal validity measures, we will focus on Ward's agglomerative clustering as an example of a standard method and on AZP with SCHC initial solution as an example of a spatially constrained cluster solution. For this, we also generate the cluster cardinalities. This is not illustrated for the other cluster solutions, but can be readily implemented using the code from previous Chapters.

14.2.1 Hierarchical Clustering

For hierarchical clustering, we preface the the code block with a `StandardScaler` command to create the standardized data set. This is not repeated in the code blocks for the other examples.

```
method = 'ward'
X = StandardScaler().fit_transform(data)

agg_clusters = AgglomerativeClustering(n_clusters = n_clusters,
                    linkage = method, compute_distances = True)
agg_clusters.fit(X)
agg_labels = tuple(int(label) for label in agg_clusters.labels_)

agg_clusters_fit = cluster_fit(data = data,
                   clustlabels =agg_clusters.labels_,
                   n_clusters = n_clusters, printopt = False)
agg_stats = cluster_stats(agg_labels)
```

Labels	Cardinality
0	16
1	26
2	29
3	9
4	14
5	3
6	26
7	11
8	20
9	4
10	15
11	10
12	1

14.2.2 K-Means Clustering

```
kmeans_clusters = KMeans(n_clusters = n_clusters, n_init = 150,
                         random_state=123456789).fit(X)
kmeans_labels = tuple(int(label) for label in kmeans_clusters.labels_)
kmeans_clusters_fit = cluster_fit(data = data,
                  clustlabels = kmeans_clusters.labels_,
                  n_clusters = n_clusters, printopt = False)
```

14.2.3 SCHC with Ward's Linkage

```
schc_clusters = pygeoda.schc(n_clusters, queen_w, data_g, "ward")
schc_labels = schc_clusters['Clusters']
```

14.2.4 SKATER

```
skater_clusters = pygeoda.skater(n_clusters, queen_w, data_g)
skater_labels = skater_clusters['Clusters']
```

14.2.5 REDCAP

```
redcap_clusters = pygeoda.redcap(n_clusters, queen_w, data_g,
                       method = 'fullorder-wardlinkage')
redcap_labels = redcap_clusters['Clusters']
```

14.2.6 AZP with Simulated Annealing

```
azp_sa_clusters = pygeoda.azp_sa(n_clusters, queen_w, data_g,
                       cooling_rate = 0.8, sa_maxit = 5)
azp_sa_labels = azp_sa_clusters['Clusters']
```

14.2.7 AZP with SCHC as Initial Solution

```
azp_schc_clusters = pygeoda.azp_sa(n_clusters, queen_w, data_g,
                           cooling_rate = 0.8, sa_maxit = 5,
                           init_regions = schc_labels)
azp_schc_labels = azp_schc_clusters['Clusters']
azp_schc_stats = cluster_stats(azp_schc_labels)
```

Labels	Cardinality
1	89
2	43

3	15
4	14
5	6
6	4
7	4
8	3
9	2
10	1
11	1
12	1
13	1

14.2.8 Max-p Regions

```
maxp_sa_clusters = pygeoda.maxp_sa(queen_w, data_g,
                            bound_variable = dfs['pop'],
                            min_bound = dfs['pop'].sum()*0.05,
                            iterations = 9999,
                            cooling_rate = 0.9,
                            sa_maxit = 5)
maxp_sa_labels = maxp_sa_clusters['Clusters']
```

14.3 Internal Validation Measures

As mentioned, in addition to the classic measures of fit, we also consider *fragmentation*, the *join count ratio*, and, for spatially constrained cluster solutions, the *compactness* and *diameter*. These measures are provided as attributes in the solution object created by `pygeoda.spatial_validation`. This requires the `pygeoda` data set, the cluster labels and the spatial weights as arguments.

We illustrate this for Ward's agglomerative clustering, with `agg_labels` as the cluster labels, and for AZP-SCHC, with `azp_schc_labels` as the cluster labels. For both, the data set is `ceara_g` and the spatial weights are contained in `queen_w`.

We store the results in, respectively, `agg_validation` and `azp_schc_validation`. These objects will then be used as arguments to the helper functions.

```
agg_validation = pygeoda.spatial_validation(ceara_g, agg_labels, queen_w)
azp_schc_validation = pygeoda.spatial_validation(ceara_g,
                                        azp_schc_labels, queen_w)
```

14.3.1 Fragmentation

The fragmentation measures are computed from the makeup of the cluster components. An ideally balanced cluster is when each component has the same number of observations. This is quantified by means of entropy and its standardized counterpart, as well as by Simpson's index and its standardized counterpart. For entropy, larger values suggest a greater balance, whereas for Simpson's index, it is the other way around.

The `pygeoda.spatial_validation` return object includes the fragmentation information in two attributes: `fragmentation` and `cluster_fragmentation`. The first contains the overall measures, as well as the number of clusters, in `fragmentation.n`, `fragmentation.entropy`, `fragmentation.std_entropy`, `fragmentation.simpson` and `fragmentation.std_simpson`. The second has the same information, organized as a list by cluster. It shows the within-cluster fragmentation for clusters that are not spatially constrained.

The `cluster_fragmentation` helper function, takes a DataFrame with the labels and cardinalities (created by `cluster_stats`), and the `cluster_fragmentation`, `fragmentation` and `spatially_constrained` attributes from the validation object. The `spatially_constrained` flag is used to limit the fragmentation output to the totals only for spatially constrained clusters.

This is illustrated for Ward's agglomerative clustering and AZP-SCHC. Note that for the latter, only the totals are given, since it is a spatially constrained solution.

The other cluster solutions can be analyzed in the same way.

14.3.1.1 Agglomerative clustering

```
agg_frag = cluster_fragmentation(agg_stats,
                   agg_validation.cluster_fragmentation,
                   agg_validation.fragmentation,
                   agg_validation.spatially_constrained)
```

```
Fragmentation
Label   N Sub  Entropy  Entropy*  Simpson  Simpson*
    0  16   9 1.751176  0.796994 0.250892  2.258026
    1  26  14 2.397937  0.908634 0.115385  1.615385
    2  29  14 2.425806  0.919194 0.109467  1.532544
    3   9  11 2.250260  0.938431 0.120000  1.320000
    4  14   9 1.923066  0.875225 0.187500  1.687500
    5   3   8 1.933810  0.929966 0.164444  1.315556
```

```
  6  26  10 2.168223  0.941647 0.132653  1.326531
  7  11   9 2.145842  0.976615 0.123967  1.115702
  8  20   6 1.609438  0.898244 0.240000  1.440000
  9   4   7 1.831020  0.940958 0.185185  1.296296
 10  15   0 0.000000  0.000000 0.000000  0.000000
 11  10   3 1.098612  1.000000 0.333333  1.000000
 12   1   0 0.000000  0.000000 0.000000  0.000000
All 184     2.351159  0.916649 0.106274  1.381557
```

14.3.1.2 AZP-SCHC

```
azp_schc_frag = cluster_fragmentation(azp_schc_stats,
                    azp_schc_validation.cluster_fragmentation,
                    azp_schc_validation.fragmentation,
                    azp_schc_validation.spatially_constrained)
```

```
Fragmentation
Label   N Sub  Entropy  Entropy*  Simpson  Simpson*
  All 184     1.599116  0.623449 0.303521   3.94577
```

14.3.2 Join Count Ratio

The join count ratio is a *spatial* measure of the degree of internal connectedness in a cluster solution. It is computed for each cluster separately as well as for the cluster solution as a whole. It is a count of how many neighbors of observations in a cluster are also members of that cluster.

The relevant measures are included in the `joincount_ratio` and `all_joincount_ratio` attributes of the `pygeoda.spatial_validation` solution object. `joincount_ratio` is a list with k entries, which are themselves objects. For each cluster (up to k), the associated attributes are `n` (the number of cluster elements), `neighbors` (the number of neighbors), `join_count` and `ratio`. The same attributes are also included for the overall cluster solution.

The result is provided by the `cluster_joincount` helper function. It takes the data frame with cluster cardinalities and the `joincount_ratio` and `all_joincount_ratio` attributes from the validation solution. We consider this for agglomerative clustering and AZP-SCHC.

14.3.2.1 Agglomerative clustering

```
agg_jc = cluster_joincount(agg_stats, agg_validation.joincount_ratio,
                    agg_validation.all_joincount_ratio)
```

Join Count Ratio

Label	N	Neighbors	Join Count	Ratio
0	16	96	20	0.208
1	26	134	26	0.194
2	29	158	64	0.405
3	9	47	6	0.128
4	14	80	8	0.100
5	3	15	0	0.000
6	26	158	30	0.190
7	11	43	4	0.093
8	20	116	18	0.155
9	4	21	10	0.476
10	15	83	18	0.217
11	10	46	8	0.174
12	1	3	0	0.000
All	184	1000	212	0.212

14.3.2.2 AZP-SCHC

```
azp_schc_jc = cluster_joincount(azp_schc_stats,
                    azp_schc_validation.joincount_ratio,
                    azp_schc_validation.all_joincount_ratio)
```

Join Count Ratio

Label	N	Neighbors	Join Count	Ratio
0	89	474	342	0.722
1	43	225	128	0.569
2	15	96	42	0.438
3	14	78	44	0.564
4	6	37	10	0.270
5	4	17	6	0.353
6	4	21	10	0.476
7	3	22	4	0.182

8	2	12	2	0.167
9	1	3	0	0.000
10	1	3	0	0.000
11	1	7	0	0.000
12	1	5	0	0.000
All	184	1000	588	0.588

Whereas the join count ratio can be computed for both classic and spatially constrained cluster solutions, this is not the case for compactness and diameter. These measures only apply to spatially constrained solutions.

14.3.3 Compactness

Compactness measures the ratio of the perimeter of the cluster to that of a circle with the same area.

The `compactness` attribute of the `spatial_validation` object is a list with k items, each an object with attributes `area`, `perimeter` and `isoperimeter_quotient`. The closer the IPQ is to one, the more compact is the cluster shape.

The helper function `cluster_compactness` extracts this information. Its attributes are the data frame with cluster cardinalities (from `cluster_stats`), the `compactness` attribute, and the `spatially_constrained` attribute. Compactness is not relevant for clusters that are not spatially constrained and therefore the helper function will yield an error message when this happens.

We continue with the same two examples.

14.3.3.1 Agglomerative clustering

```
agg_compactness = cluster_compactness(agg_stats,
                                     agg_validation.compactness,
                                     agg_validation.spatially_constrained)
```

```
Error: Compactness is only applicable to spatially constrained clusters
```

Since the solution for Ward's agglomerative cluster does not impose spatial constraints, an error message is generated.

14.3.3.2 AZP-SCHC

```
azp_schc_compactness = cluster_compactness(azp_schc_stats,
                        azp_schc_validation.compactness,
                        azp_schc_validation.spatially_constrained)
```

```
Compactness
 Label  N          Area     Perimeter       IPQ
     0 89 8.672968e+10 1.536222e+07 0.004618
     1 43 2.797625e+10 6.198588e+06 0.009150
     2 15 1.053291e+10 2.220946e+06 0.026834
     3 14 1.138704e+10 2.122643e+06 0.031759
     4  6 4.038275e+09 9.257796e+05 0.059209
     5  4 3.085985e+09 5.499120e+05 0.128238
     6  4 1.779537e+09 4.240068e+05 0.124386
     7  3 9.969357e+08 3.168568e+05 0.124782
     8  2 1.474872e+09 3.229358e+05 0.177718
     9  1 6.171934e+08 1.199243e+05 0.539283
    10  1 7.908164e+07 5.056877e+04 0.388616
    11  1 8.449201e+08 1.739887e+05 0.350738
    12  1 4.124364e+08 1.255397e+05 0.328855
```

14.3.4 Diameter

The diameter of a spatially constrained cluster is an alternative measure of compactness, based on the network structure reflected in the spatial weights.

The diameter of a cluster is the number of steps in the spatial weights graph that corresponds with the longest shortest path between any pair of observations (Newman 2018). Since this number will increase with cluster size, it is also standardized by dividing by the number of cluster members. Note that when a cluster is a singleton, the diameter will be zero.

The `diameter` attribute of the `pygeoda.spatial_validation` object is a list with k items, one for each cluster, as an object with attributes `steps` and `ratio`. The helper function `cluster_diameter` extracts this information as a DataFrame. It takes as arguments the cluster cardinalities (from `cluster_stats`), and the `diameter` and `spatially_constrained` attributes from the `pygeoda.spatial_validation` object.

Again, we use the same two examples.

14.3.4.1 Agglomerative clustering

```
agg_diam = cluster_diameter(agg_stats,
                            agg_validation.diameter,
                            agg_validation.spatially_constrained)
```

```
Error: Diameter is only applicable to spatially constrained clusters
```

As in the case of compactness, an error message is generated for clusters that are not spatially constrained, such as Ward's agglomerative clustering.

14.3.4.2 AZP-SCHC

```
azp_schc_diam = cluster_diameter(azp_schc_stats,
                            azp_schc_validation.diameter,
                            azp_schc_validation.spatially_constrained)
```

```
Diameter
 Label  N  Steps     Ratio
     0 89     22 0.247191
     1 43     17 0.395349
     2 15      6 0.400000
     3 14      7 0.500000
     4  6      3 0.500000
     5  4      3 0.750000
     6  4      2 0.500000
     7  3      2 0.666667
     8  2      1 0.500000
     9  1      0 0.000000
    10  1      0 0.000000
    11  1      0 0.000000
    12  1      0 0.000000
```

14.3.5 Overall Comparison of Internal Validation Measures

We conclude our discussion of internal validation measures with an overview of the main non-spatial measures for all the cluster solutions considered above.

```
clusters = [
  agg_clusters_fit, kmeans_clusters_fit, schc_clusters, skater_clusters,
  redcap_clusters, azp_sa_clusters, azp_schc_clusters, maxp_sa_clusters
]
labels = [
    agg_labels, kmeans_labels, schc_labels, skater_labels,
    redcap_labels, azp_sa_labels, azp_schc_labels, maxp_sa_labels
]
label_names = [
    'Hierarchical', 'K-Means', 'SCHC', 'SKATER',
    'REDCAP', 'AZP', 'AZP_Initial', 'Max-p'
]

results = []

# Run pygeoda.spatial_validation for each label set
for cluster, label, name in zip(clusters, labels, label_names):
    result = pygeoda.spatial_validation(ceara_g, label, queen_w)

    try:
        wss = np.round(cluster['Total within-cluster sum of squares'],
                                                    4)
        bss_tss = np.round(
           cluster['The ratio of between to total sum of squares'], 4)
    except:
        try:
            wss = np.round(cluster["WSS"], 2)
            bss_tss = np.round(cluster["Ratio"], 2)
        except:
            wss = None
            bss_tss = None

    spatially_constrained = result.spatially_constrained
    all_join_count_ratio = np.round(result.all_joincount_ratio.ratio, 4)
    entropy = np.round(result.fragmentation.entropy, 4)
    simpson = np.round(result.fragmentation.simpson, 4)

    results.append({
        'Method': name,
        'Spat. Const.': spatially_constrained,
        'WSS': wss,
        'BSS/TSS': bss_tss,
```

```
        'Join Count': all_join_count_ratio,
        'Entropy': entropy,
        'Simpson': simpson
    })

validation = pd.DataFrame(results)
print(validation.to_string(index = False))
```

```
      Method  Spat. Const.      WSS  BSS/TSS  Join Count  Entropy  Simpson
Hierarchical         False 349.0000   0.6800       0.212   2.3512   0.1063
     K-Means         False 334.3800   0.7000       0.240   2.3213   0.1112
        SCHC          True 568.0173   0.4827       0.668   1.6394   0.2730
      SKATER          True 604.2209   0.4497       0.784   1.3661   0.3901
      REDCAP          True 562.7003   0.4875       0.660   1.6109   0.2769
         AZP          True 617.0010   0.4381       0.526   1.9521   0.2016
 AZP_Initial          True 538.3477   0.5097       0.588   1.5991   0.3035
       Max-p          True 745.2474   0.3213       0.496   2.4175   0.0959
```

14.4 External Validation Measures

External validation measures are designed to compare a cluster solution to a *truth*, but they can also be employed to compare several cluster solutions to each other. The validation indices reveal how close the cluster solutions are. We consider two measures, the *Adjusted Rand Index* and the *Normalized Information Distance*.

14.4.1 Adjusted Rand Index (ARI)

The adjusted rand index is based on counting how many pairs of observations are in the same grouping for two cluster solutions. It can be computed by `sklearn.metrics.adjusted_rand_score`. The two arguments are numpy arrays of the labels of the *reference* (first argument) and the labels of the cluster to be compared. Note that we need to convert our `labels` solution to a numpy array for this to work.

For example, the ARI between Ward's agglomerative solution and K-Means is found by passing numpy arrays for `agg_labels` and `kmeans_labels`. The result of 0.392 is smaller than 0.5, which suggests only low correspondence.

```
ari = adjusted_rand_score(np.array(agg_labels), np.array(kmeans_labels))
print(np.round(ari, 3))
```

```
0.392
```

We can now compute all pairwise indices with a simple loop. We first recreate the **labels** and **label_names** lists from above (so this can be run without the internal validation measures).

```
labels = [
    agg_labels, kmeans_labels, schc_labels, skater_labels,
    redcap_labels, azp_sa_labels, azp_schc_labels, maxp_sa_labels
]
label_names = [
    'Hierarchical', 'K-Means', 'SCHC', 'SKATER',
    'REDCAP', 'AZP', 'AZP_Initial', 'Max-p'
]
```

In a simple loop, we compute all pairwise indices and populate a matrix. This is then turned into a data frame and printed. Note that the matrix is symmetric and the diagonal values of 1.0 can be ignored.

```
h = len(labels)
allari = np.zeros((h, h))

for i in range(h):
    labi = np.array(labels[i])
    for j in range(h):
        labj = np.array(labels[j])
        allari[i,j] = adjusted_rand_score(labi, labj)
dfari = pd.DataFrame(allari, columns = label_names,
                     index = label_names)
print(np.round(dfari, 3))
```

	Hierarchical	K-Means	SCHC	SKATER	REDCAP	AZP
Hierarchical	1.000	0.392	0.131	0.079	0.145	0.160
K-Means	0.392	1.000	0.176	0.095	0.184	0.205
SCHC	0.131	0.176	1.000	0.424	0.918	0.504
SKATER	0.079	0.095	0.424	1.000	0.384	0.258
REDCAP	0.145	0.184	0.918	0.384	1.000	0.516
AZP	0.160	0.205	0.504	0.258	0.516	1.000
AZP_Initial	0.155	0.165	0.735	0.452	0.727	0.577
Max-p	0.089	0.091	0.194	0.173	0.185	0.218

```
             AZP_Initial  Max-p
Hierarchical       0.155  0.089
K-Means            0.165  0.091
SCHC               0.735  0.194
SKATER             0.452  0.173
REDCAP             0.727  0.185
AZP                0.577  0.218
AZP_Initial        1.000  0.163
Max-p              0.163  1.000
```

As in Chapter 12 of the *GeoDa Cluster Book*, the matrix reveals a much closer correspondence among the non-spatial solutions and the spatial solutions respectively. The greatest correspondence is between SCHC and REDCAP, with an ARI of 0.918.

14.4.2 Normalized Information Distance (NID)

The second external validation measure is based on information-theoretic considerations, such as entropy. In Chapter 12 of the *GeoDa Cluster Book*, the Normalized Information Distance is introduced (NID). A close counterpart can be computed by means of `sklearn.metrics.adjusted_mutual_info_score`. The arguments are the same as for ARI. However, in contrast to NID as presented in the *GeoDa Cluster Book*, a higher value for the adjusted mutual information score indicates closer similarity.

We first illustrate this for Ward's agglomerative clustering and K-Means, passing numpy arrays of `agg_labels` and `kmeans_labels`.

```
nid = adjusted_mutual_info_score(np.array(agg_labels),
                                  np.array(kmeans_labels))
print(np.round(nid, 3))
```

```
0.614
```

Finally, we run the same loop as for ARI to compute all pairwise NID scores.

```
allnid = np.zeros((h, h))
for i in range(h):
    labi = np.array(labels[i])
    for j in range(h):
        labj = np.array(labels[j])
        allnid[i,j] = adjusted_mutual_info_score(labi, labj)
dfnid = pd.DataFrame(allnid, columns = label_names, index = label_names)
print(np.round(dfnid, 3))
```

	Hierarchical	K-Means	SCHC	SKATER	REDCAP	AZP
Hierarchical	1.000	0.614	0.257	0.219	0.267	0.306
K-Means	0.614	1.000	0.300	0.244	0.308	0.328
SCHC	0.257	0.300	1.000	0.548	0.897	0.581
SKATER	0.219	0.244	0.548	1.000	0.496	0.425
REDCAP	0.267	0.308	0.897	0.496	1.000	0.595
AZP	0.306	0.328	0.581	0.425	0.595	1.000
AZP_Initial	0.317	0.322	0.727	0.545	0.727	0.646
Max-p	0.177	0.191	0.388	0.423	0.372	0.445

	AZP_Initial	Max-p
Hierarchical	0.317	0.177
K-Means	0.322	0.191
SCHC	0.727	0.388
SKATER	0.545	0.423
REDCAP	0.727	0.372
AZP	0.646	0.445
AZP_Initial	1.000	0.367
Max-p	0.367	1.000

As for ARI, we find the closest correspondence between SCHC and REDCAP.

14.5 Practice

We now have all the available tools to compare the various cluster solutions obtained in earlier Chapters. In addition, when an administrative regionalization is available (e.g., subdistricts in a city), the various cluster solutions can be compared to that *truth*.

References

Algeri, Carmelo, Luc Anselin, Antonio Fabio Forgione, and Carlo Migliardo. 2022. "Spatial Dependence in the Technical Efficiency of Local Banks." *Papers in Regional Science* 101: 385–416.

Amaral, Pedro, Lucas Carvalho, Thiago Rocha, Nubia Silva, and Joao Vissoci. 2019. "Geospatial Modeling of Microcephaly and Zika Virus Spread Patterns in Brazil." *PLoS ONE* 14.

Anselin, Luc. 2024a. *An Introduction to Spatial Data Science with GeoDa - Volume 1, Exploring Spatial Data.* Boca Raton, FL: CRC/Chapman & Hall.

———. 2024b. *An Introduction to Spatial Data Science with GeoDa - Volume 2, Clustering Spatial Data.* Boca Raton, FL: CRC/Chapman & Hall.

Anselin, Luc, and Xun Li. 2020. "Tobler's Law in a Multivariate World." *Geographical Analysis* 52: 494–510.

Assunçao, Renato M., M. C. Neves, G. Câmara, and C. Da Costa Freitas. 2006. "Efficient Regionalization Techniques for Socio-Economic Geographical Units Using Minimum Spanning Trees." *International Journal of Geographical Information Science* 20: 797–811.

Campello, Ricardo J. G. B., Davoud Moulavi, and Jörg Sander. 2013. "Density-Based Clustering Based on Hierarchical Density Estimates." In *Advances in Knowledge Discovery and Data Mining. PAKDD 2013. Lecture Notes in Computer Science, Vol. 7819*, edited by Jian Pei, Vincent S. Tseng, Longbing Cao, Hiroshi Motoda, and Guandong Xu, 160–72.

Campello, Ricardo J. G. B., Davoud Moulavi, Arthur Zimek, and Jörg Sandler. 2015. "Hierarchical Density Estimates for Data Clustering, Visualization, and Outlier Detection." *ACM Transactions on Knowledge Discovery from Data* 10,1. https://doi.org/10.1145/2733381.

de Leeuw, Jan. 1977. "Applications of Convex Analysis to Multidimensional Scaling." In *Recent Developments in Statistics*, edited by J. R. Barra, F. Brodeau, G. Romier, and B. van Cutsem, 133–45. Amsterdam: North Holland.

de Leeuw, Jan, and Patrick Mair. 2009. "Multidimensional Scaling Using Majorization: SMACOF in R." *Journal of Statistical Software* 21.

Duque, Juan C., Luc Anselin, and Sergio J. Rey. 2012. "The Max-p-Regions Problem." *Journal of Regional Science* 52: 397–419.

Ester, Martin, Hans-Peter Kriegel, Jörg Sander, and Xiaowei Xu. 1996. "A Density-Based Algorithm for Discovering Clusters in Large Spatial Databases with Noise." In *KDD-96 Proceedings*, 226–31.

Gan, Junhao, and Yufei Tao. 2017. "On the Hardness and Approximation of Euclidean DBSCAN." *ACM Transactions on Database Systems (TODS)* 42: 14.

Guo, Diansheng. 2008. "Regionalization with Dynamically Constrained Agglomerative Clustering and Partitioning (REDCAP)." *International Journal of Geographical Information Science* 22: 801–23.

Guo, Diansheng, and Hu Wang. 2011. "Automatic Region Building for Spatial Analysis." *Transactions in GIS* 15: 29–45.

Hinton, Geoffrey E., and Sam T. Roweis. 2003. "Stochastic Neighbor Embedding." In *Advances in Neural Information Processing Systems 15 (NIPS 2002)*, edited by S. Becker, S. Thun, and K. Obermayer, 833–40. Vancouver, BC: NIPS.

Hubert, Lawrence J., and Phipps Arabie. 1985. "Comparing Partitions." *Journal of Classification* 2: 193–218.

Kaufman, L., and P. Rousseeuw. 2005. *Finding Groups in Data: An Introduction to Cluster Analysis.* New York, NY: John Wiley.

Kolak, Marynia, Jay Bhatt, Yoon Hong Park, Norma A. Padrón, and Ayrin Molefe. 2020. "Quantification of Neighborhood-Level Social Determinants of Health in the Continental United States." *JAMA Network Open* 3 (1): e1919928–28. https://doi.org/10.1001/jamanetworkopen.2019.19928.

McInnes, Leland, and John Healy. 2017. "Accelerated Hierarchical Density Clustering." In *2017 IEEE International Conference on Data Mining Workshops (ICDMW)*. New Orleans, LA. https://doi.org/10.1109/ICDMW.2017.12.

Newman, Mark. 2018. *Networks.* Oxford, United Kingdom: Oxford University Press.

Openshaw, Stan. 1977. "A Geographical Solution to Scale and Aggregation Problems in Region-Building, Partitioning and Spatial Modeling." *Transactions of the Institute of British Geographers* 2: 459–72.

Openshaw, Stan, and L. Rao. 1995. "Algorithms for Reengineering the 1991 Census Geography." *Environment and Planning A* 27: 425–46.

Sander, Jörg, Martin Ester, Hans-Peter Kriegel, and Xiaowei Xu. 1998. "Density-Based Clustering in Spatial Databases: The Algorithm GDBSCAN and Its Applications." *Data Mining and Knowledge Discovery* 2: 169–94.

Schubert, Erich, Jörg Sander, Martin Ester, Peter Kriegel, and Xiaowei Xu. 2017. "DBSCAN Revisited, Revisited: Why and How You Should (Still) Use DBSCAN." *ACM Transactions on Database Systems (TODS)* 42: 19.

van der Maaten, Laurens, and Geoffrey Hinton. 2008. "Visualizing Data Using t-SNE." *Journal of Machine Learning Research* 9: 2579–2605.

Vinh, Nguyen Xuan, Julien Epps, and James Bailey. 2010. "Information Theoretic Measures for Clustering Comparison: Variants, Properties, Normalization and Correction for Chance." *Journal of Machine Learning Research* 11: 2837–54.

Index

About the Authors

Luc Anselin is the Founding Director of the Center for Spatial Data Science at the University of Chicago, where he is also Stein-Freiler Distinguished Service Professor of Sociology, Data Science and the College. He previously held faculty appointments at Arizona State University, the University of Illinois at Urbana-Champaign, the University of Texas at Dallas, the Regional Research Institute at West Virginia University, the University of California, Santa Barbara, and The Ohio State University. He also was a visiting professor at Brown University and MIT. He holds a PhD in Regional Science from Cornell University. Over the past four decades, he has developed new methods for exploratory spatial data analysis and spatial econometrics, including the widely used local indicators of spatial autocorrelation. His 1988 *Spatial Econometrics* text has been cited about 20,000 times. He has implemented these methods into software, including the original `SpaceStat` software, as well as the widely used `GeoDa`, and as part of the Python `PySAL` library for spatial analysis. His work has been recognized by several awards, including election to the U.S. National Academy of Sciences and the American Academy of Arts and Sciences.

Pedro Amaral is an Associate Professor at the Department of Economics and the Center for Regional Development and Planning (Cedeplar) at the Federal University of Minas Gerais, Brazil, and a Senior Fellow at the Center for Spatial Data Science at the University of Chicago, where he has also served as a Visiting Professor since 2020. He holds a Ph.D. in Land Economy from the University of Cambridge and is currently Deputy Editor-in-Chief of *Regional Studies, Regional Science*. He co-leads, with Prof. Luc Anselin, the development of `spreg`, the spatial econometrics module of `PySAL`, an open-source Python library for spatial analysis. His contributions to the field have been recognized with several honors, including the Distinguished Service to Regional Studies Award from the Regional Studies Association, the Peter Nijkamp Research Encouragement Award from the Regional Science Association International, the Tinker Visiting Professorship at the University of Chicago, and the Nathaniel Lichfield Award from the Regional Studies Association.

Made in the USA
Las Vegas, NV
03 November 2026

57424838R00150